# BETWEEN
# GOD AND BEAST

BETWEEN

# GOD

AND

# BEAST

*An Examination of Amos Oz's Prose*

*Avraham Balaban*

*The Pennsylvania State University Press*
*University Park, Pennsylvania*

An earlier version of this book was published in Hebrew
(Tel Aviv: Am Oved, 1986).


Library of Congress Cataloging-in-Publication Data

Balaban, Abraham, 1944–
   [Ben El le-Ḥayah.   English]
   Between God and beast : an examination of Amos Oz's prose /
Avraham Balaban.
      p.    cm.
   Translation of: Ben El le-Ḥayah.
   Includes bibliographical references and index.
   ISBN 0-271-00851-2
   1. Oz, Amos—Criticism and interpretation.   I. Title.
PJ5054.O9Z5913   1993
892.4'36—dc20                                                         92-5896
                                                                                               CIP


Copyright © 1993 The Pennsylvania State University
All rights reserved
Printed in the United States of America

Published by The Pennsylvania State University Press,
Suite C, Barbara Building, University Park, PA 16802-1003


It is the policy of The Pennsylvania State University Press to use acid-free paper for the first printing of all clothbound books. Publications on uncoated stock satisfy the minimum requirements of American National Standard for Information Sciences—Permanence of Paper for Printed Library Materials, ANSI Z39.48–1984.

## CONTENTS

| | |
|---|---|
| Author's Note | vii |
| Preface | 1 |
| 1  Between Klausner and Oz: A Biographical Note | 11 |
|     A Memory: Man Toward Man a Fearful Porcupine | 31 |
| 2  Introduction to Oz: The Early Stories | 33 |
|     A Memory: First Encounter with "Where the Jackals Howl" | 78 |
| 3  Between God and Beast: Religious Aspects of Oz's Work | 79 |
|     A Memory: A Desire to Belong | 137 |
| 4  Water and Sky: Water Images and Female Characters | 139 |
|     A Memory: Oz as a Soccer Player | 177 |
| 5  War and Peace: The Element of Synthesis | 179 |
| Appendix: On the Structure of *Where the Jackals Howl* | 241 |
| Bibliography | 251 |
| Index to the Works | 257 |

# AUTHOR'S NOTE

Since the Hebrew version of this study was published in 1986, Amos Oz has published three more novels. In the process of revising my research for publication in the United States, I have added detailed discussions of the latest novels.

Twelve of Oz's fourteen books have been translated into English. In order to enable the reader to follow the quotations, each one is followed first by a page number referring to the Hebrew version and then the page number of the English version. Most of Oz's books have been translated with many condensations. When the page number of the English version does not appear, it means either that the book has not been translated yet, or that the quotation under discussion does not appear in the English version. The English edition is also ignored when the original text has been translated in such a manner as to significantly alter the phrasing. In several quotations I have rewritten the English translation, mainly in cases where a recurrence of a word or image had been omitted.

The original stories of *Where the Jackals Howl* (1965) were rewritten by the author and published in 1976. The 1976 edition is the one translated into English (1981). Therefore the discussion of the first edition of this book refers to the Hebrew edition only.

# PREFACE

In interviews he gave on the occasion of the publication of his first book, *Where the Jackals Howl* (1965), Amos Oz said:

> I don't believe that the focus of human misery lies in the social realm, and I don't believe that setting society right means uprooting that misery. (1965b)
>
> One who assumes that man's main problems are in the social realm might assume that there is a solution to these problems. Certainly then misery appears less awesome, because somewhere, at least in some distant utopia, an existence without misery is hinted. . . . One who assumes that the focus of misery originates in the tension between man and the basic components of human existence—the soul, the urges, death, even the unexplained sadness—such a man cannot promise himself even a distant utopia. (1965c)

The notion that human misery originates in the human "soul" appears repeatedly in Oz's interviews in which he compares societal problems to a chain of hills above which loom "crests of mountains of the main existential problems: death, Eros, the other" (1968b, 1978d). This metaphor also appears in Srulik's journal in the final pages of *A Perfect Peace*: "I say 'the battle'—yet as soon as I say it, I sense, staring down at me through the thin curtain of ideology, the peaks of savage mountains of a suffering far more primeval. The very suffering that drives all of us to look constantly for battlefields, for 'challenges,' to fight, to defeat, to win" (1982, 371; English edition 1985, 363).

The notion of ideology as but a thin film ("a curtain") over primordial urges is conveyed throughout Oz's work. "The peaks of savage mountains," the primeval forces in the human psyche, have spellbound Oz from his very start as a writer. His protagonists set out again and again on journeys with the desire to understand these peaks and the forces throbbing within them, and to attempt to learn to live with them. Yet these journeys take place, in general, in their psyche and not in the external world.

The story "Before His Time" (1962b), the earliest of the stories in *Where the Jackals Howl*, depicts social and political tensions, the problems of kibbutz society, and the Arab-Israeli conflict. Beneath the external plot hides a psychic drama whose pinnacle is the protagonist's discovery that human beings cannot eradicate or tame the savage forces hidden within their soul. This drama, which is the core of the story, is illustrated by means of very subtle symbols and motifs. Such a structure has served Oz in most of his subsequent works.[1] Against the background of kibbutz life and the reality of Israel, his protagonists continuously struggle with "the peaks of savage mountains" within this primeval, unconquerable world of the psyche. A careful reading of these works reveals that the social and political reality reflects the forces that exist in this primordial, timeless world.

Few of Oz's critics have set off with his protagonists on the journey to "the peaks of savage mountains." In spite of the fact that Oz repeatedly emphasizes in his works, articles, and interviews that one's true struggle does not take place in the sociopolitical arena, his critics have tended to focus on the sociopolitical aspects of his work.[2] Several factors have apparently contributed to this development. Before Oz, no one had depicted kibbutz society and its familial and social dramas in the way he did. These dramas caused vehement disputes within Israeli society and drew attention to this aspect of the works. In addition, Oz was identified as a political animal from the beginning of his literary career. When his first story was published in 1961, he was an active member in the Min ha'Yesod ("From the Beginning") movement, whose campaign against David Ben-Gurion was accompanied by a vigorous controversy in Israeli society. Furthermore, throughout his literary career Oz has supported several left-wing movements (the Movement for Peace and Security, the Committee for Israeli-Palestinian Peace, the Sheli movement, the Peace Now movement). Another explanation of this phenomenon is the simple fact that problems concerning Israel and the kibbutz are expressly described in his works,

---

1. In Chapter 2 I deal extensively with the structure of "Before His Time" as a model of most of Oz's subsequent works. Following the earlier publication of Chapter 2 as an essay (1984), Oz wrote me that indeed in this story he had found a narrative model which he was to use repeatedly later on (letter dated July 2, 1984).

2. Needless to say, I speak of a tendency only. Several Israeli scholars have described, from different points of view, the deeper layers of Oz's work, notably Shaked (1970) and Gertz (1980).

whereas their psychological core is conveyed by means of a highly elaborate system of allusion and symbols.

Critics' tendency to focus on the sociopolitical level of Oz's work is even more prominent in Europe and America. Most of his fourteen books have been translated into English (and many of them have been translated into more than twenty other languages), thus gaining wide popularity. Yet the reviews accompanying their publication have usually dealt with problems related to the kibbutz society, the tensions typifying the Israeli scene, and so forth.[3] It would seem that the vast interest the West has developed toward Israel and its social experiments, notably the kibbutz, as well as the clear political identity of the author and his frequent references to the Israeli political scene, has drawn critics' attention to the sociopolitical aspect of Oz's works.

As already noted, Oz himself has repeatedly emphasized in his articles and interviews that one's true struggle is with "the peaks of savage mountains" in the world and in one's soul. To the best of my understanding here lies the kernel of all his works. This study accompanies Oz's characters in their journeys beyond "the chain of hills of societal problems."

## *Between Oz and Jung*

Upon reading Oz's first stories, I once again recalled the ideas of Carl Gustav Jung, which I first encountered during my high school years at Kibbutz Hulda. Rereading Jung's major works confirmed my growing conviction regarding the deep affinity between Oz's fiction and Jung's psychological theory. I elaborate on these findings in Chapter 2, and use them in discussing Oz's earliest stories. In his letters to me following the initial publication of that chapter (1984), Oz confirmed my findings several times: "Indeed, you have touched on the heart of the matter. Indeed, I was 'Jungian' even prior to reading one line of Jung, and indeed, the things that interested me thirty years ago, when I was a boy of fifteen, are principally the things that have interested me to this day and apparently, they will concern me until I am taken to them" (letter dated July 2, 1984).[4] In that letter he added:

---

3. Among the scholarly works in English worth noting is Robert Alter's discussion of Oz's fiction (1977a, 1977b). Alter describes very accurately the forces struggling in the souls of Oz's protagonists. For in-depth interpretations of some of Oz's works, see Aschkenasy (1986) and Cohen (1990).

4. For an explanation of Oz's attraction to Jung's ideas, see Chapters 1 and 2.

"I know that Jung's ideas are not popular right now in the West. Yet, I think that his Copernican revolution has had a tremendous impact on our understanding of human nature."

Like many other modern writers, Oz prefers implicit, allusory description. The world depicted in his work is one of contradictions and oppositions that defy any direct and clear-cut formulation. Moreover, the experiential world he conveys is frequently located beyond the borders of culture and consciousness, beyond words. A symbol is sometimes the only way through which this hidden world can be expressed. In order to understand Oz's frequent use of symbols, many of them unfamiliar to much of his readership, we must also remember the literary norm that reigned in Hebrew literature in the 1950s and early 1960s. Agnon's fiction dominated Hebrew literature, and its influence on the novelists who started writing at that time is well-known.[5] Agnon's work is overloaded with symbols and allusions, and the best Israeli literary scholars were kept occupied trying to decipher the intricate code of his works. In his first two stories Oz imitated Agnon's style. Although in his later stories he has moved from the metarealistic mode to a more realistic one, he has not given up the use of a highly condensed net of symbols and allusions.

As I mentioned, the more I read Oz's prose, the more I realized that one of the main keys to his highly complicated texts was in Jung's work. Jung's writings, and to a great extent his interpretation of alchemist texts, have provided Oz with an unending reservoir of symbols. Oz uses these in combination with other symbols taken from various mythological traditions (Christianity, Judaism, Greek mythology)—a general pattern in his work. In fact, most of the mythical symbols, as elaborated in the following chapters, are employed by Oz in keeping with Jung's interpretation of them. Thus, for example, Oz's second story, "Purple Coast" (1962), describes a group of travelers sailing on the ocean. The group of travelers includes, among others, Dita and Mordu. It is easy to see that the names Dita and Mordu hint at Aphrodite and Marduk (the creator of the world in the Babylonian myth, "Anuma Elish"), and the story concretizes this possible allusion in various ways. The ocean, illustrated in the story as a mighty entity full of desires, carries all the features granted by Jung to the ocean. Thus, a reader who is unfamiliar with the significance ascribed to the

---

5. In a conversation I had with Oz in the early 1960s at Kibbutz Hulda, at the beginning of his literary career, the author emphasized the influence of Agnon on the younger generation of Hebrew novelists. Agnon, he said, is like a big bank with many cashiers. Oz himself stands by one of these cashiers, A. B. Yehoshua stands by another, Appelfeld stands by still another, and so on.

ocean by Jung is likely to overlook a part of the meaning of the story, just as a reader unaware of the references to Greek and Babylonian mythology misses some of the significance of the work.

This is even more true of symbols less prevalent than water. A reader familiar with Jung's discussions of the uroboros will understand why Noga (in *Elsewhere, Perhaps* [1966a; English edition, 1973]) and Rimona (*A Perfect Peace* [1982; English edition, 1985]) are described as impregnating themselves, and will recognize the relationship between this image and the function of these protagonists in the novels. The interpretation given by Jung to the unicorn enables the reader to understand the connection between Yonatan's hair combed forward "like the horn of a charging animal" (*A Perfect Peace*, 1982a, 219; 1985, 207) and the nickname Re'em (the Hebrew name of an animal Jung identifies with the unicorn), which Rimona calls Yonatan in her thoughts (180). The significance of mercury in Jung's writings is likely to explain why the moonlight is associated so frequently with mercury in the climactic scene of *A Perfect Peace*. This significance may also clarify the nature of the experience Yonatan undergoes in this situation and the connection between this experience and his previous appearance as a unicorn. In other words, Oz uses many symbols discussed by Jung, in addition to other traditional symbols, to create implicit levels of meaning. A reader who ignores the hidden levels of Oz's work might be left with only its sociological shell.

Oz conceives of the primal forces within the "soul" as concrete entities, forces that have existed in the world since its very beginning. These forces inhabit his world as archetypes or Platonic forms. He does not always take great pains to re-create them in his work. Often he is content with merely pointing out these forces, usually by means of one or two Jungian symbols, assuming that they are as powerful and meaningful in the reader's world as they are in his own. I elaborate on this issue in my *Toward Language and Beyond* (1988a).

Oz's use of symbols as examined by Jung may be pictured from another angle. Many writers have a cluster of notions that they take as self-explanatory, universally accepted. These notions are often connected to a group of writers (novelists, philosophers, psychologists) to whom one has been exposed as a youth, and who constitute the immediate intellectual and experiential world of a specific author. This is the writer's personal myth (to refer to Barthes's use of the term). From several conversations that I had with Oz in the summer of 1987, a year after the Hebrew version of this study was published, I realized that Oz knows Jung's writings even better than I had surmised. I received the palpable impression that Jung and his disciples (notably

Erich Neumann), the writings of the alchemists, notions such as the great mother, the uroboros, and the *prima materia* of the soul, are part of his immediate personal myth.

Jung's ideas are expressed in Oz's work in two other principal areas. First, in the conception of the structure of the psyche: the ego is depicted as a weak and unstable point at the pinnacle of a pyramid whose main volume is the collective unconscious; the collective unconscious is conceived of as a reservoir of primordial urges, creativity, and supreme sagacity. Second, the major psychic processes that are depicted throughout Oz's prose are typically Jungian. For instance, the "self" is achieved when the protagonist is reconciled with the dark recesses of his soul; the "self" reveals the image of God in man; the treasure hunt or quest typifies the search for "self." These processes, conveyed by typical Jungian symbols, compose the core of most of Oz's stories and novels, and they are expressed in his work from its very beginning.

Oz's psychological approach has reached its peak in *Black Box* (1987a; 1988). The Hebrew name of the female protagonist of the novel is Ilana, and her name in Poland, where she was born, was Halina, an implicit allusion to Helen, one of the four typical anima figures discussed by Jung. Indeed, Ilana is characterized as a typical anima figure. Ilana's husband, on the other hand, carries all the features of a Jungian animus figure (an elaborate discussion of the novel is included in chapters 4 and 5). Oz's next novel, *To Know a Woman* (1989; 1991), reveals a shift in emphasis; employing symbols taken from the alchemists' search for the philosophers' stone, the novel has a powerful epistemological facet.[6] The latest novel to date, *The Third Condition* (1991), is to a large extent a continuation of *To Know a Woman*. Interestingly enough, the psychological concept reflected in this novel is a Kabbalistic one, according to which an understanding and mutual affinity can be established only between souls who belong to the same "root."[7] The novel represents a dramatic change in Oz's worldview: the synthesis sought by the protagonist is achieved not by reuniting with the dark recesses of his psyche, but rather by coalescing with the world's primal light.[8]

---

6. G. Avigur-Rotem persuasively argues that the protagonist's attempts "to know a woman," indicated by the novel's title, actually are meant to know the world around him, to decipher its rules (1990). The importance of this issue in the novel is also illuminated by Nitza Ben-Dov (1990).

7. For the Kabbalistic notion of the soul, see Gershom Scholem (1965, 1987). Jung amply discussed the ties between Kabbala and alchemy (mainly in 1953b, 1963, 1968).

8. The Kabbalistic aspect of the novel is discussed in my review of the book (1991)

It is easy to see how Oz's psychological ideas have shaped his political views as expressed in his three books of essays (1979a, 1983, 1987b) as well as in his political activities. His explanations of the lasting Arab-Israeli conflict (tribal fears projected on each other by the vying parties; each party creates its own "shadow") are a direct extension of his Jungian worldview and terminology. Oz's constant demand for an Arab-Israeli peace agreement is parallel in its structure, terminology, and implications to the struggle waged by his protagonists who desperately try to find a synthesis between the forces at war within themselves.

It goes without saying that even after realizing the deep connection between the works of Oz and the thought of Jung, such an approach to Oz's fiction must be taken merely as a working hypothesis and must not be imposed relentlessly. Moreover, Jung is not the only relevant psychological framework evident in Oz's work. For example, Oz's first novel, *Elsewhere, Perhaps*, reveals strong Freudian influence (see Chapter 5).

As is well known, the theories of Freud and Jung have elicited a wide range of psychological approaches in the interpretations of literary texts. These interpretations, as fascinating as they may be, have at times tended to impose prefabricated psychological models on literary works, while ignoring specific textual details (a review of various applications of the psychoanalytic theory in literary research and examination of its achievements can be found in Skura [1981] and Felman [1982]). It seems to me that there is a fundamental difference between psychological analysis and a close reading of a text produced by an author who presumably applies a particular psychological theory to his work, using its symbols or concepts to create his fictional worlds. In the first case, in one way or another, the researcher applies a psychological theory to the text, using this theory as his tool of analysis. In the second case, the psychological theory is not the method of analysis. Rather, it becomes the subject of interpretation as it emerges through symbols and motifs along with other experiential processes and thematic implications. The psychological theory is employed in this case just as the Bible or the Talmud are used to illuminate textual allusions or concepts, disregarding the scholar's own religious belief. Therefore in this case, it is discussed irrespective of the critic's own view of it, along with a discussion of other aspects of the text (structure, rhetoric and narration, motifs).

---

and in Dorit Zilberman (1991). For a more elaborate examination of that aspect, see Chapter 5.

I originally set out to write a chronological study on the works of Amos Oz: a chapter on *Where the Jackals Howl*, a chapter on *Elsewhere, Perhaps*, and so on. After realizing the tremendous complexity of each of his works, it became clear to me that this approach would not succeed. In order to deal with Oz's work in a chronological manner and to interpret his books thoroughly, I would have been forced to write as many books as Oz himself had written. Therefore, I set out to deal with several topics that shed light on important aspects of his works. The religious element basic to these books intrigued me; I deal with this issue in Chapter 3. In the course of writing the next chapters, the importance of this element became even clearer to me. I realized that the subjects of these chapters (the sea and female characters, the element of synthesis) are to a large extent but variations of the religious issue. The halo around the female heads (Noga in *Elsewhere, Perhaps*, Rimona in *A Perfect Peace*, and others) alludes to their holiness on the one hand, while on the other it is also connected to the sea symbols (the ring and the snake eating its own tail). The unity of opposites characterizing the religious sphere is also expressed in the significance of the water: the sky and the sea were one entity before they were parted and each still preserves elements of the other. Oz's conflict-ridden protagonists seek the lost harmony, a synthesis where all the forces acting in them would live at peace with each other. Importantly, the quest for this synthesis is repeatedly described as a typical religious quest. Thus, the structure of the book is a spiral, and one central theme is dealt with. I decided to retain this structure if only to clearly illustrate the different facets of this one theme.

The short biographical chapter was written after I had completed the four major essays of the book. In the course of reading Oz's works and writing about their major theme, I became very curious about the man behind them. In this short chapter I looked for answers to satisfy this curiosity. I have known Oz from the time he came as a fourteen-year-old boy to Kibbutz Hulda where I was born. As a high school student I used to show him my poems (he had already finished his service in the army and was a student at the Hebrew University). Our acquaintance has always been a literary one: Oz was more than happy to read my poems and to suggest some changes, or to talk about newly published books. An extremely introverted person, he has never shared his private life or childhood memories with me. Thus, trying to map his formative years, I had to rely heavily on his numerous interviews and articles. There are many gaps in this information.

Often I could satisfy my curiosity only by means of intuitive guesses that were supported by experiences and motifs recurring in Oz's works, among other things. Needless to say, the possible connections between the author and his work are often merely speculative.

# 1

# BETWEEN KLAUSNER AND OZ
## A Biographical Note

In "A Note About Myself" Amos Oz wrote:

> Until his dying day, in October 1970, my father, Yehuda-Arieh Klausner, continued to deal with literary comparisons in fifteen languages. Only Fanya, my mother, could not bear her life, and in 1952 she committed suicide out of great despair and longing. Something hadn't gone right. Two years after her death, when I was fourteen, I arose and left my father's home, the good manners, and the wisdom, changed my family name from Klausner to Oz, and went to work and study at Kibbutz Hulda. I truly hoped to turn over a new leaf in my life, and not in Jerusalem. (1979a, 207)

As these lines suggest, his mother's suicide planted a seed that would later sprout and bear fruit in Oz's life. The psychological changes he experienced during the two years between his mother's suicide and his departure from home apparently dictated the direction his literary production was to take, creating the psychic tensions we find expressed there. Fourteen-year-old Amos Klausner changed his name of his own volition and initiative to "Oz" (meaning "power," "vigor"), a name containing a complex of oppositions and contradictions. How could he reconcile going to the kibbutz, which proffers a sane, moderate way of life, with such a heroic name?

## Childhood Under the Sign of the Hero Myth

Oz's works and interviews provide clues to his reasons for choosing such a name. In a candid moment during an interview held at the time of the signing of the peace treaty between Israel and Egypt, Oz said: "What did I want to be when I was a child? I wanted to be a hero, all kinds of heroes, like everyone else. But the discovery that I was not a hero was a hard one and remains so to this day" (1977a). Indeed, Oz's heroic aspirations have not faded and the myth of the hero is found throughout his writings.

Amos Klausner grew up in a world where the hero myth was part of reality.[1] The children's stories he was told concerned Jerusalem's past, the fallen Jerusalem "either in heroism or helplessness" (1979a, 210). Similarly, he found corresponding stories in elementary school: "My parents chose to send me to a Hebrew elementary school with strong religious and national tendencies, where they taught us to long for the glory of the ancient kingdoms of Israel and to aspire to restore them in blood and fire" (ibid., 206).

Moreover, daily life in Jerusalem during the 1940s invited heroic visions: "I think about it against the background of Jerusalem. The 1940s. We were children in a dramatic world: underground, bombings, arrests, curfew, searches, the British army, Arab gangs, the impending war, dread" (ibid., 195). Those visions were nurtured and fortified by the films of the epoch:

> If, in the long run, we were unperturbed and even enthusiastic, and fearless, it was in large measure because of the movies about Tarzan, Flash Gordon, and cowboys we saw constantly. For example, it was clear and self-evident that the weak would triumph—always, and unconditionally—over the strong, and that the few would overcome the many: that was the way of the world, and the opposite was simply impossible. Woe to the

---

1. Neumann, following Jung, claims that the hero myth is a necessary stage in the child's development as he matures. The ego achieves individuation through the struggle with the dragon, the unconscious (1973, the chapter "The Original Unity" and elsewhere). As an adult, Oz will replace the fight against "external" dragons with that against "inner" ones.

strong. Woe to the many. Thus all those movies fit in marvelously with the Zionist education we were given. (ibid.)

When describing his feelings at the outbreak of the Six Day War, Oz indicates the lasting impression of these movies: the actual war did not seem real to him because there was no background music accompanying the armies' movements (ibid., 199).

Oz was taught the heroic myth—the central myth of his childhood—at home, in school, and in the streets of Jerusalem. Its powerful influence is evident in his youthful poems about the heroism of the Jewish people (see Gertz 1980, 27), as well as his stories about childhood. Two of them, "Mr. Levi" and "Longings" (1976b; 1978), describe a "crazy" child, constantly immersed in dreams of redeeming Jerusalem from the British, and of discovering a secret weapon that would completely change the balance of power. The title character of *Soumchi* creates fantasies wherein he and his puppy accomplish heroic deeds:

> I pulled him and walked and walked and walked and pulled, while my spirit was borne far, far away, to the tangled forests and impenetrable jungles, where, surrounded, I made a brave and hopeless stand against a mob of shrieking cannibals, covered in war-paint and brandishing javelins and spears. Alone and weaponless, I struck out on all sides, but for every one of them I felled with my bare hands, a host of others swarmed yelling from their lair to take his place. Already my strength was beginning to fail. But then, as my enemies closed in on me with cries of joy, their white teeth gleaming, I gave one short, shrill whistle. From out of the thicket leaped my own private wolf, menacing, merciless, rending their throats with his cruel fangs until my enemies had scattered in all directions, bellowing with fear. (1978a, 45–46; 1980, 45)

This myth is found in stories other than those about childhood. A hero with great physical strength, mighty on the battlefield and in bed, appears as a central figure in several of the stories in *Where the Jackals Howl* ("Before His Time," "The Trappist Monastery," "All the Rivers") and in the novels *Elsewhere, Perhaps* and *Black Box*, among other places.[2] Many of his characters dream of personal heroism and

---

2. In the description of protagonists with great physical force, one can sometimes sense how literature is a compensation for what was denied to Oz in life. From his works it emerges that he was a weak child, completely untalented at sports and certainly not

seek to achieve it in a devious fashion (Gideon Shenhav in "The Way of the Wind," Nahum Hirsch in "The Trappist Monastery"). Other characters seek a solution to the problem of the Jews through the development of sophisticated weaponry ("Late Love," *A Perfect Peace*, and elsewhere). Dr. Emmanuel, one of the saner figures in "Longings," mocks those who expect him to find a formula for "a mighty explosive" (1976b, 119; 1978, 139). He continues his "modest" experiments to find such a formula, however, and gradually becomes convinced that he will succeed.

At the age of fourteen, two years after his mother's suicide, and two years after writing enthusiastic poems of heroism, Amos Klausner turned his back on the world of his childhood. His transfer from a religious school to a secular one, and from the right-wing Beitar youth movement to the Scouts (where his group leader was none other than A. B. Yehoshua), prepared him for that transition. Oz reveals little about himself directly, particularly regarding those tormented years after the death of his mother. How did his mother's suicide affect him? How did it affect his attitude toward everything he had absorbed and received from his parents? From his stories and articles it appears that his mother was a romantic figure, who because of her longings for what was distant in time and space, rejected the here and now. Apparently, his mother's suicide led the young Klausner to conclude that romantic dreams, whether in their political, Revisionist guise, or in personal form, meant just one thing: destruction and doom.[3] Consequently, to survive he had to choose a sane and realistic way of life, and thus, he revolted against everything his parents had stood for. First, he left behind the name Klausner, a name with a rich Zionist and cultural past, and second, he chose a way of life antithetical to that of his parents. Years afterward, in describing his attitude toward Ben-Gurion, he recounted:

> On the one hand stood everything I learned in Hulda, to which I had fled from Revisionism: that it was preferable to trust

---

fit for heroism on the battlefield (see *My Michael*, "The Hill of Evil Counsel," and *A Perfect Peace*, all of which have a strong autobiographical element). Of course Oz's relation to those heroes remains ambivalent. They stem from the root of his yearnings and wishes, but their society is not his, their sensitivities are not his, and their language is not his. He describes them with a mixture of admiration and esteem on the one hand, and mockery and criticism on the other. As Oz said in reference to the films of his childhood: "It's a broken myth, the breaking of which cost me great anger, irony and longings" (1979a, 199).

3. That subject is covered well by Gertz (1980).

reason rather than the instincts. Yet, on the other, it was impossible to attenuate the struggle within me between the exalting, seductive, and overwhelming—and the good. The good was prosaic, even narrow-minded, and evil was colorful and gripping. Though one's relationship towards that evil was liable to be that of the moth to the flame. If the moth is wise, he looks ahead, from a distance, and, as stirring as the flame may be, he has to fill his little mouth with a droplet of water and douse it instead of racing forward and getting burned up, for fire is not for us. (Gertz 1980, 28)

In the most elaborate interview he has given in recent years, Oz talked about the need to be resigned to the idea that he will always live with "the spell of blood and fire," "the spell of death," "the spell of something bigger than life in which you can melt completely" (1989b, 164–65). He added: "I will always see this spell, and always from afar. One should not come close to it." Describing this attraction to blood and death as a disease, he remarked: "Apparently, all my life I have been attracted to the Crusades, to blood and snow, to the big gestes of throwing away one's life. Apparently, these are my Revisionistic genes. And as long as I have the power, I'll resist it and denounce it, and I'll fight against it in the political arena, and depict it in stories" (ibid.).

## A Double Agent

Here the contradictions begin. To abandon the hero myth, Klausner rebelled against his home and his father—an act typical of heroes. Doubtless, Oz was aware of this contradiction, having read fables and mythical tales throughout his childhood, some of which were interpreted by his father.[4] Moreover, while apparently abandoning the heroic myth, young Klausner adopted the name Oz, a name synonymous with heroism. This choice reveals much about Oz's contradictory world. His revolt, though it appeared total, was actually only partial. The change of name clearly signifies the setting aside of his father, his norms and beliefs; however, the new name preserved a central element of his parent's world and of Oz's childhood. Oz did not leave these

---

4. On the literary work of his father, Yehuda-Arieh Klausner, see Oz's article, "An Introduction to My Father's Collected Works" (1979a, 201–4).

childhood myths behind him, but became what he frequently refers to as a foreign agent:

> I have been here in Hulda since the age of fourteen. But that is quite an adult age, the patterns were already laid down. I come from an old Revisionist family, and I think that that sharp transition permits me to be a "foreign agent" both in Hulda and Jerusalem. (1968b)
>
> If I am a foreign agent, I am one that was planted here years ago, and my connections with the foreign power from which I come, and for the moment I don't wish to call it by name, or to describe it, are no less complex than my ties to the power I was trained for, where I was sent to act. (1980)[5]

The agent, foreign both in Jerusalem and in Hulda, is in fact a double agent.[6] This spiritual position requires a dual relationship with both of the powers employing the agent, resulting in a tug of war that manifests contradictory feelings: the need for closeness and belonging, on the one hand, and bitter criticism on the other. In his stories and novels, Oz time and again depicts a dualistic world in which light and darkness or nature and culture struggle with each other. However, the forces at war have two faces—awesome and enchanting, brilliant and somber. Like the witches in *Macbeth*, Oz's protagonists might say: "Fair is foul, and foul is fair." Because of the double agent's divided soul, Oz cannot speak directly or unequivocally. Thus, ambivalence and irony become important stylistic elements of his works, as well as essential components of his fictional world. A central theme of Oz's stories and novels is the search for harmony between opposing sides, a continuous effort to find some synthesis between the agent's two employers.[7]

As a double agent, Oz will recoil from all those who advocate radical views, from all those who believe in absolute truths, and certainly from those who attempt to impose them upon others:

---

5. In *Elsewhere, Perhaps* Zechariah-Siegfried Berger introduces himself as a "spy sent by an enemy power" (1966a, 271).

6. In reaction to my remarks on the cunning of the narrator in this novel, Oz wrote to me: "True, the narrator in *Elsewhere, Perhaps* is almost like a 'mole,' a secret agent planted deep, and at the same time, like U.S. Ambassador Lewis in Tel Aviv, enamored in his own way with the soil in which he was planted. So in a sense he's a double agent" (letter of June 15, 1984).

7. This element has not received sufficient attention from Oz's critics, who tend to emphasize the split and conflicting nature of his world. A detailed discussion of that subject appears in Chapter 5.

> For a few years I worked a little in the kibbutz fields and I studied in a free, socialist classroom, where we sat barefoot all day long and learned about the source of human evil, the corruption of society, the sources of Jewish pathology, and how to overcome them all through labor, a simple life, cooperation, equality, and the gradual improvement of human nature. To this day I accept those views, although sometimes with a certain sadness, and sometimes with a slight smile. In the name of those views I still reject all radical doctrine, whether within socialism, Zionism, or current political life in Israel. (1979a, 207)

Describing Palestinian and Zionist fanatics he writes: "The heroes of tragedies, men consumed with desire for justice and purity, destroy and ravage each other unto death with the force of consistency, like fire compressed within their bones. Those who seek round, complete justice actually desire death, not life" (1979a, 84). In an interview held at the time *Soumchi* was published, Oz related his career as a writer to that complex situation:

> I have also changed positions in my own life. . . . But the truth is that in that argument between the child Soumchi and the engineer, Inbar, I don't want to take any clearly defined position and say that one or the other is right. Both of them are right. Soumchi speaks in the name of the absolute world, where there need be no compromise or concession—nor can there be. The engineer, Inbar, speaks of a relative world, and he cannot do otherwise. (1978b)

He goes on to say: "If I could simply be for or against things, I wouldn't write stories; I would write posters and campaign slogans, maybe I would enter the political arena and do battle against all comers" (ibid.). This approach is typical of Oz's articles in which he rejects polarized stands, seeking to effect a compromise between them.[8] It led him to

---

8. With regard to this notion, the Order of the Day written by Oz for General Israel Tal is exceptional. It was distributed to the soldiers of General Tal's regiment at the beginning of the Six Day War:
    SOLDIERS OF THE "REGIMENT OF STEEL"!!
  The sign has been given.
  Today we go forth to smash the hand that has reached out to throttle us. Today we go forth to throw open the southern gate, which was sealed by the Egyptian aggressor.
  Our armor will carry the war to the depths of the enemy's territory. We did

support skeptical leaders who do not "hear voices" and who are not absolutely certain they know what they have to do: Levi Eshkol and not David Ben-Gurion, for example.[9] The eulogy he wrote for his friend Monia Mendel is characteristic of his attitude:

> not seek this battle. The enemy desired it. The enemy began it. The enemy will get his full share of it.
> Remember:
> • This is the third time the Egyptian dagger has been brandished at us. This is the third time the enemy has given himself over to a mad illusion: the hope of seeing Israel prostrate.
> *With blood, with fire, and with steel we shall once more uproot that malice from his heart.*
> Also remember:
> • We are not at war with Egyptian civilians. We do not covet their land or their property. We have not come to destroy their land or expropriate it.
> • We drive forward to crush the concentrations of the enemy which were intended to threaten our well-being.
> • We drive forward to tear the gates of the Egyptian blockade from their hinges.
> • We drive forward utterly to destroy the evil desire to destroy us.
> "And the Earth shall tremble beneath it."
> (Quoted from the original Order of the Day, preserved in Oz's archives in Arad)

No, here we have no ironic reconciliation and compromise, but a war cry, the release of repressed desires. Notwithstanding, there is a clear expression of the author's declared political views in the Order (the section beginning "We are not at war with Egyptian civilians").

9. For an explanation of Oz's political preferences from a different point of view, see Gertz (1980, 29). Of course those preferences result from an incessant inner struggle, demonstrated by the tension between Oz's linguistic preferences in social and political life and the style of his writing. In explaining his affinity for Yitzhak Rabin (Israel Chief of Staff during the Six Day War, later Minister of Defense and Prime Minister), Oz wrote:

> Once, many years ago, before the outbreak of the Six Day War, I was shown a secret mimeographed document in which was written, among other things: "There are enormous concentrations of Egyptian military forces in eastern Sinai." Someone had crossed out the word "enormous" and written above it, "very large." I, as though stung by an adder, scurried about and investigated. I could not rest till I discovered whose handwriting that was. It turned out, of course, that it was the Chief of Staff, Yitzhak Rabin, who had done the crossing out and the writing in. Since that day I have been fond of him. (1979a, 29)

That preference for restrained diction is in open conflict with the hyperbolic style of the Order of the Day that Oz wrote at the same time (n. 8). The tension between Rabin's style and Oz's can also be found in a change Oz made in his story, "Before His Time." In the original version Oz speaks of the "big searchlights" placed by the enemy to prevent Ehud's comrades from removing his body from no man's land (1965a, 63). But

I saw him as a sober social democrat, and many of the ideas in which he believed, the ideas of the kibbutz, of the labor movement, of humanistic socialism, of clear-sighted Zionism, passed through the filter of his soul and emerged without any fringes of hatred or fanaticism. Perhaps because he always harbored deep doubt as to the urges of the human heart and its weaknesses. He would translate ideals and ideas into his Galician language, and that translation emerged in moderate, ironic, skeptical form, far indeed from slogans, constantly taking account of the "perhaps," the "in spite of," and the "now." (1974, 187)

Describing the hidden civil war within the history of the Zionist movement, between Russian and Polish trends, Oz frequently refers to the Galician middle ground: "If I were to be asked where I stand in that hidden civil war: my heart would respond with that minor melody sung by the Galicians here, on condition that one extends the borders of Galicia not only from Buber to Agnon, but also from Artur Rupin to Eshkol, Lavon, and Aran" (1979b, 6). The complexity of Oz's world is manifested, among other things, by the fact that most of his protagonists reject that "Galician" compromise and are drawn to the absolute, darkness, and death. Moreover, in many cases Oz attacks in his political articles attitudes that typify his own protagonists. Thus, for example, in an article published in 1987, he argues that between the War of Independence and the Six Day War many Jews in Jerusalem longed for pre-1948 Jerusalem, then under British mandate. He describes the elements of this feeling in great detail: "The rustle of the pine trees, the mist around the towers on the crest of the hills, the sound of the churches' bells . . . the dark alleys, the slopes of olives and rocks" (1987c, 9). In this article he mocks this nostalgia and its clichés as they appear in literature. And yet, which writer has given this kind of nostalgia its most powerful literary expression if not Oz himself, in *My Michael* and elsewhere? By the same token, when he attacks religious fanatics in his articles, one could sense at one and the same time Oz's deep fascination with them. Thus, Oz's work is a spellbinding example of a person's attempt to shape himself according to convictions and beliefs reached as an adult; at one and the same

---

in the second version, those "big" searchlights became "tremendous" (1976a, 69; 1981, 21). However, that change is not typical of the many differences between the two versions of *Where the Jackals Howl*.

time his prose manifests the failure of such an undertaking. This issue is further elaborated in the introduction to Chapter 5.

As noted, choosing a heroic surname such as "Oz" demonstrates that Oz's rebellion against his father was only partial. This choice also suggests that latent motivations, rather than conscious "official" ones, were behind his move to the kibbutz. Thus Oz says of Hannah Gonen, the female protagonist of *My Michael*:

> True, Hannah wished to belong to a great hero, Michael Strogoff, to a world-shaker, but on the other hand she also wanted to belong to a stable, solid scholar. That's what she wanted, and that's what she got. . . . She needed Michael's protective hand to provide a solid launching pad for all of the dream-rockets she sent out into space. . . . Perhaps she was going downstairs, and then she tripped, and perhaps she knew what she was doing. Perhaps the fact that she married Michael gives her room and freedom to be both protected and wild at the same time. (1974)

Was Hulda, too, meant to be a kind of "launching pad for dream-rockets"? It seems that Oz never completely gave up his childhood dreams of heroism, the desire to be a world-conqueror, a discoverer, longing, like Soumchi, for the source of the Nile or the Zambezi; but at an early age he impeded his own progress along this adventuresome path. It is difficult to determine when that decision became a conscious one, but there is no doubt that in the course of his high school studies, after he was exposed to the ideas of Schopenhauer and Nietszche and the concepts of Freud and Jung, Oz resolved to maintain his main Jerusalemite childhood dreams: to be a writer and a "hero" (a discoverer of new continents, a conqueror). This combination of writer and hero is a typical expression of the double-agent situation. It meant that Oz retained his childhood ambitions while changing the arena in which the struggle would take place. First, the hero's feats would not take place in the outside world but in stories and novels. These stories and novels would convey, on the one hand, romantic dreams about death and heroism, about "another place" (this is the literal translation of the Hebrew title of Oz's first novel), and, on the other hand, they would criticize these dreams and preach for the acceptance of the here and now. In other words, retaining his childhood dreams, Oz would be able to have the cake and eat it too. Another aspect of this situation is the tension between Oz's fiction and non-fiction writings. Second, in his writings Oz would travel to "lands where white man has not trod," as the saying goes, yet the journey would not take place in the jungles of Africa; most frequently it would be an inner or a psychic journey.[10] The heroism of his characters would not be expressed in actual journeys, but in the discovery of deep worlds of darkness, which would seduce them with magic and dread and where they would fight in solitary combat against the dragons hidden there. The role of this topic in Oz's work will be dealt with in the coming chapters.

Another reason for the journey would be the "treasure hunt," the search for inner wholeness (for a detailed discussion of the treasure hunt, see Chapter 3). Oz stresses the similarity between the inner voyage and the outer one in an interview held upon the publication of *Soumchi*. In response to a question about Soumchi's yearnings for the Zambezi River, the Himalayas, and other unexplored places, the author states:

> Those are traces of what I might call "holy places," and when I was a boy those places were holy sites not only because of Nahum Gutman's books, but also because of a thousand other books, because of the maps hanging in the classroom at school, because of the movies we saw, because of the dark, strange world we wanted to discover, we wanted to lay it bare, because it was a world where people obtain glory and lose their lives. That's the game. The boy in the story, Soumchi, sets out to discover the world. He goes toward distant places and reaches slightly less distant ones, *but he really does discover a little of the world.* (1978b; italics mine)

He goes on to say:

> The point is that I'm talking about yearnings, about exotic places. And Soumchi gets to fantastically exotic places. Maybe

---

10. In answer to a question as to what distinguishes the novella "Crusade" from his other works, Oz states that all of his stories are tales of journeys:

"Crusade" is not different. No, I take that back. I'm not saying this in pride now, or regretfully. People go and look for complete harmony or redemption, or for saving the world or some joy that doesn't belong to this world or for some liberation; they go and seek that liberation somewhere else, or at least they dream of looking for it somewhere completely different from the place where they are. A few of them take their journeys on horses and kill Jews on the way; others make those journeys in visions, and they recline upon evenings of visions along the way. All of them, more or less, discover, in the end, that that aspiration to get out of their skin by means of a journey is based on an error. (1978c)

> not exactly to the Zambezi, but he gets to a house like nothing he's ever seen, and he gets into a confrontation, a struggle, a war such as he had never before experienced. He loses what he had never lost before and finds what few people have ever found, even older and wiser people. Thus, ultimately, he actually does take a *very long voyage in this story, from the beginning to the end.* (ibid., italics mine)

Later in the interview Oz clarifies the relationship between inner reality and external reality:

> I do not agree that this work is some kind of new leaf. I wrote stories about life and this story is about life too. Whether we go up in a plane and travel, let's say, to Newfoundland or New Caledonia, or make that journey in the evening, by ourselves, at our window, in the autumn, it's still the same thing. I know, in one case you buy a ticket, in the other you don't. There are all sorts of technical details. But it's still the same thing. (ibid.)

Evidently Oz, too, transfers the desire for a remote and strange world from the arena of external events to the inner world. He would seek fame not as a discoverer of lost continents but as a writer, yet as a writer who delves into the regions of the psyche's dark side.

The "double agent" situation is responsible to a large extent for the intricacy of Oz's prose. The tension between the author's Apollonian and Dionysian tendencies has paved the way for a literary text in which every statement that is explicitly embraced by the narrator is implicitly negated by the implied author. Moreover, in several of his works the narrator's point of view quickly changes. Thus, for example, in the opening chapters of *Elsewhere, Perhaps* the narrator is presented as a kibbutz member who espouses the kibbutz ideology and its struggle against the Arabs and the jackals. Yet later in the novel he depicts himself as one of the jackals (1966a, 279). Thus the reader cannot identify the narrator's set of norms nor can he rely on his evaluative statements. This issue is further elaborated in the next chapter.

## "They Say There Is Love in the World"

The traumatic response to his mother's suicide is apparent in "The Hill of Evil Counsel," one of Oz's most autobiographical stories. At the climax of the story the mother of the boy-narrator escapes with an English officer, an escape implicitly compared to death. In response, the child tries to end his own life (1976b, 35; 1978, 59). A fascination with death characterizes many of Oz's protagonists (*Elsewhere, Perhaps, A Perfect Peace, Black Box*, and elsewhere). In fact, one of the tensions in Oz's work lies in the fact that many of his characters experience life as a flat, deathlike existence, whereas death is thought of as a lively, seductive situation, or at least as a restful, peaceful condition.

It seems that his mother's untimely death will have a long-lasting effect on Oz's world. Oz's stories of childhood and his autobiographical essays depict his mother as a charming yet capricious and irrational figure. Her suicide, at an age critical for the formation of relations between the sexes, prevented Oz from coming to terms with her world. His mother's world will remain inaccessible to him, a source of both infinite fascination and obscure dread. His work clearly manifests this notion: first, as we shall see in Chapter 2, the tension between yearnings for the all-embracing womb on the one hand, and the fear from this deadly embrace on the other, establishes one of Oz's main themes. All of his female characters are clearly "anima" figures, dragonlike representations of the Great Mother who are intimately bound up with the frightening world of nature and darkness; for example, all of them are connected to the sea, the life-giving womb and the grave (see Chapter 4).[11] It is not by chance that the moon, a common symbol of the Great Mother, appears on the cover of *Where the Jackals Howl* (1965a) and *A Perfect Peace* (1982; 1985), and it is not by chance that Yonatan Lifshitz shoots at the moon at the high point of *A Perfect Peace* (see Chapter 3). Second, the men in his fiction feel horror and fascination when facing women, and are unable to create a relationship based on equality and mutual sharing. In *Black Box* Manfred Zakheim writes to Michel Sommo about Ilana's new contacts with her ex-husband, and shares with him this observation: "Women, my dear Michel, are in my humble opinion very much like us in certain respects, but in others they are astonishingly different" (1987a, 99; 1988, 107). The protagonist's father repeats almost the same phrasing in *The Third Condition*, Oz's latest novel to date (1991, 125).[12] We also find this theme expressed in Oz's protagonists who have difficulty

---

11. Jung discusses the subject of the anima in all of his works (detailed discussions of the topic are found in Jung 1956, 1959a.)

12. In an interview, Oz said that he had heard the same observation from his ninety-five-year-old grandfather (1989b, 156).

falling in love. Some of the protagonists wonder what love is. "I still haven't understood love. I'm sure I won't get to know it now," writes Srulik in his diary, in the final passage of *A Perfect Peace* (381). The inability of others to love is indirectly conveyed by the way they become aware of their "love": "When they were alone, he [Professor Wertheimer] warned Father obliquely not to complicate his private life unnecessarily. And it was precisely these words that brought Father to inner certainty that finally love had happened to him" (1976b, 21; 1978, 22). It is no coincidence that several of Oz's main characters are "confirmed bachelors" (Dr. Kleinberger in "Strange Fire," Segal in *Elsewhere, Perhaps*, Srulik in *A Perfect Peace*, among others). Indeed, in *The Third Condition* the protagonist dreams of establishing a "commune" for men only (1991, 223).

## *Hulda: Double Parenthood, Jackals, and Arabs*

Amos Oz reached Kibbutz Hulda at the age of fourteen. Decades later, upon reading *A Perfect Peace*, his classmates on the kibbutz would remember his tireless efforts to impress them and make himself well-liked. The novel tells the story of Azariah Gitlin coming to the kibbutz, a strange outsider who wants to win the love of the kibbutz members immediately. The age of fourteen becomes a determining one in several of Oz's works. Jephthah the Gileadite starts seeing signs when he is fourteen ("Upon This Evil Earth"), Michael has not been ill since he was fourteen (*My Michael*), and the young poet, Ido, is also fourteen (*Elsewhere, Perhaps*).

In Hulda, Oz was adopted by the family of Ozer Hulda'yi, the principal of the local school and one of the central figures of the kibbutz. For Oz that adoption was in direct correlation to the stories of his childhood: did not all of the heroes have two sets of parents? Was not double parenthood one of the most common identifying marks of the hero?[13] Double parenthood will become a typical characteristic of many of his protagonists ("Where the Jackals Howl," "Strange Fire," "Upon This Evil Earth," "The Way of the Wind," *Elsewhere, Perhaps, A Perfect Peace, Black Box, The Third Condition,* and others), and it is linked to the central topics of his stories: the duality of human existence, the inseparable sanctity and sin that characterize it, and

---

13. On this subject, see Rank (1959) and Neumann (1973).

the desire to break out of the social framework with its stultifying taboos.[14]

The layout of Kibbutz Hulda (the dining room, the swimming pool, the cultural center, the youth group buildings, the barns, and the rest), the fields around it (the vines spreading out beneath the "hills to the east," the orchard to the west of the kibbutz, behind which were the railroad tracks), provided the model for descriptions of the kibbutz in many of Oz's works. It should also be remembered that before the Six Day War the Jordanian border was but a few kilometers from Hulda, and Arab terrorists infiltrated the kibbutz only days before the Sinai Campaign, blowing up one of its buildings. The enemy who sits "on the hills to the east" (*Elsewhere, Perhaps*, for example) was a real presence in Hulda during the 1950s. The Arabs who had terrified Amos Klausner had the same effect on Amos Oz. Hulda was not, then, a well-protected, tranquil place of refuge. Gertz writes of the transition from Jerusalem to Hulda:

> The private history of Amos Oz revolves around two geographical axes: Jerusalem and Hulda. . . . Those two geographical areas became two regions in the child's consciousness, and later in that of the adult. The house in Jerusalem was a memory of everything that was whole, beautiful, full of enchantment, but also of something that ended in disaster. The world of the kibbutz, in contrast, was one which had to be retained at any price, for there was nowhere else. (1980, 25)

Gertz's argument that these two geographical areas came to represent two separate regions in Oz's consciousness is a difficult one to accept. Even if we had not read modern psychology, which emphasizes the importance of the early childhood years, or if we had not read Oz's comments on having reached the kibbutz at a relatively advanced age when "the patterns were already laid down," we would still find that claim hard to accept. In Oz's autobiographical notes and from his stories of childhood, the house in Jerusalem does not appear as "a memory of everything that was whole, beautiful, full of enchantment." He describes the world of Jerusalem as threatening and full of unstable elements. This instability manifested itself in his inner world where opposing forces vied with each other, in a home dominated by a

---

14. This subject, which has not been mentioned by any of Oz's critics, is worthy of separate discussion. Some of the topics connected with it are discussed in Chapter 5.

mother who was not at peace with herself or those around her, and culminated in the constant threat posed by the Arabs:

> I was born in Jerusalem. I lived there during my childhood. When I was nine I underwent the siege and bombardment of Jerusalem. It was then that I saw a dead man for the first time. . . . For many years I hated that man because he used to come back and frighten me at night in my dreams. I knew that Jerusalem was surrounded by powers that desired my death. (1979a, 209)

Later in that piece about the city of his birth Oz writes:

> A ring of hostile villages surrounded the city on three sides: Shuafat, Wadi Joz, Aisawiya, Silwan, Azariya, Tsur-Bahar, and Beit-Sefafa. It seemed that they had only to close their fists and the city would be crushed. At night during the winter it was possible to feel how a kind of malicious intention flowed from there to here. . . . From over there, on the other side of the ceasefire line, a kind of angry threat was directed at me throughout most of my life: "Wait, wait, we aren't done yet, we'll get you." (ibid., 210–11)

Life in Hulda was far from a complete contrast to that of Jerusalem, but in large measure, an extension of it. Oz's adoptive parents were a sharply drawn variation on the figure of his parents, and among his classmates there were not many with whom he could feel comfortable (his class was composed of very few children born on the kibbutz; most of them were refugee children from Europe, children who had experienced hard knocks and could give them out as well).

I am trying to recall Kibbutz Hulda in 1954 when Amos Oz arrived: it was cut off from the nearby settlements, and beyond the faint glow of the lights on the fence, after nightfall, there was total darkness. In the kibbutz itself the darkness was thick, attenuated only by the lights of the dining room and the children's houses. When night fell, the air was full of the howling of jackals, prolonged howling ceasing for a moment only to start again, howls heard both far away and very close, as if voiced from within the kibbutz. In time, Oz was to use that image as a metaphor for the structure of the human soul, an illuminated area in the center surrounded by deep and threatening darkness ("Where the Jackals Howl," "Before His Time," and others).

Doubtless, the "angry threat" that Oz had felt in Jerusalem he also experienced in Hulda; the jackals surrounding the kibbutz and the nearby Jordanian border posed such a threat. No, Jerusalem and Hulda did not become two separate areas of consciousness. They were rather grafted upon each other in a kind of spiritual double exposure, as when a photographer forgets to advance the film between pictures. Consequently, Oz would attribute a religious attitude similar to the one he had grown up with to the members of the kibbutz (see Chapter 3), and the Arabs and jackals would come to represent a single threatening entity (*Where the Jackals Howl* and *Elsewhere, Perhaps,* for example).

The key to Oz's world is not in the contrast between Jerusalem and Hulda, for his existence in both places was characterized by inner division and oppositions. A better key is hinted at by Oz's ambivalence toward the Arabs. Along with the maliciousness that he had feared from the ring of hostile villages surrounding Jerusalem, and the angry threat of Arab Jerusalem, we find the following observation: "Across the way, for all those years, was the other Jerusalem, the city that surrounded mine: from which strange voices flowed to us, guttural sounds, and fragrances, the pale lights glimmering at night, and the frightening cry of the muezzin at dawn. One might say: Atlantis, a lost continent" (1979a, 211). Strangely, Arab Jerusalem, with its angry countenance, its threatening "Wait, wait, we'll get you yet," is, at the same time, Atlantis, a lost continent, a focus of yearnings and hidden longings. This ambivalence—one of the cornerstones of Oz's world—also emerges in his view of the unconscious (a source of both destruction and health), and in his protagonists' attraction to jackals and death.[15] In this schema, the Arab represents that which is primal and natural—destructive and fecund simultaneously (*Elsewhere, Perhaps, A Perfect Peace,* and elsewhere). When Oz discovered in his early twenties that the struggles common to external reality (the kibbutz and its tensions, the Arab-Israeli conflict) were parallel to those within himself, his worldview was complete.

## *Schopenhauer, Nietzsche, and Jung*

At the kibbutz Oz proved to be a brilliant student with strong conceptual and analytical abilities, which led his teachers to treat him as a

---

15. That ambivalent relationship finds a natural extension in the situation of the double agent (see above).

colleague. From his youth he aspired to be a writer: Dov Sadan reports that he found a typed sign on the six-year-old boy's door, stating: "Amos Klausner, Author" (Oz, 1968b). He wrote poems and stories in his early elementary school years, and he was a voracious reader (ibid.). In Hulda a new element was added to his intense reading: Fridays were devoted to three subjects: philosophy, psychology, and sociology.[16] He was stimulated by his encounter with German romantic philosophy and with the theories of Freud and Jung.[17] Jung's ideas were especially influential because Oz's desire to be a writer, a redeemer, had been in conflict with other desires and instincts since his elementary school days. In Oz's stories of childhood his protagonists feel shameful desires that they deny:

> "Stop showing off. You have no secret except the same as all the other boys that come and want me to touch them and feel it. . . ." "You're no different," said Bat-Ami sadly, "you're just the same as the others. Just take a look at yourself, you're shaking like a leaf. You're a boy, Kolodny, and you're just the same as all the other boys and you want the same thing as them only you're too scared to say so. Look, you've even got pimples on your face. What's the matter, why are you running away? What's wrong? What are you running away for, what have I said? You're nuts." (1976b, 82–83; 1978, 94–95)

Oz found distant brothers in Schopenhauer and Nietzsche, who mock the pride of consciousness, describing it as a mere crust that has solidified upon the seething mass of natural instincts and primal urges.[18] His encounter with the psychological doctrines of Jung gave him a complete model of the strange drives and forces vying within him. In the first place, Jung did not condemn the primary urges of the

---

16. On Fridays a special teacher would come to the kibbutz from Tel Aviv to teach those subjects. Generations of students at the Hulda High School retain fond memories of that teacher, Yehezkel (no one seems to remember his family name).

17. Among the popular textbooks were those of Will Durant, *The Story of Philosophy* (translated into Hebrew, 1953), and that of Nissan Turov, *Contemporary Psychology* (Hebrew, 1939). Durant's book contains detailed chapters on the doctrines of Spinoza, Schopenhauer, and Nietzsche; Turov's book presents a summary of Freudian and Jungian psychology. Oz's excellent mastery of English enabled him to expand his knowledge in areas that aroused his interest.

18. Both of them were highly influential in shaping Oz's worldview. An important element of Nietzsche's struggle with Schopenhauer appears in Oz's books. It is not a coincidence that Oz felt a "genetic affinity" with Berdyczewski (1979a, 30) whose strong affinity with Nietzsche is well known.

heart, the shadow side of the soul. On the contrary, he emphasized the vitality, intelligence, and creativity embedded in the unconscious. Moreover, in his view, a person cannot achieve wholeness or individuation without being reconciled with the primal forces latent within him (this topic is discussed at greater length in the following chapters).

Oz, feeling himself rent asunder by contradictory forces, torn between his Apollonian and Dionysian sides, found a redemptive message in Jung's doctrine: rather than making war against one's urges and drives, one must seek them out and come to terms with them. Other possible reasons for Oz's affinity with Jung are discussed in Chapters 2 and 3. Oz accepted Jung's views regarding the structure of the human soul, the processes of its development, and his symbols.[19] Oz's works depict the central psychic processes described by Jung, and consistently include symbols from Jung's repertory. Notably, however, he does not ignore Freud (see the discussion of *Elsewhere, Perhaps*, in Chapter 5).

Oz's worldview reached maturity when he discovered a relationship between the ideas of Schopenhauer, Nietzsche, and Jung.[20] The process of finding individuation will be the axis of his first story, "A Crack Open to the Wind" (1961b): the protagonist travels to Tel Aviv seeking assistance from an influential relative to mend a crack in the wall of his house. Upon his return to the kibbutz at night, he meets a wet jackal puppy, holds him up against his chest, and lays him down to sleep under the steps of his house. Having become reconciled to the jackal within him, he closes up the crack in his wall with his own hands, certain that in the future he will be able to preserve the wholeness of his home. Seeking and recognizing the jackals in one's soul and becoming reconciled with them becomes a central thematic structure in most of Oz's works.

---

19. One might surmise that his father's literary work prepared Oz psychologically for Jung's concepts. From Oz's descriptions it emerges that his father's research was decidedly Jungian in character:
> Every night, by the light of a table lamp in a remote corner of the apartment, he would sit till dawn, investigating and describing the flow of myths, motifs, heroes, and ideas from tribe to tribe, from language to language in antiquity. The second volume of his studies, *The Middle Ages*, appeared in 1952, and it too concentrated on revealing the links and transitions, which were sometimes hidden and indirect, from both remote and nearby cultures and literatures: the trickling down of legends, figures, fears, and hopes, changing costume and "wandering" in disguise from literature to literature. (1979a, 203)

20. On the role of Spinoza and Schelling in the development of Oz's religious views, see Chapter 3.

As noted, the kibbutz was well suited to the childhood patterns Oz brought to it. At the time he was coming of age, Israel too, regretfully, fit that pattern. The "shadow" and the "enemy," to use Jungian terms, were constantly evident in the image of the prolonged conflict between Israel and the Arab states and the perpetual cycle of wars. That reality has provided, among other things, a fine alibi for the death wish characterizing quite a few of Oz's characters (as in, for example, *Elsewhere, Perhaps* and *A Perfect Peace*). It also established a parallel between Oz's inner conflicts and his external reality—a parallel that appears throughout his works.

The affinity between Oz's inner world and Israeli society has another important characteristic. When Oz moved to the kibbutz, attempting to turn his back on his father's home, Oz made himself a reflection of the Kulturkampf that had been raging in Israel for the past decades. The forces at odds with each other in his experiential world—romantic Revisionism and "enlightened," "sane" socialism—are also the primary forces trying to capture the allegiance of Israeli society. In his political essays Oz repeatedly attacks "Messianic yearnings" and "Messianic madness" of right-wing parties, yet this messianic fervor is well known to him from his own childhood and his own yearnings. In turning to the kibbutz, Oz made himself, unconsciously, a faithful mirror of Israeli society, tormented by the struggle for identity. The parallels between the structure of Oz's personality and that of Israeli society contributed to his great popularity in Israel, making him the most widely read Israeli author during the past three decades.[21] Of course, his uncommon literary talents also played a role in that success.

---

21. A description of that parallel from a different point of departure can be found in Gertz (1980, 29).

# A MEMORY
## Man Toward Man a Fearful Porcupine

I had intended to spend the year granted me upon receiving the Prime Minister's Award for Creativity writing about Amos Oz's work. For many years I had not particularly liked his books. During the year 1982, at the Kibbutz Movement Teacher's Seminar in Tel Aviv, I taught his stories and two of them—"Before His Time" and "A Hollow Stone"—suddenly revealed to me that the mannerist style and the traditional, worn-out oppositions between light and darkness, culture and nature, hid a much more complex and intricate experiential world. Consequently, I decided to devote my sabbatical year to satisfying the great curiosity that this work had created in me.

Prior to my departure for Boston, in the summer of 1983, I had several questions I wished to ask Oz. In our many conversations, we had never discussed his work. En route to the kibbutz of my childhood, a few days before flying to Boston, I wondered whether this time he would be willing to deviate from his habit.

Seemingly at ease, we sit on the swinging lounge chair that stands in Oz's well-tended garden. It is a gloriously beautiful dusk hour. The air is a darkening blue and a band of birds is heralding the approach of evening from a nearby tree. In the distance are the kibbutz vineyards, the olive orchard, and the tall row of palms leading to the forest. Suddenly my childhood closes in on me (I know every tree, every path in the landscape spread before us as a child knows his own bedroom), and my heart aches with longing. In the falling darkness Oz is also wrapped in his thoughts. Nili, his wife, serves a bowl of grapes. Seemingly eating, we are two darkening lumps. The questions I had wanted to ask now seem superfluous. Here, touch it, this is what there is: falling darkness, shrieks of a distant train, a row of palms, a heart punctured by longing, and man toward man—a fearful porcupine, desperate.

Exchanging parting words, we both know that something was not said, will not be said.

# 2

# INTRODUCTION TO OZ
## The Early Stories

Amos Oz's first book, *Artsot haTan* (*Where the Jackals Howl*, literally "The Lands of the Jackal" [1965]), consists of nine stories written between 1962 and 1965. The earliest of these stories, "Before His Time" (1962b), was preceded by two others, "A Crack Open to the Wind" (1961b) and "Purple Coast" (1962a), which were not included in the later collection.[1] An analysis of these two early stories and the transition to "Before His Time" reveals the consolidation of Oz's literary concepts. Clearly, in "Before His Time" Oz created a fictional model that satisfied his various needs and to which he has remained loyal through most of his literary career. This model includes the main drives and the main concerns of the protagonists, the complex of symbols serving them, and the multilevel structure that parallels all areas of human experience (psychic processes as well as familial and sociopolitical ones).

## "A Crack Open to the Wind"

In his first article for the daily press in which he attacked David Ben-Gurion's interpretation of the kibbutz and its values, Oz defended the

---

1. These stories are reprinted in the appendix of the Hebrew edition of this study (1986). The following references are to that edition.

"unnaturalness" of kibbutz values: "The essence of man, the deepest content of his human existence, is the struggle against nature, and not adaptation and submission to the laws of nature" (1961a). After discussing the external aspect of that war, the domination of the forces of nature and applying them to human uses, he added: "There is another level in that struggle, a latent and inner struggle, but one which is no less heroic than the outer one. That is man's war with his own nature, with his urges and instincts, the beast within him, that which is 'natural' in his soul." This internal war, which threatens to rip the individual apart, and the effort to bring the two warring sides to a peaceful coexistence will later prove central in Oz's works. In fact, his first story, "A Crack Open to the Wind," written at the time the aforementioned article was published, takes up that struggle.

The narrator of "A Crack Open to the Wind" is a kibbutz member; a large crack has opened in the wall of his room, and the story revolves around his attempts to have it repaired. First, he addresses Tishbi Eliahu, the kibbutz builder, who demands the authorization of the Secretary of the kibbutz. The Secretary, Sashka, is of the opinion that the completion of new houses should take priority over repairing cracks of various sorts, but in the end he agrees to bring the matter before a general meeting of the kibbutz. The narrator, who falls ill because of the winter winds blowing through the crack, is not satisfied with this response. Consequently, he decides to go to the city and bring the matter up before his influential relative, Barukh Makhtesh, who will help him leave his kibbutz and find a decent place in the city for him and his wife. On his way to Barukh Makhtesh's house, the narrator meets an old shoeshine man and a peddler who sells pornographic pictures. They ask him to speak for the residents of the streets around the Central Bus Station before the authorities, for their souls "are shattered with the oppressive noise and tumult" (197).

The narrator comes to their assistance by leading a demonstration to the city hall. He begins a dispute with the Municipal Planner and other officials, and eventually breaks into the office of the "city father." The receptionist tries to convince him of the futility of his mission, but the narrator is not convinced and pounds on the "city father's" door. When no one responds to his knocking, he interrogates the receptionist as to the identity of the "city father." She informs him that the "city father" is none other than Barukh Makhtesh, whose advice he has come to solicit.

At the end of the story the narrator returns to his kibbutz, covering the end of the journey by foot. On his way through the dark fields a small jackal starts to follow him: "As I walked, tired and withdrawn, on the straight-edge road, like a scratch in the flesh of the moist fields, a small jackal attached itself to me. He walked after me and cried. I stamped my foot. He recoiled and burst out in a jackal's laugh. I walked faster. He ran. I threw a stone at him. His eyes flashed in rebuke. I leaned over and patted him. He rubbed against me. I picked him up and wrapped him in my coat" (202). The narrator reaches the kibbutz, spreads out a dry bed of sacks for the jackal, and goes to Tishbi Eliahu for the key to the storeroom. He mixes a bucket of cement and plugs the crack in the wall of his room by himself.

The story is written in Agnon's metarealistic style, as in "Sefer Hama'asim" (1942).[2] The crack around which the story revolves metaphorically represents the rift in the protagonist's personality: instead of saying that a central element in his personality has been undermined, threatening his existence, the protagonist speaks of the weakening of the "central column" of his house and of the huge crack that has opened in the wall of his room. What is the meaning of that crack? What is the nature of the rift that threatens the protagonist? Undoubtedly, one of the main causes of the crack is the opposition between "nature" in man—the overwhelming forces of the instincts, the jungle urges—and the civilized elements of his being. The forces of nature—the movement of the earth, "the mighty currents of water"—have created the crack, depriving the protagonist of the protection of civilization and exposing him to the winds and rain.

The opposition between nature and civilization frequently emerges in the story. The world of nature is depicted here as a living, breathing essence with its own soul. Moreover, that soul is hostile to the narrator and conspires against him. After his wife has plugged the crack with old newspapers, he comments: "Our dwelling is exposed to the fierce and prolonged storms of the month of Tevet [December/January], and a ball of old newspapers is no obstacle for the wind, which knows its own will. One day the wind broke in, carrying away my dear wife's barricades, and scattering scraps of paper all over the room, bits of out-dated news that no longer interested anyone" (192). The word "barricades" indicates the struggle that took place, and the narrator immediately goes on to describe the wind further; it "comes through the crack and laughs at me, aggravating my illness" (192).

The opposition of the vital world of nature to that of civilization emerges in a number of short natural descriptions. We recall, for example, that the protagonist makes his way home at night "on the

---

2. The term "metarealistic" is used here in the sense suggested by Hillel Barzel (1974).

straight-edge road, like a scratch in the flesh of the moist fields" (202), and while he is in the city he recounts that he has often seen "a jet plane leaving behind a white scar in the flesh of the blue sky" (193). Both of these descriptions show human activity as wounding the forces of nature, as cutting into its flesh. Those metaphors, describing natural forces as if they were animals, will appear repeatedly in Oz's later works, pointing to a central aspect of his world: many of his protagonists attribute life, soul, and will to natural phenomena.

The arena of the battle between nature and culture is, of course, the psyche of the protagonist. The relationship between the two poles of his being is clarified by the conclusion of the story: on his way home the narrator adopts a wet jackal, warms him up in his bosom and then gently places him on a pile of dry sacks. Undoubtedly, the personified jackal represents the forces of nature within the protagonist. Now that he has become reconciled with the jackal within him, he can apply himself to the task of plugging up the crack that has threatened the integrity of his home. Yet Oz presents a rather weak version of the struggle between man and beast in this story. The jackal is a wet and miserable puppy with human attributes: he cries, laughs, and rebukes. In Oz's later stories the jackal loses his humanity and becomes a malevolent beast, drooling saliva and emitting foul odors. Nevertheless, the effort at reconciliation with the jackal, the aspiration for inner harmony, will mark all of Oz's works, a subject discussed at length in the concluding chapter of this study.

Another central natural force is the protagonist's sexual drives. Oz discussed the problem of erotic urges in an interview published when *My Michael* first appeared in Hebrew: "I think that human relations, a priori, are a sad business. Our adaptation to the cosmos is far from complete, and if one may speak of biological logic, man is a doubtful creature, full of contradictions in the essence of his being. . . . Moreover, we are the only creatures in nature for whom Eros is a problem. Throughout nature Eros is merely a reflex, a mechanism. With us it's a problem" (1968b). The problem of Eros is presented in this story through the unexpected, violent response of the main character upon seeing the filthy pictures offered to him for sale (195). Eros is one of the main forces in Oz's world, disturbing his young heroes (in "The Hill of Evil Counsel," "Mr. Levi," and others) as well as the mature characters. Eros is the key principle in the entire cosmos (in his first novel, *Elsewhere, Perhaps*, Oz describes the Jordan Valley rift as the "primeval crack," an image with vaginal overtones [1966a, 40; 1973, 32]), and within the human psyche it represents one of the forces of nature that has been preserved in all its primal power, mighty and somber.

The mere pictures that upset the protagonist's equilibrium attack and mock him like the wind that laughs at him and aggravates his illness. The "crazed fury" he experiences reminds us of the story of the man whose "mind was swallowed up" because of the cracks that opened up in his house (198). The importance of these pictures appears again at the end of the story. Before he leaves the office of the "city father," the narrator takes a large piece of paper and writes: "A peddlar named Sultanian circulates in the alleys around the Central Bus Station. He sells pornographic pictures. I am honored to propose his candidacy for the office of city father" (201). Before his final reconciliation with the jackal, the narrator, in his madness, proposes the cult of Eros in place of the cult of God, which has lost its effectiveness.

When the narrator loses his faith, another "crack" in the story appears—his feeling of being cut off from God. The "city father" is depicted here as if he were God: "In the days of the city's creation the man served as its father, the first of its fathers. Some say of him that he is the founder of this city. Who can get to the bottom of those old matters fluttering on the border between legend and twilight?" (198). His office is in "the room at the end of the numbers" (a metaphorical representation of the concept of infinity that characterizes the idea of God), and the narrator addresses him in terms taken from the vocabulary of hymns and prayers: " 'My Lord, the Father of the City,' I shouted, 'Open thy door for me, open it for me, have pity on me and open thy door' " (201). When he receives no response to his cries, he asks the city father's secretary in a "cracked voice": " 'Who is it that sits within? Who is he? Is there a man there, or is an empty desk placed there, or is this the city orphaned of its father? . . . But who is he, miss, who is he? . . .' I shouted, and the shout overwhelmed the shouter and shook his whole body. 'Barukh Makhtech,' Yardena answered in slight wonderment" (201).

The narrator's questions concern the very order of the world, or, in other words, the existence or nonexistence of God: does the city have a father who governs it and guides its activities, or is it perhaps governed without a master plan, without any providence? The fact that Barukh Makhtesh is the city father, or at least that is what his secretary claims, does not provide an unequivocal answer to the narrator's puzzlement. The name "Barukh" (meaning "blessed" in Hebrew) might appear to support the secretary's contention that the city father actually exists. It appears frequently in prayers and hymns, and is used as an epithet for the name of God ("Blessed art Thou, O Lord," "Blessed who says and does," "Blessed is God every day," "Blessed be He and Blessed be His name," "Blessed be the Name"). On the other hand, the family name "Makhtesh" (meaning "mortar" or "crater") indicates a lack, a big hole defined by the walls around it. This family name supports the narrator's feeling that the city father's office is empty. Furthermore, even if he does work in his office, his secretary quickly explains: "He is very old, and hard of hearing. Perhaps he is immersed in his work. Perhaps he is thinking. Perhaps he has fallen asleep" (200).

The protagonist finally understands that no help will come from this quarter. He returns to the kibbutz and, with his own hands, plugs up the crack that had opened in the wall of his room. "In my whole life I never worked at construction, and I had little faith in my own hurried handiwork. Certainly I would have to plug the crack up again. That is what I shall do. I shall plug the crack up again and be more stubborn than the crack, until a main column settles in its place. One day or another the house has to settle in its final position, the one naturally meant for it" (202). The narrator had played a heroic role earlier by representing the residents of the Central Bus Station area before the municipal authorities. Now he takes a no less honorable role upon himself: a constant struggle against the crack, until the house finds its final resting position. The conclusion of the story demonstrates the process of individuation, of finding one's self as discussed at length in Jung (1956, in the chapter "Conscious, Unconscious, and Individuation" and elsewhere). The only way that a mature person can experience the feeling of unity and fulfillment is through the recognition of his shadow side, the bestial element within him, and through reconciliation with that aspect of himself. This process brings about individuation comprising all the powers of the soul, the dark and light, resulting in the unification of opposites—a divine unity (a detailed discussion of this issue appears in the following chapter). When the narrator of "A Crack Open to the Wind" is reconciled with the jackal within him, he promises to persevere and plug up the crack in the wall of his room until the house "settles in its final position, the one naturally meant for it" (202). This final, natural position is presented here as a substitute for redemption by God. Indeed, after filling the crack, the narrator removes his shoes and enters his home as one enters a holy place.

The influence of Agnon's "Sefer Hama'asim" on "A Crack Open to the Wind" is notable in the allegorical names given to the characters (Tishbi Eliahu [i.e., the Prophet Elijah the Tishbite], Barukh Makhtesh) and streets (Barukh Makhtesh lives in the "Twisted Fork" neighborhood on "Almost Certain Lane"), in the complex of forces that motivate the plot (the crack, the narrator's illness), and in the surprising coincidences that dictate its course (a hole in the wall that needs to be fixed, leading to the protagonist's trip to his native city, is found in the first story in "Sefer Hama'asim"; in subsequent stories one finds descriptions of Tel Aviv, the noisy Central Bus Station and other annoyances, as well as frequent allusions to the protagonist's pains and illnesses). Oz's next story continues this trend, but deviates from it in important ways.

## "Purple Coast"

Oz also uses a metarealistic framework in his second story, "Purple Coast." Exploiting the possibilities of this style to the fullest, he erases all indications of time and place. The story does not take place within the realistic setting of the kibbutz, but against an abstract, allegorical background: a boat with passengers sails the ocean on an aimless voyage. Oz thus gives radical expression to another tendency notable in Agnon's "Sefer Hama'asim": the Jungian symbols so common in Agnon's book (crossing a bridge, the sea, and many others) become reality in "Purple Coast." Yet he departs from Agnon's style in one central area. The framework of the Jungian worldview left no place for Agnon's allegorical protagonists. Adhering to the notion that the power of the ancient levels of the psyche is as great in the present as it has been in the past, Oz began to adopt archetypal figures with a mythological background. All his subsequent works, the short stories as well as the novels, were to be influenced by that decisive change.

The narrator of "Purple Coast" is one of a group of travelers passing their lives on an endless cruise on the ocean. However, the narrator, unlike the other passengers, cannot share in the atmosphere of gay abandonment and complacency on the ship. Strange visions visit him nightly, disturbing his tranquillity:

> I went back to my cabin and slept for two hours. Nearly at daybreak alertness descended upon me. I arose from my bed and pressed my face against the glass of the porthole. Then the thing came. It always sneaked up on me. Every night I saw the visions, and every night the visions drew me towards them, incomplete and unredeemed. I alone saw the visions. I

have no witness but the visions, and the visions have no witness but me. Dita, I whispered loudly, and my lips stuck to the chilly glass of the porthole. Dita, I see land. I see islands. A purple coast. There is nothing in the ship purple as those coasts. I never saw purple like that purple. (206)

The narrator wishes to bring the news of the existence of those purple coasts to the attention of the other passengers, but the ship's captain takes this wish as a rebellion. The protagonist does not give up, yet the revolt is stillborn. Passengers flee to their cabins, and the narrator is declared dead by the ship's physician and captain. His effort to persuade the people around him that he is alive is in vain. At the captain's orders, the protagonist is flung into the ocean in a "burial at sea." Surprisingly, he does not drown immediately, but floats on the surface of the water. The story ends with a description of the ship slowly sailing away from him.

Like its predecessor, this story concerns the structure of the human psyche and the tensions within it. However, in "A Crack Open to the Wind" the scope of the story's concerns is rather limited (the crack appears only in the wall of the narrator's room, and it is the hero's "fault" for choosing to live in an outside room of the house; the other rooms were not damaged). In "Purple Coast" Oz comments on the human condition in general. The main characters of the story represent various stages in the hypothetical development of history: starting with gods and Titans, progressing through the Biblical Nephilim and giants, and ending with man, whose consciousness seeks to free itself from the ocean of primeval, natural, unconscious forces and reach out to the bright coast of consciousness.

A key figure in the story is Dita, the hero's beloved, whose name alludes to Aphrodite. Dita, like Aphrodite, represents the ocean in the story, the Great Mother, dark and unknown. She is the source of life and she is its end.[3] Aphrodite was born of the sea, thus representing its infinite depths and breadth, and Dita is constantly described in terms related to the sea. Here, Oz compares Dita's hair to the sea foam from which Aphrodite was born according to the myth: "Always, always Dita would dance in the center. Her hips moved slowly like the waves. Her soft, bright hair was dispersed like the foam at the crest of

---

3. On Aphrodite as the Great Mother and the ocean, see Neumann (1973, 48, 89, 178, and elsewhere). Another work by Neumann is entirely devoted to the Great Mother (1963). For more on this subject, see Jung, "Psychological Aspects of the Mother Archetype" (in Jung 1959a).

a wave" (203). Similarly, like the waters of the sea "slowly flowing," Dita's hand "slowly flows" and "seeps" into the narrator's veins. Dita's association with the ring also reveals her affinity with the ocean. Throughout, Oz juxtaposes the "feminine principle," symbolized by the ring, and the "masculine principle," symbolized by the straight line. That subject previously appears in the beginning of the story when the narrator "breaks through a joyful ring of women and girls" to approach the captain and ask him if his boat "is tracing a straight route on the surface of the sea" (203). The captain avoids giving a direct answer: " 'Perhaps a circular route, perhaps a looping route,' said the captain, looking at me with concern and affection" (ibid.). When the narrator persists in asking his question, the captain's affection for him disappears. He becomes convinced of the seriousness of the narrator's "disease" and sends him to the ship's physician.

The contrast between the ring and the straight line occurs frequently throughout the story. The captain, a kind of Zeus ruling his world highhandedly, throws his cigar away "in a purposeful trajectory, straight as a ruler" (204). When he hits the tennis ball, it also flies in a trajectory as "straight and purposeful as a ruler" (208). In contrast, the ball that Dita hits "traces a fancy bow in the air" (208). The importance of this issue becomes evident at the end, when the narrator, floating on the surface of the water after his burial at sea, reflects: "I shall never know whether my flaccid body is drawing a straight line on the surface of the sea or a circular route, or perhaps a looping one" (210).

What is the significance of that question asked at the end of the protagonist's life, disquieting him even in his final moments? The ring, like the ocean, represents a fullness, including both its beginning and its end, bringing to mind an image of the great dragon with its tail in its mouth, eating its own flesh, fertilizing and pregnant with itself.[4] The ring stands for the dark forces of nature, the unconscious, existing in an inviolate wholeness, unchanging and stable. The association of the symbolic ring with the snake eating its own tail reappears in Oz's later works (see the discussion of *Elsewhere, Perhaps* and *A Perfect Peace* in the following chapters). In contrast to the ring, the masculine principle is bound up with activism, with purposefulness, and with change.[5] Thus, throughout the story the narrator wonders whether

---

4. The uroborus, the snake with its tail in its mouth, is one of the widespread symbols discussed by Jung (see, for example, 1953b, 1959a).

5. The meaning of the straight line was brought out by Cooper (1984, 162) and Cirlot (1983, 131).

human history shows any development, any true distancing from its jungle origins, whether the human soul possesses sufficient force to contend with bestial, biological energies and can deflect them in other directions. The character of Dita, indissolubly connected to the ocean and the ring, is the model of all the women in Oz's works. She is directly related to the figures of Tanya and Galila (in "Where the Jackals Howl") and to Noga Harish (in *Elsewhere, Perhaps*) and Hannah Gonen (*My Michael*), Rimona (*A Perfect Peace*) and Ilana (*Black Box*).

The affinity between Dita and the ocean is mutual. Just as the woman is compared to the ocean, the ocean represents a feminine element. Thus, for example, the prow of the boat slices the waters "as if it were cutting soft silk" (203) and the story ends with a description of the bow of the ship "delicately embracing the silk of the sea" (210). Like Dita, seducing the narrator, the waters are also full of desire: "The talons of the ship's propellers scratched the sea, and the waters replied with a wavy whisper. The desire of the water seeped into the ship and hovered over the decks like a thin vapor" (202). The couple's tumultuous movements as they make love embody the sea's desire. The significance of the sea, the fact that it symbolizes the unknown world of the depths of the unconscious, is implied by its black color, which swallows all light that comes near it (205). In many traditions, the color black stands for a stage in primary, fetal development;[6] Jung repeatedly uses the sea as a central symbol for the unconscious.[7]

The story places Dita and the ocean waters in contrast to the figure of the captain and to the continent and islands seen by the protagonist. Unlike Dita, the representative of the dark waters, the captain is associated with light. His stare moves "like a searchlight" (203), a simile that combines the motif of the straight course with that of light; the cigar thrown from his hand flies "like a falling star" and is swallowed noiselessly by the sea (204). The protagonist's vision of the purple islands is a central element in the story, and it is in their behalf that he rebels, in their name that he is thrown into the sea and buried there. They, in turn, keep his body afloat on the water: "I am not strong, Dita. But those visions live within me, and I am floating. I am floating, Dita" (210). In contrast to the water with its instability, its hidden, threatening depths, the islands are terra firma, to be leveled and worked. Even from the point of view of the development of the

---

6. See Cooper (1984, 39–40), de Vries (1981, 50), and Cirlot (1983, 57).

7. Information on that topic is widely dispersed in Jung's many writings. For detailed definitions of the sea, consult, for example, 1953b, 1956, 1959a.

animal kingdom, life on land is a more advanced step than life in the sea. In certain cultures the color purple symbolizes spirituality and sublimation, a fact which supports the notion that the islands stand for the principle which is essentially opposite to that of the ocean: the principle of the spirit, or of consciousness.[8]

In summary, the author presents two realms of experience, two principles of existence as a basis for judging the human condition. On the one hand, the feminine principle, symbolized by the ocean, the ring, darkness, and unconsciousness; on the other hand, the masculine principle, the dry land, a straight course, light, and consciousness. From the story we see that these forces are neither equal in strength nor in degree. The ocean is reality, living and breathing, and the islands are merely visionary sights, uncertain, seen only by a single man. Moreover, the protagonist wishes to report the message of the islands, of light, to mankind. He proclaims its existence, but when he calls for revolt, the "howl of a jackal" bursts from his lips (209). In other words, even the hero has not yet distanced himself from the primal, bestial level of existence, and when he sets out to do battle with it, it overcomes him. The primal condition, then, is the ocean, the unconscious existence of the natural world, the primal realm, complete within itself and unchanging.

We find this topic illustrated in another way. The name of Mordu, the first mate, recalls the name of Marduk, the creator of the universe in the Babylonian myth "Anuma Elish." Mordu's fear of opening the chimneys of the heavens (205–6) is a reference to this myth: after splitting Tiamat and creating the firmament with half her body, Marduk stationed watchmen to prevent Tiamat from releasing her waters. In "Purple Coast" the watchmen fail in their appointed task, and Marduk loses control over the world he created. The ocean is viewed as a deluge (see below), and Marduk fears a second flood. In other words, Tiamat is as powerful as ever.

The story reflects several stages of historical development. Representatives of the gods (Mordu, Dita, the captain), representatives of the Titans, and human beings are found on the ship. In Greek mythology the Titans, the second generation of gods, symbolize the savage, unchecked forces of primal nature. They were the first rulers of the

---

8. The various connotations of the color purple are exemplified in this story. On the one hand it is a feminine color connected to water and the moon (de Vries 1981, 488), and on the other hand it is the color of penitence (Cooper 1984, 40; Ferguson 1961, 152). The purple light cast on the dance floor is connected to the first significance of that color, whereas the purple color of the coast and land seen by the narrator recalls the second significance.

world, subdued by the order-loving Olympian gods. Their representative on the ship is "Titan," the captain's dog.

The narrator refers to the subjugation of the Titans by the gods when speaking to the dog: "Watch out, Titan. Remember the fate of your predecessor. The dog raised by the captain before you died a strange death. The captain buried him at sea. It happened before you were born. At night his body was thrown into the sea, sinking to the depths like a stone. Watch your step, Titan, keep your eyes open. You're a good dog" (206).

However, the dog Titan also illustrates the active, rebellious element latent in the protagonist himself. In fact, the dog is the only one who sorrows or mourns the failure of the narrator's attempted rebellion: "Titan came over and sniffed my face. How gray the dog's eyes were. There was sadness in the dog's eyes. Finally the dog emitted a long, mournful howl" (209). Importantly, the narrator's fate is that of the captain's first dog: burial at sea.

The essence of the human being is defined in the opening sentences of the story, describing the ship's navigator: "With shielded eyes the sailor on watch would cling silently to the wheel and stare at the dark sea. Naked to the waist he would stand, his mouth open and two sharp teeth gleaming whitely from inside it" (202–3). The sailor's animal-like fangs show that he has not yet progressed far beyond his natural, bestial origins. The other voyagers on the ship are similar to him. The narrator, who wishes to convince at least one of the travelers of the existence of the purple visions, surveys the passengers and sees men-beasts before him:

> My eyes wound among the deck chairs and sought faces. A place to cast anchor. There's the wise woman, a mole-face. The nearsighted old man is reading a holy book, and his nose wriggles among the faded pages like a worm. The boy stretching his muscles by doing handstands, seeking to bathe in some of Mordu's glory. So cheeky, a little monkey! The grandson stretched out in the sun like a turtle. The band of husky wolves bunched together and exchanging dirty jokes. The pair of chess-playing foxes ignoring the entire ship, and wound up in their own cunning calculations. Dita, her cat-hips. (208–9)

The narrator himself is astonished to hear "the jackal's howl" burst from his throat when he cries out to the voyagers in order to incite them to rebellion.

The closeness of human beings to the primal world of nature, the world of animals, is illustrated in another way in the story. Throughout, the ship is compared to Noah's Ark, and the people are compared to the beasts Noah gathered on it: "Every night the Ararat Orchestra would flood the halls with the joyous strains of jazz, and we would cling to each other in dances, male and female, male and female (cf. Genesis 7:15–16).

The meager progression of the human race beyond its first bestial origins is further exemplified. Human development depends upon the person of high abilities, the hero, who discovers an illuminated shore and seeks to bring all people to it. Like Prometheus, the narrator seeks to bring humanity to the shores of light, but no one helps him in his elevated task. Moreover, the captain of the ship is like Zeus, who wanted to leave mankind in ignorance and who punished Prometheus. He wants the passengers to continue their life of indolence, complacency, blissful ignorance, and unconsciousness. Yet the end of the story is not completely somber. The protagonist, thrown into the sea, does not drown immediately despite his physical weakness: "I am not strong, Dita. But those visions live within me, and I am floating. I am floating, Dita. Isn't that surprising! A dove I'd like to see. A dove should come. I want my body to be reconciled to the water. I am reminding my body of the vision. Perhaps it won't disappoint me" (210).

The dove, a reminder of the story of Noah's Ark, demonstrates the existence of the shore and of the islands that the protagonist sees every morning. The story, surprisingly, does not completely deny the possibility of the dove's appearance; as long as the hero has not yet drowned, it might yet appear before his eyes. The great similarity between the narrator and the prophet Jonah supports that possibility (perhaps also hinted at by the Hebrew homonym of Oz's image, for "yonah" is both "dove" and the name of the prophet Jonah): the narrator's cry for rebellion echoes that of Jonah in Nineveh, and like Jonah he is thrown into the sea, but does not drown. The underlying Biblical reference might, therefore, suggest the hero's possible redemption. The story thus vacillates between "and God said, I shall wipe out man, whom I created, from the face of the earth" (Genesis 6:7), and "and God saw their actions, that they had repented of their evil, and God repented of the evil He had intended to do to them, and He did not do it" (Jonah 3:10). The author's pessimistic outlook on the human race, then, finds temporary relief at the end of this story, which does not completely deny the possibility of human redemption, the possibility of putting our natural origins behind us.

Oz has retained this idea of the human being throughout his entire literary career up to the present. It is consistent with Jung's worldview, which sees the human soul as a pyramid with, at its base, essentially the major part of its volume, the collective heritage common to mankind and to all of nature. The ego, in that view, is merely the narrow, flat point at its summit. According to Jung, the ego grows out of the depths below it, and it is in constant danger of invasion from those depths, which threaten to occupy its territory (cf. the protagonist's reaction to the sight of the pornographic pictures proffered to him in "A Crack Open to the Wind"), or in danger of total withdrawal into those depths. Let us recall, furthermore, that Jung did not see the unconscious as merely a negative factor, and he frequently emphasized the wisdom and intelligence latent within it. The vitality and creativity stored up in the darkness of those depths will appear repeatedly in later stories (see Chapter 5). That concept of the psyche, already inherent in the early story under consideration here, shows that the metaphorical image of the human soul as a pyramid is more complex than one might at first think. Progress from the base of the pyramid to its summit is progress from utter darkness toward light, toward consciousness and culture, but at the same time it is a process of dilution, of limitation, and of distancing from the root: the broad foundation where man is at one with nature and with its gods becomes a narrow point, cut off from its origins. The transition from darkness to light is, among other things, a transition from vital existence, where one enjoys contact with the sources of power, intuition, and mystical union, to one of separation, alienation, and barren intellectualization.

Thus, the metaphor of the pyramid implies a double structure in which upon the first pyramid (for the sake of brevity, "the cultural pyramid") a second, inverted pyramid is superimposed, with its base touching the top of the standing pyramid and its summit pointing downward ("the natural pyramid"). In other words, the more one retrogresses, from the point of view of culture and the development of consciousness, the deeper one plunges toward the base of the pyramid of culture, the closer one comes to the apex of the inverted natural pyramid. Conversely, the more closely one approaches the illuminated peak of the cultural pyramid, the more one distances oneself from the apex of the natural pyramid. The worldview expressed in "Purple Coast" implies that the summit of the natural pyramid does not represent only blind urges, base drives, but holiness as well: Dita is both a goddess and an offspring of the primal ocean. Hence, one of the main implications of this double pyramid is that the closer one comes to his natural origin, the closer he comes to his primal, divine sources.

The essential affinity between the holy and the impure, as demonstrated in "Purple Coast" by the character of Dita, appears frequently in Oz's work. The double pyramid challenges the very notion of historical or cultural "progress"—for progress within one pyramid is retrogression in the converse pyramid. This double structure demands reexamination of our previous definitions. Since human beings' bestial origin is at one and the same time their godly origin, Oz's notion that people are still very close to their origin is not necessarily a "pessimistic" one. Actually, every phenomenon in Oz's world is approached from two contradicting points of view, thus being affirmed and negated simultaneously. The far-reaching meanings the double pyramid has with regard to language are discussed below.

The double pyramid implies constant vacillation between the lifeless light and the powerful darkness, between consciousness and the roiling depths below, between secure existence defended within the bounds of society and the seductive and threatening life beyond them. This vacillation provides the axis of most of Oz's subsequent stories and novels.[9] Yet the role of the protagonist will change completely. In "Purple Coast" Oz does not present his entire worldview, preferring to retain the figure of the hero who bears a message, the hero who might be capable of redeeming human beings. Thus, in total contrast to the view expressed in the body of the story, one finds at the end traces of the old humanism, glorifying man, his mastery over his own fate and world, the power of his will, and the determination of his decisions. In Oz's following stories all traces of that humanism will disappear. Whereas in "Purple Coast" the protagonist seeks to bring light to humanity, henceforth Oz's characters will repeatedly give themselves over to the darkness. They will not seek light, but will plunge deeper and deeper into the darkness of the depths within themselves. True, in the final analysis those two tendencies coincide: for the exposure of the dark recesses of the soul implies, among other things, bringing them to light, enlarging the regions of conscious control. Three decades would pass before Oz's protagonist would again seek light in *The Third Condition* (1991).

It is noteworthy that "Purple Coast," like Oz's first story, concentrates on the qualities of the forces active within the human psyche. The importance of this point cannot be overemphasized: the central concerns of Oz's works have been decidedly psychological and metapsychological from the start.

---

9. For a description of that phenomenon from another point of departure, see Gertz (1980, 51).

In order to fully understand "Purple Coast," we must look beyond its scriptural background (the deluge, Noah's Ark, and the prophet Jonah). The story deploys at least two other mythological structures: Greek (Dita, Zeus) and Mesopotamian (Mordu). Those three mythological complexes in the background of the story are all encompassed by the ocean waters, which bear a decidedly Jungian stamp. The multileveled background creates a textual density which, along with the mythic-psychological meaning of the various details, creates a mutual bond between the separate mythological structures. We find this mythic and psychological layering evident in Oz's later work as well.

## "Before His Time": The Starting Point

Oz's next story, "Before His Time," was the earliest to be included in *Where the Jackals Howl*. One might wonder why this story differs so markedly from "Purple Coast." It would appear that after his first two stories Oz discovered that too many of his primary concerns had been left unexpressed. Moreover, the stories created no real dialogue between himself and his immediate audience, the ranks of the kibbutz movement.

It seems that these questions were plaguing him: how was he to express the Dionysian and Apollonian urges vying within him? And how was he to express the complex of emotions bound up in his relations with his parents? How was he to give voice to the emotions and feelings stored up within him, including a good deal of bitterness toward the kibbutz society where he lived? Oz's involvement in social and political issues from an early age necessitated that he find a literary model through which he could express those concerns as well. Another level of concern was the metaphysical one, the seriousness of which is already evident in "A Crack Open to the Wind." As for his readers: how could he address the kibbutz community without giving up Agnon as a potential reader, as well as Agnon's readership? He also had to consider the issue of subject matter and structure. It would seem that at this point Oz decided that he no longer wished to write a book made up of a number of independent stories, each one standing by itself; rather he sought to produce a single, comprehensive statement about human nature, a statement comprising all the stories, each shedding light upon each other, either complementary or contrasting.[10]

---

10. This issue is dealt with in the appendix.

The conclusion demanded by all of those combined pressures was, first of all, a return to the background of the kibbutz as described in "A Crack Open to the Wind." The kibbutz, its characters and landscapes, would give the author the necessary continuity for the entire collection. Through the characters of the kibbutz, he could also express his frustrations regarding family tensions and respond to the political situation as well. A second conclusion determined his presentation of the kibbutz. In order to give human validity to his characters, their doubts and struggles, and in order to give the story true force, he had to forgo the metarealistic mode and describe the kibbutz, at least on the level of the overt plot, as a real place that the reader could recognize, identifying with the characters or despising them. The symbolic meaning of the characters had to arise from the plot or be conveyed in the background by means of well-camouflaged hints, and not through the names of the protagonists. This manner of depicting the kibbutz also responded to the various expectations of his readership, both the immediate one on the kibbutz and the sophisticated one, expert in the connotative language of Agnon, Kafka, and Joyce.[11] These considerations seem to be the complex of factors shaping "Before His Time," making it a model of Oz's later works.

"Before His Time" develops along two plot axes. One of them concerns the fate of Samson the bull, and the second describes the last night of the story's main character, Dov Sirkin. Samson the bull, "the pride of the kibbutz dairymen, glorious product of the valley" (1965a, 59), loses his "generative powers" when bitten by a rabid jackal. The story begins with the night of the bull's slaughtering and the sale of his skin to Rashid Effendi. The buyer intends to turn the skin into "souvenirs for rich tourist ladies, colorful pictures on parchment: the alley where Jesus lived; his carpentry shop with Joseph in the background; the angels playing timbrels and announcing the birth of the redeemer; and finally the infant himself, his forehead radiating light—everything done on parchment, a splendid creation" (59).

The protagonist of the story, Dov Sirkin, once worked in the orchards and he was one of his kibbutz's "pillars." Previously, he did battle with the jackals who surrounded the kibbutz gates at night, and he was certain that in the end he would overpower them: " 'He laughs best who laughs last,' Dov used to say in the old days, before leaving his family and his kibbutz to roam about the country, putting the imprint of his fingers on it" (62). After leaving the kibbutz, Dov took up various lines of work, finally settling in Jerusalem where he became

---

11. Gertz (1980) commented extensively on this aspect of Oz's work.

a geography teacher. Two heart attacks made him leave his post and stay home.

Dov's son Ehud took part in all the reprisal raids carried out by the Israel Defense Force during the 1950s and finally died in one of them. His body remained in no man's land. It was only on the fourth night that his comrades succeeded in rescuing his corpse, but not before the jackals had eaten his flesh. The story describes Dov's last night: he is sitting as usual, sketching an imaginary world several times larger than the earth, when he hears the steps of a stranger climbing up the stairs to his apartment. Those footsteps arouse obscure anxieties within him, and he closes up his house tightly—the shutters, the windows, and the door. In the end he realizes that just as he had been unsuccessful in keeping the jackals out of the kibbutz fence, he cannot avoid meeting the stranger outside. Seeing that he is fighting a lost battle he goes to the door, to his final meeting with his son, who has come to take revenge on him, and collapses. Hearing the howl of the jackals, he knows that he has lost his war against them: "I am the last, and I am not laughing" (74).

The realistic nature of the story is evident in the abundant use of precise description and details—more than is necessary for the purpose of conveying symbolic meanings. Thus, for example, the reader can follow the slaughter of the bull and Dov's collapse step by step, see the kibbutz fruit trees in their various species, and observe Dov tirelessly reading the dozens of reports written by his pupils. Clearly, Oz took a good deal of trouble to fortify the illusion of reality in this story. Many of the details serve that end alone, and the symbolic meaning of other details does not deprive them of their realism, but rather complements that realism as another level of meaning.

The difference between the present story and Oz's previous ones can be demonstrated by his treatment of Dov Sirkin. The name Sirkin has a firm realistic basis (it is common among German Jews), and the connection between it and the Biblical Cain, although the name Cain is spelled in Hebrew exactly like the second syllable of Sir*kin*, is less immediate than the connection between Dita and Aphrodite or between Mordo and Marduk. The name Dov, meaning "bear" in Hebrew, does hint at the protagonist's bearish nature, but on the other hand it is a common Hebrew name, and it is given variety and richness through the external description of the man. Dov is portrayed in great detail (his physical appearance in the past and in the present, his actions on the kibbutz and in the city, the series of meetings with his son Ehud), and some of these descriptions are devoid of any symbolic meaning. The reader, then, can view the protagonist as a gnarled authoritative figure who is hard on himself as well as others, a personality who exhibits a child's naïveté along with an adult's pragmatism and an old man's obstinacy; there were more than a few people like that among the founding generation of the kibbutz. Yet, the increased realism of the story did not change Oz's writing technique significantly: beneath the realistic veil of the story one finds many other levels of meaning. Indeed, the same conflicts that were expressed in the timeless plot of "Purple Coast" are found in the present-day Israel of "Before His Time."

The story reaches its climax during the visionary encounter between Dov and his son and in Dov's final reflections. Dov, hearing the stranger's footsteps reach his threshold, rises from his chair and steps toward the door with stooped shoulders. At this point we find a long description of Dov's struggle against the jackals, and of the jackals' revenge against Dov's son Ehud; only afterward does the narrator return to Dov, full of dread, gripping the brass handle of his door (73). Thus, the description of Dov as he goes to open the door of his house is accompanied by a kind of parenthesis, which replays the earlier struggle with the jackals, suggesting that the jackals are described from Dov's point of view. At last he understands that it is impossible to fence the jackals' path. It is impossible to keep the jackals on the other side of the kibbutz fenceposts, in the darkness. For they are found in the very heart of the well-lit kibbutz. In his last moments Dov realizes that the contrast between light and darkness, between nature and culture, is only an external, apparent contrast. Indeed, after the description of the jackals roaming around the kibbutz fence, and before he returns to Dov, who is clutching the handle of his door in dread, the narrator adds: "An eternal curse lies between house dwellers and those who inhabit the mountains and streambeds. Sometimes, during the night, a sleek house-dog hears the voice of his cursed brother. The sound does not come from across the fields. The dog's enemy dwells within him. From the depths it sends out volleys of greenish laughter" (73).

This passage, a typical dianoia, to use Aristotelian terminology, is the thematic axis of the entire story. The jackal, says the narrator, preceded the domestic dog, and its characteristics carry on a latent existence within the dog. The difference between the two is not one of kind, but merely one of degree. An outer layer has grown over the primal traits of the jackal, yet the jackal's traits have not been completely effaced: they continue to exist inside the dog, attacking him occasionally from within. Plants, too, which have been pruned and cultivated, preserve their natural traits. Thus, the furniture in Dov's house is not an assemblage of lifeless objects: "Entering the room, one falls into a roaring maelstrom of flocks of furniture bleating with thick voices" (64–65). That view is also expressed in other stories in *Where the Jackals Howl*, such as the title story, "The Trappist Monastery," and "A Hollow Stone."

In his article "Man is the Sum of His Sins and of the Fire Lurking in His Bones," Oz elucidates this idea in a discussion of Berdyczewski:

> Berdyczewski was not an anti-ideologist after one of the fashions of his times, and he was not ignorant of the major ideological trends, both in Europe and among the Jewish people of his generation. He knew them well, and he was involved with them, supporting some and condemning others; however, when he came to write a story, his attitude became somewhat skeptical. That is, young men maintain all sorts of notions, but their ideas are merely a restrained and dignified version of primal forces, just as the domestic dog is the tame descendant of timber wolves, and if you remove his restraints, the dog will revert to being a wolf again. Only then does a Berdyczewskian story achieve its full force. (1979a, 30–31)

Those remarks, it might be superfluous to note, apply equally well to the works of Oz himself.[12]

This view of the nature of the world and of human beings is the same as the one expressed in Oz's earlier story, "Purple Coast." Oz also uses metaphors similar to those in that story. Like the sunrise in "Purple Coast" that plows "a deep scar in the flesh of the ocean," the lanterns along the fence in "Before His Time" are described as "lashes of light whipping the flesh of the fields" (72). Similarly, the islands seen by the narrator of "Purple Coast" find kinship with the description of the kibbutz as an island in "Before His Time":

> The jackals walk about on tip-toes, with their moist, sniffy noses, and they dare not approach the fence. They swarm all around, clustering as in a rite, a ring of quivering jackals circulating at the edges of the ring of shadow enclosing the island of light. With the morning light they saturate the air

---

12. The description of a dog as a wolf, as seen by a child, is repeated frequently in *Soumchi* (1978a).

with the sounds of wailing, and their hunger shatters in waves on the shores of the illuminated, fenced-in isle. (73)

We find a similarity between that metaphor, the kibbutz as an island with the jackals and darkness compared to waves breaking on its shores, and the main symbols of "Purple Coast" (cf. the repeated appearance of the ring and the circle). Thus one finds that in the story's struggle the jackals are not in an inferior, pitiable position. As the representatives of the night world, the jackals are part of the "ocean," part of the primal natural world that continues to exist, undisturbed and intact. The narrator emphasizes this quality: "Generations of jackals have passed since then, but the young ones maintain the tradition of their fathers, not given to innovation" (64). The kibbutz, in contrast, is an island rising from the depths of the sea, a constantly endangered island, threatened by the ocean waves and by the danger of sinking completely beneath the water. In other words, human beings emerge out of the world of nature, and remain connected to nature by their navels. Even their "human" traits are drawn from the world of nature, and their existence in their own right is weak and unstable. The areas of the soul where consciousness reigns, the "illuminated" regions of the soul, are small and limited, and, beneath them, the dark, threatening depths are constantly churning.[13]

The image of water once more emerges in Dov's thoughts before he loses consciousness: "True, when the kibbutz was founded, Ehud, we wanted to inaugurate a new order, until things cried out that they were incorrigible. I said, it will be enough for me if I do good and decent actions, and I didn't know, Ehud, that the imprint of our fingers doesn't last on a *watery* surface" (74, italics mine). Dov reconfirms the narrator's words: one's attempt to alter his nature is like trying to stamp one's seal on water. Water is an eternal natural force, unchanging, which can be neither overcome nor tamed. The founders of the kibbutz sought to create a new character, a logical, sane personality, whose behavior would not be dictated by the instincts and drives at work in the natural world. For a while it did seem as if the attempt was succeeding "until things cried out that they were incorrigible." The "things" "cry out" in rage, because of the attempt to reshape them, to impose a rein and bridle on them, or even to drive them out of existence.

---

13. The image of the development of consciousness in the course of history or individual life as an island rising out of the sea is one frequently found in the writings of Jung and his followers.

## The Law of the Conservation of Energy

"Before His Time" is a story of a fall. In the fight between man and jackal, the jackal has the last laugh. The law of the conservation of energy rules in nature. The primal forces of the psyche, the jackal-like powers, have not departed from the world; they have only changed their form for a while. The effort to stifle them completely restores their fangs and claws and stirs them up again. Dov Sirkin is not alone in his fall but is accompanied by his son Ehud and Samson the bull.

The bull, the archetypal symbol of masculinity in nature, is defeated by the jackal, the representative of darkness, the symbol of the Great Mother, the ocean.[14] Thus, the struggle between the masculine and feminine principles has passed from the ocean of "Purple Coast" to the earth of the kibbutz in "Before His Time." As in "Purple Coast," where the protagonist's rebellion against the Great Mother failed, so too in "Before His Time" the principle of the jackal and the night is the eternal and victorious one. "Samson," the name of the bull, also bears witness to that struggle and its outcome. His fate is like that of the Biblical Samson, who was defeated by a woman.

A series of parallels link Dov Sirkin and Samson the bull, identifying them with the same principle in the story. For example, both were "in their prime" (59, 67), and both die before their time because of a bodily defect; both of them rest "with head bent" (60, 65), and both are tired by the struggle and accept death as a blessing, as though it were a return to the womb (61, 74).

Similarly, Ehud, the brave warrior, finally succumbs to the Arabs and the jackals. Like Samson the bull, he too is unable to avoid the fate of castration (his castration is symbolized by the jackal's eating of his face).[15] The verb "to be harvested" is used twice in the story to describe Ehud's death (62, 70), and it is one that might well recall the fertility rites of the harvest time when the bull, the beloved son of the Great Mother, was sacrificed. Ritual plays a significant role in this story: the jackals "cluster as if in a rite" around the kibbutz (73), and before biting into Ehud's flesh they are like "festive priests at a

---

14. In some traditions the bull has "feminine" characteristics (see de Vries 1981, 68–70; Cooper 1984, 26–27; and Cirlot 1983, 33–35). However, they are not alluded to here. On the bull as a father figure, see Jung (1956, 261). Neumann points out that in ancient fertility rites the bull served as a symbol of the beloved son of the Great Mother, and it was brought forth as a sacrificial offering. The beheading of the bull was a kind of ceremonial castration (1973, the chapter "The Great Mother").

15. The connection between the head and the phallus and the symbolic interchange between them are discussed at length by Neumann (1973, in "The Great Mother").

mourning ceremony" (73). Ehud is described as a "sorcerer" as he "busies himself with the coffee with whispers and charms. . . . From the day Ehud was harvested, the secret of the coffee ritual was forgotten, the ritual order of the tiny stream, the laws of the precise ceremony" (62).

The story places the world of the men in opposition to that of the women and jackals. Parallel to the story of Samson, who is victimized by Delilah, Zeshka, Dov's divorced wife, is described as Yael, the wife of Heber the Kenite, who killed Sisra. The repetition and detail in the description of the china cup ("Zeshka gave Yosh sweet hot milk to drink, from the china cup. . . . The thick, clumsy china cup" [61]) and of the milk in it ("a hot and fragrant vapor rises from the cup, a fatty skin floats on the surface of the water") can only be justified by the Biblical story of which they are reminiscent ("He asked for water and she gave milk, in a mighty cup she brought butter." Judges 5:25). The description of Zeshka, "like a pocket knife with its blade folded and a rounded back" (63), also hints at the destructiveness of women. Geula, Zeshka's daughter, is like a jackal: "Geula is not like the rest of her friends, the daughters of the kibbutz. They have plump, tanned legs. Her legs are thin, pale and her arms have hairy, black fuzz. They have round faces and dark eyes, lively eyes, and Geula's face is thin and elongated; her eyes are a turbid blue" (62). This conception of women as the representatives of the Great Mother, the creative and destructive world of nature, is reiterated throughout Oz's works.

True to a worldview which maintains that the primordial forces of the psyche have lost none of their power, the main characters of "Before His Time" are archetypal, primordial figures. Thus, like the bull, called "a mighty bull" (59), Dov throws his son skyward "with a mighty heave" (63), and he draws "the ships of the Nephilim" prepared to devour "mighty chunks" (66). Although he lives on the kibbutz, which stands for an egalitarian society, Dov is described as a "ruler" (63) and as a "master" (64). In his drawings one finds a combination of mythic consciousness making contact with the primal forces of nature, ignoring any restrictions of size and proportion, and modern consciousness, in which his visions are detailed in "precise calculations of the raw materials, the costs of constructions, the paving and the transportation" (72).

Dov's room metonymically reflects his primal, archaic existence:

> Entering the room one falls into a roaring maelstrom of flocks of furniture bleating with thick voices. That was because of that wild amalgam of colors: the hubbub of the light, pink

curtains and the antique bureau, the round table, leaning on dinosaur legs, and the battered black cabinet. Like a riotous splash the red and blue floral bedspread cried out in the midst of all that, and the black lamp *hovers* over the *chaos*, one of his forefathers' lamps. In a large flowerpot in the corner of the room the twisting snakes of an African cactus grow. (64–65, italics mine).

The reference to the chaos that existed before creation (the text uses exactly the same words as the second verse of Genesis) is developed in the following section, which describes Jerusalem at night: "A silent crust on the earth, and a bluish mist rises before him from the openings of the sewers" (67; cf. Genesis 2:6, "And a mist arose from the ground and watered the whole face of the earth"). The dinosaur and the African cactus with its twined snakes contribute to the creation allusion. The "flocks of furniture" seem to become what they were before they were made into lifeless objects.

Dov's room, like the world of the jackals, points to a realm of experience with no change or development, an existence with "interminglings" and "maelstroms" of various noises, of "lust" and "riot," of "neighing" (a word applied to both Dov and the jackals) and of "lamenting." The primordial chaos of the room relates to the protagonist's name, Dov ("bear"), and to the lead in his body (67, 68, 71). For alchemists the lead symbolized the chaotic, primal matter they tried to turn into gold (Jung 1953b, 340; 1968, 74, 105).

The chaos of Dov's room suggests that the primordial, original situation was not one of purity and tranquillity. Rousseau's "noble savage" never existed. At the root of everything lie dark urges, lust, and riot. Yet urges and creativity are synonymous (in Hebrew the former is *yetzer* and the latter is *yetzira*, i.e., they appear to be based on the same three-letter root, Y-TZ-R). Dov Sirkin represents that primordial situation but falls victim to it. In Dov, an idealist who protects his kibbutz from the jackals at the gate, there is a hint of Satan: the description of him as one who abandoned "his family and kibbutz to roam about the country" (62) alludes to Satan, who comes to a meeting with the sons of God and with God "from roaming on the earth and walking up and down on it" (Job 1:7). Dov's nocturnal drawings recall the primitive, wild atmosphere of his room ("a thicket of roads, tracks, bridges, and paths intertwines like an angry tangle of snakes" [66]), and they are characterized by the "chaos" preceding the creation, which contains power, creativity, and destruction (67–68). Dov is thus described as having primordial bestiality and as maintaining a mutual affinity with the forces of nature. Indeed, in the morning hours he "usually looks out through the window to the east, exchanging searing glances with the sun rising over the mountains of Moab" (71).

The kibbutz would seem to be an ideal solution to the multifarious forces at work in such a character. At first Dov attempts to channel his vitality into the ideological framework of the kibbutz, which called for a return to the earth and to nature. For a while it seems as if that is his place (see the descriptions of his work in the orchards, accompanied by "broad neighing" in section IV). But that original experience, as noted, is not tranquil and harmonious. Indeed, the strong contradictions within him ultimately drive Dov from the kibbutz: the attempt to return to nature is accompanied by the effort to change it. The founders of the kibbutz advocated return to nature, and at the same time they wished to "inaugurate a new order," to form a new image of the human being. But while the return to nature means giving free rein to the primal forces of the psyche, the pretentious attempt to "inaugurate a new order" entails the strict control of those forces. Thus Dov, who enjoys the renewal of his contact with nature, at the same time fights against it (as embodied by the jackals), and thus, against himself. The juxtaposition of his struggle with the jackals and his leaving the kibbutz is not coincidental (62).

Acknowledging the superiority of the primordial, jackal-like forces of the psyche, Dov leaves the kibbutz while adopting the accepted social morality as a last line of defense: "True, when the kibbutz was founded, Ehud, we wanted to inaugurate a new order, until things cried out that they were incorrigible. I said, it will be enough for me if I do good and decent actions, and I didn't know, Ehud, that the imprint of our fingers doesn't last on a watery surface" (74). The verb "cried out" is used again in connection with Dov's room ("Like a riotous splash the red and blue floral bedspread cried out in the midst of all that") showing the "riotous" nature of the things that are irreparable. Dov's last line of defense is also penetrated, and before his death he realizes he has lost the battle: "I am the last, and I am not laughing" (74).

"Before His Time," then, is a story of self-discovery: in his last moments Dov understands that the jackals against whom he battles are flesh of his flesh and cannot be uprooted. The narrator's earlier words regarding the eternal curse between home dwellers and those who live in mountains and ravines, also point to this painful contradiction. For on the one hand, there seems to be cruel, implacable hostility between the two camps, yet on the other hand there is a blood connection between them ("the voice of his accursed brother"), a family tie stronger than all others.

Dov, then, falls victim to the tragic contradiction inherent in the human condition. Human beings have grown out of nature, and their characteristics—drives, instinctual urges, creative and destructive vitality—derive from the living world. Yet in the development of consciousness, a pathological barrier grew between them and their natural origins, and ethical conventions turned those origins into a "shadow," an enemy burrowing in the depths, biding its time, an "accursed brother."[16] The development of consciousness inflicted damage on human beings in two ways simultaneously: their bonds with the world of nature remained sufficiently powerful to frustrate any human attempt to create a character completely separate from the primal forces of nature, and on the other hand, those bonds are not sufficiently strong to give one a sense of kinship with nature, a feeling of harmony with the cosmos.[17] Thus, humanity remains deprived of any possible or satisfactory realm of existence. Life lived according to natural principles has a kind of vitality and creativity, but also an instinctiveness and destructiveness that leaves no room for coexistence with morality. Conversely, daily life in the orderly reaches of society are like a pale, pitiful, and barren imitation of the living, natural world (cf. the discussion of the inverted pyramid, above).[18] Thus, in the concluding section the narrator draws a parallel between daily life in Jerusalem and the decorative objects and holy pictures made of the bull's skin. Those objects are truly made out of "the skin of a real bull, brave and primitive," but these two adjectives no longer apply to the objects made from his skin. In "Man is the Sum of His Sins and of the Fire Lurking in His Bones," Oz makes certain explicit remarks on this subject. He describes the major forces at work in his own world through an analysis of Berdyczewski's stories:

> In his work there are two possible structures of experience: there are the powerful, primary experiences, and there are the secondary ones, pale, pitiful, and threadbare. The primary experiences are always linked to throwing off the reins and

---

16. On the deep connection between the shadow and the twin rival, see Neumann (1973, 352–53).

17. The feeling of reduction, of dilution, of separation accompanying the growth of consciousness is described at length by Neumann. That feeling is a central aspect of the theory of the personality as developed by Shoham (1980, 1982).

18. Nurit Gertz discussed that tension from a different point of departure (1980, 50–51).

instinctual release: love, hate, envy, friendship, destruction, and burning ambition, the defiance of fate. . . . They are all primary experiences that take a heavy toll (madness, death), but which have the life spirit. In contrast, there are secondary feelings: making a good impression, social success, the ability to get along in life, and the like, making oneself popular. (1979a, 36)

This opposition is the pivot of Oz's world. Typically, Oz finds this tension in all the works discussed in *Under This Blazing Light* (1979), the writings of Brenner and Agnon, as well as Emily Brontë's *Wuthering Heights*.

## *The Jackals: Ceremonial Priests*

It is no coincidence that the Biblical background of the story is limited to the four opening chapters of Genesis. Keep in mind that with the birth of Enosh came the first teachings of religious faith: "Then people began to call upon the name of the Lord" (Genesis 4:26). Unlike "A Crack Open to the Wind," which entertains the possibility that God rules and guides his subjects from on high, in the degraded world of "Before His Time" there is no place for monotheistic faith. Here, a mythic experience emerges that preceded monotheism. The religious conception of this story contains both pagan and pantheistic elements. God is revealed in the world itself, and the nature of God, then, is that of the world. Merciful and wicked, He destroys and creates. God and the jackal are merely two sides of a single entity.

At the beginning of the story, the narrator describes a strange bond between the church bells and the wild, riotous chorus: "Last but not least the station broadcast the boldest of melodies. Wild and riotous the melody was sent forth, and the church bells accompanied it as with cymbals" (59). "Wild" and "riotous" describe both Dov's room and the howl of the jackals. The author takes pains to strengthen that possible connection in several ways. First, just as the church bells of the Christians in Jerusalem "exchange confessions" with those of Bethlehem (66), so the jackals of Jerusalem reply to those of Bethlehem (68). Moreover, in the final passage of the story the earlier parallel becomes a direct and mutual connection between the two camps: "How ceremonial are the monastery bells. How contemptible and shamefully wild are the jackals, responding to the message of the bell clappers with twisted laugh, the mockery of fools. Their hearts harbor incitement to malice, malice and blasphemy" (74). That final passage is patently ironic. On the previous page the jackals are given the epithet of "priests," linking them to the world of churches and monasteries, and are described as "ceremonial," a word that refers in the final paragraph to the sound of the bells: "slowly, like ceremonial priests in a mourning ceremony, they approach the young man's corpse" (73). Oz is not content with this implied analogy and twice describes the entire pack as a congregation (Hebrew: *kahal* and *aidah*). Apparently, the opposition between the ringing of the bells and the howls of the jackals resembles the conflict between the domestic dog and its "cursed brother." It is not an opposition in kind but simply one of degree, a partial and temporary contrast between two camps related by blood, by ancestry, and by tradition.

The religious conception latent in the story suggests an essential closeness between holiness, being as near as possible to the "world soul," and impurity and sin. In order to unite oneself with the god-beast, a person must return to his primal, bestial origins. This topic, one of Oz's central concerns, will be treated at length in the following chapter.

To return to "Before His Time," it is impossible to summarize the story's religious concepts without mentioning the holy pictures made by the aged effendi from Samson's hide (59). What place does Jesus, the redeemer, have here in this dark and gloomy story? Not incidentally Jesus' birth is told by pictures made of the bull's hide. Jesus shares the fate of the male characters in the story, as well as that of their analogue, the bull. Contradicting the Christian belief that redemption has already come in the figure of Jesus, Oz holds that redemption is still far off. Jesus, who was supposed to herald a new stage in spiritual life, a change in human consciousness, has not fulfilled his appointed task. The human condition is still close to its primal chaos.

## *Language: Between Elevation and Self-Abnegation*

The last paragraph brings the story to one of its major themes. However, this theme is not the overt conflict between the monastery and the jackals, but the complete rejection of the evaluative language that brings about this opposition. Oz gathers the choicest fruits of the Hebrew language to stress the baseness of the jackals, yet the entire story serves to contradict the ideas and the language of this paragraph.

Throughout the story, the narrator describes the external appearance and voices of the jackals (62, 64, 68, 71, 73). In the final paragraph, however, evaluative language replaces the descriptive language that has characterized the story heretofore. This language divides the world into beautiful and despicable, righteous and corrupt, good and evil. The similarity between the description of the monastery bells and the description of the jackals, however, undermines the validity of this evaluative language. The contemptible jackals, the polar opposites of the monks and their message, are at the same time their potential brothers. It becomes clear that the bells have no "pure" message, and that the jackals are not contemptible. Language here opposes itself, negating its own declarations.

There is a fundamental contradiction between language and the realm of experience that spellbinds Dov Sirkin. He seeks a world of primal existence in which contradictory forces merge, coexisting through struggle and reconciliation, whereas language consists of fixed signs that achieve their meaning through distinctions and differentiations. This principal discrepancy is far more noticeable in the case of evaluative language, which imposes on the world a fixed set of contradictions between "good" and "bad."[19] The dual pyramid mentioned above signifies that the values reflected in language are falsified and distorted. The jackal has "negative" and "positive" elements simultaneously. Moreover, the jackal is not only the mortal enemy of the house-dog, but he is also his distant brother, and from him the dog draws his vitality. Thus, the complexity of existence thwarts any clear division between "good" and "evil." The dual pyramid implies that an individual who reunites with his primal, base origins unites at the same time with his godly origins. The apex of the "cultural pyramid" represents, among other things, a life of alienation, detachment, and distance from the sources of fertility and vitality. Language disregards this complexity and creates a world of its own, oversimplified and misleading.[20]

---

19. This issue is one of the main topics of my *Toward Language and Beyond* (1988a).

20. In his last words, Dov Sirkin admits that the kibbutz ideology could not cope with the elemental forces of the human psyche (see above). It is interesting to compare the protagonist's idea to the comments Oz himself has expressed regarding the kibbutz: "This too is the revenge of the world on the redeemers of the world from days of yore, this is the ancient revenge of man's soul against all who try to redeem it. The necessary distance between words, formulas, theories and the deeds is exposed. 'Life' bursts the fences through its infinite complexity which shatters even the most witty and most comprehensive ideologies" (1979a, 178).

## "Before His Time" as a Model

With the writing of "Before His Time," Oz consolidated his literary concepts. Here, he found the literary method that fulfilled his various needs. In order to express the complexities of his world and the various levels of conflict comprising it, the story was structured as a wheel within a wheel, centered upon a psychological conflict, a psychic drama. That drama, the struggle between the ego and its shadow, or between the illuminated regions of the soul and the dark ones, is the kernel of the story; it dictates the structure, the course of the plot, the character of the protagonist, the social background, and the landscape. Upon that inner ring is constructed a family drama, a mere projection of the tensions within the psychic drama, which is surrounded by the circle of society and landscape. Having noted the generative character of the innermost kernel, it is not surprising to find that the conflict within it is found both in the circle of society and the landscape (the kibbutz and the jackals around it) and in the political circle beyond (the war against the Arabs; Arab Jerusalem and Bethlehem, the sound of whose church bells and jackals is heard in Hebrew Jerusalem). The outermost sphere is the divine one, manifesting the same forces as those within the psychic drama: light and darkness, creation and destruction. However, the opposing forces act in unity and harmony within the divine sphere. That fact, in addition to the primal vitality churning there, explains why Oz's protagonists, all of whom suffer from being divided within themselves, are always so desperate to join this sphere. In his later works Oz suggests that holiness can be achieved through unifying the opposing forces within the soul, a unity comparable to that which occurs within the divine sphere.

As I have shown above, Oz's early stories scrutinize the human psyche and the nature of the forces within it. The circular structure described here reaffirms the importance of that particular concern. Undoubtedly, the psychic drama (the tension between the various forces seething within one's psyche and the search for the possibility of synthesizing them) has remained the central axis of Oz's work throughout his career.

Because of the circular structure of Oz's schema, the various circles correspond metaphorically, giving the story dense textual complexity. That complexity is increased by the fact that a section lacking in a given ring may be replaced by the corresponding section of another ring. Oz makes use of that structure in all his subsequent work, expressing the various forces within, giving voice to the turmoil regarding his relations with his parents and permitting him to sharply criticize the world of the kibbutz while responding to various other phenomena in Israeli society. This structure also allows him to address various audiences: some readers are satisfied with family or kibbutz dramas, while others discern the multiple circles of meaning and their interrelatedness.

This story also solved two other sorts of problems for Oz. We saw that in the character of Dov two forms of consciousness are at work, mythic and modern, or two principles of existence, "Dionysian" and "Apollonian." From this point of view the figure of the protagonist is similar to the author. Oz's protagonists all show that a Dionysian element exists in their author as well, an attraction for the archetypal, the dark and savage, for the instinctive and sensual, for drunkenness and madness. Yet these qualities exist alongside decidedly Apollonian elements (in his articles the author consistently advocates a life of equilibrium and sanity, and the rejection of extreme solutions). While Dov Sirkin expresses the author's Dionysian side, Oz's Apollonian side emerges in his portrayal of Dov, in the complex literary structure, in the linguistic allusions that create bonds of significance within the story, and in the way the Biblical and mythic background is deployed. The Dionysian element of the author is expressed in the character of Dov, who remains attached by his navel to the Great Mother; the Apollonian element of the writer placed that figure in the framework of human experience, interpreted it, and gave it significance.

Further, this story hints at the direction of Oz's future work. In his subsequent stories Oz expanded on various aspects of "Before His Time." In "The Trappist Monastery" (1962c, 1965a) he pondered the nature of the silence of the cosmos that is frequently depicted in "Before His Time" (66, 67, 74), and in "Where the Jackals Howl" (1963a, 1965a) he returned to the kibbutz and the struggle against the jackals surrounding it. In the following stories later included in *Where the Jackals Howl*, he concentrated on various topics that emerge from the worldview latent in "Before His Time."

Henceforth, the basic outline of Oz's works was to be as follows:

1. *The cosmos is driven by instinctual and creative forces.* The nature of God is like that of the world, that of the Great Mother: creator and destroyer, desiring evil but sublimely merciful. The world, with the animal, vegetable, and mineral kingdoms within it, is an all-inclusive pantheistic entity where there is a free and mutual flow among the various beings. The only being who is cut off from that all-inclusive realm of experience is the human being:

> What is the hidden thread that joins the lifeless to the living? We look for the end of this thread in despair, in rage, doubtful, quivering, screaming, clenching jaws, gnashing teeth, biting our lips till they bleed, squinting madly. The jackals know that thread. Sensuous, pulsating currents are alive in it, flowing from body to body, from being to being, vibration to vibration. ("Where the Jackals Howl," 1965a, 15)

The words "current" and "thread" appear with this connotation in many other stories in *Where the Jackals Howl*, such as "The Trappist Monastery," "All the Rivers" (not included in the English translation), "A Hollow Stone," and "Strange Fire," as well as in Oz's later novels.

2. *Human consciousness grew out of the great ocean of the unconscious.* That ocean is far stronger than consciousness, which it fascinates with its huge, mysterious power and its forces of creativity and destructiveness. Thus, the human being remains deprived of a sufficient existential space offering him peace and harmony. On the one hand, the development of consciousness was accompanied by an acute feeling of inner division, of reduction and separation. Conscious life within the limits of action of human society is merely a sorry echo of primal existence. On the other hand, one cannot respond to the siren call of nature, for to respond in such a way would mean destruction and loss. That subject, the struggle with nature (represented time and again by the symbols of the Great Mother) and the attempt to cut oneself off from the area of its influence, and the desire to be joined with nature and to enjoy the pantheistic plenty that characterizes its being, is the axis of Oz's existential world.

Many of Oz's main characters discover that the only way one can be united with the all-encompassing existence of the world is by breaking through the limits of consciousness (in "Where the Jackals Howl," *My Michael*, and other works). In most of these the adjective "strange" ("a strange sound," for example) refers to the primal forces that come back and overcome consciousness.

Oz's fascination with the primal strata of the psyche reached its peak in *Black Box* (1987a; 1988). In his subsequent two novels one can discern a clear shift of emphasis in his interest. In *To Know a Woman* (1989; 1991) we find an influence of post-Freudian object-relationship theories. In his previous work, children were described either as a by-product of some inner, natural forces that had nothing to do with a child's family (*Elsewhere, Perhaps, A Perfect Peace*, and elsewhere), or as a static totality of his parents' character (*My Michael, The Hill of Evil Counsel*). *To Know a Woman* is Oz's first novel where the family is conceived of as a dynamic unit, whose members, parents and children alike, shape each other by way of interaction and symbiosis. In Oz's latest novel to-date, *The Third Condition* (1991), we find the schism between parents and children, an element well known to any reader familiar with *Elsewhere, Perhaps* or the stories of *Where the Jackals Howl*. Yet the novel offers a new line of connection, that of the souls which, according to Kabbala theories, belong to the same "root." In these two novels Oz has not left behind his familiar themes (the tension between daily, safe routine and the intensive, life-threatening experience; the wish to reunite with the cosmos' all-encompassing entity), yet he examines them from decidedly new angles. One should add, though, that the new emphasis given to Kabbalistic notions in *The Third Condition* has come at the expense of psychological depth. The psychological observations of Freud, Jung, and their followers explain the complexity of human behavior and human relationships better than any Kabbalistic theory.

3. *The total severance of consciousness from the primal forces and the complete acceptance of society's regulations and expectations are likely to lead to the sudden outbreak of repressed forces, or to the total death of the soul.* The point of departure for *A Perfect Peace* (1982; 1985) is the death-in-life of Yonatan, the faithful and cuddled son of the kibbutz society. With his last remnant of vitality, Yonatan responds to the voice urging him to find "life," and he is saved. We find the same point of departure in *The Third Condition*, whose protagonist uses Pascal's discussion of "the death of the soul" to characterize his own situation (1991, 163, 199, and elsewhere).

The way to live with the world of the depths is to acknowledge its existence, to be nourished by the creative forces bound up within it, and to try to stave off its instinctual murderous nature. Two of the later stories of *Where the Jackals Howl* are devoted to the possibility of achieving a synthesis: "A Hollow Stone" and "Strange Fire," as well as the final chapters of *Elsewhere, Perhaps, A Perfect Peace*, and *Black Box*. A character like Srulik, one of the main characters of *A Perfect Peace*, knows how to draw upon the world of the depths without being victimized by it. Yonatan also realizes that possibility after scorching his wings in the desert. On the other hand, the novel also tells the story of the domestication of Azariah, the soaked jackal who emerges from the night.

4. *The conception of the existence of primal, eternal forces within the psyche will lead Oz to portray characters as mythic or bestial figures.* Oz compares all his characters to animals, frequently using symbols discussed by Jung. The characters who are umbilically con-

nected to the world of nature will be characterized by constant inner movement, inner twitching. Such is Tova: "nervous currents move her lips" and impart a "hidden quiver" to them ("All the Rivers," 1965a, 93). Noga, the protagonist of *Elsewhere, Perhaps*, moves constantly in "an inner dance" (1966a, 30; 1973, 23) and her uncle, Zechariah-Siegfried Berger is typified by the "nervous twitching" of his mustache (264; 205 and elsewhere). The thighs of Pitdah, the mother of Jephthah the Gileadite, are described repeatedly as "dancing a repressed, inner dance," and the same movement characterizes the hips of Jephthah's daughter (1976a, 241; 1981, 235). The same image recurs in *To Know a Woman* (1989, 50). The novel *A Perfect Peace* revolves around, among other things, the way in which Azariah Gitlin finds relief from the nervous squint that scurries about his eyes.

5. *In human society the Great Mother is represented by the figure of the woman.* Neumann's generalization—woman is nature, man is culture (1973, 140–44)—is most applicable to Oz's world. Thus, the father of the protagonist in Oz's stories of childhood ("The Hill of Evil Counsel," *Soumchi*, and others) stands for a life of balance, correct proportion, and sanity, whereas the mother is driven by hidden urges and impulses. Most of the female figures in *Where the Jackals Howl* belong to that category, as does Eva Berger and her daughter Noga in *Elsewhere, Perhaps*. Ilana, the female protagonist of *Black Box*, is an extreme example of this dynasty. Rimona, one of the main characters in *A Perfect Peace*, is repeatedly described as withdrawn within herself, as if pregnant with herself, like the dragon with its tail in its mouth. Separation from the oceanic realm of experience and the desperate desire to return to it are the major forces active in Hannah Gonen's life (*My Michael*).

Of course, one of the implications of the double pyramid discussed above is that the one who is connected to nature, to the oceanic world, is still close to his divine origin as well as to sources of supreme intelligence and intuition. Indeed, many of Oz's female characters are depicted as holy figures (in *Elsewhere, Perhaps* and *A Perfect Peace*, for example). Many of them are endowed with unerring intuition (such as Rimona in *A Perfect Peace* and Netta in *To Know a Woman*).

On the surface, Oz repeatedly resorts to binary oppositions such as nature and culture, human being and jackal, female and male, life and death, light and darkness, Jews and Arabs. Yet, this dichotomy is constantly deconstructed in his works. It turns out that Nature has both feminine and masculine features, and just as it represents aggression and death it is also the source of life and resurrection. As for culture, it brings about a barren, lifeless existence, and life is sought after not in the lit kibbutz but rather in the dark underworld (see the discussion of *A Perfect Peace* in Chapter 3). Furthermore, the opposing forces contain elements of their rivals; they long to merge with each other or to metamorphose into each other. Thus, in Oz's work, these traditional dichotomies are continuously negated by the implied author; here, such dichotomies are not linked to any judgmental values, nor do they refer to actual political strife or events. The Arabs in *Where the Jackals Howl, Elsewhere, Perhaps*, and *A Perfect Peace* are projections of psychic forces.[21] In his political essays Oz has dealt time and again with the rights of the Palestinians and with their need for a homeland. He was the first Israeli writer who, immediately after the Six Day War, argued that Israel should withdraw from the newly occupied territories. All these issues are never directly addressed in his fiction. Still, whereas the author has not examined the Arab-Israeli conflicts in his stories and novels, he has definitely dealt with the war between the sexes (see Chapter 4). And in this war the woman has remained an archetypal other, awesome and admired. In the previous chapter I mentioned that Oz's mother committed suicide when he was twelve years old; I offered that traumatic event as a possible explanation for his male protagonists' attitude toward female characters.[22]

6. *The author is like the witch doctor of an ancient tribe, the creator of myth*. Oz has expressed that view repeatedly in interviews, and it is strongly bound up with his conception of human beings as subject to primal natural forces.[23] The mythic backgrounds of his stories are, therefore, not only metaphors. That background is not erected only to give historical depth to the characters or to shed new light on the plot, its development, and the ties among the characters. Similarly, that background does not simply provide an additional viewpoint from which the present is judged and evaluated (cf. the use made of the mythic background by writers such as James Joyce, T. S. Eliot, Ezra Pound, and others). Oz's worldview removes the mythic background from its metaphorical-interpretive status and makes it an essential part of his fictitious world. Nevertheless, his approach to the mythic world remains ambivalent, a result of the struggle between the Apol-

---

21. This topic is exemplified in Chapter 3 in the discussion of *A Perfect Peace*. Some aspects of this issue are dealt with by Ramras-Rauch (1989).

22. Esther Fuchs (1987) argues that Oz's portrayal of women reflects a general attitude in contemporary Israeli fiction. See note 3 in Chapter 4.

23. Cf. "For Me Writing is the Conjuring Up of Spirits" (1971b), "Writing is the Conjuring Up of Spirits" (1968c), "The Figure of the Author as the Tribal Witchdoctor" (1973b). Oz returns to that conception in other articles and interviews.

Ionian man within the author and his "accursed brother," the Dionysian.

The mythic figures in his stories often have Jungian significance and not, as noted, incidentally. Jung based his theory on the existence of early strata of the soul that have lost none of their power during the thousands of years of human development, and he saw myth as the verbal projection of that hidden strata. For a creative artist with a worldview like that of Amos Oz, Jung was a natural choice. Later in interviews, Oz's incorporation of Jung's theory would emerge in his explanations of human nature and in the nature of his images. Thus, for example, in an interview held with him at the time of the publication of *Unto Death*, he said:

> My daughters are more frightened of wolves than of cars. Why is that? Is there any real danger that wolves will devour them? The threat of cars is a hundred times more real and likely. However, fear of wolves is an ancient legacy existing within the collective structure of the human imagination. It is impossible to ignore that structure. It exists within the person, and I find it most fascinating in my writing. (1971b)

Clearly, there is a connection here between Oz's views and the Jungian concept of the collective unconscious. A similar idea appears in Oz's remarks about Israeli life: "When all is said and done, what we find here is not exactly 'negligence' or 'slackness,' but ancient tribal urges, the action of forces from the depths, collective history and traumas with which the tribe is afflicted" (1979a, 150). Those concepts, which have a decidedly Jungian quality, appear repeatedly in Oz's articles and interviews. In his explanation of the Arab-Israeli conflict he also uses Jungian concepts. Jung discusses at length the process through which one projects a shadow upon the other, one's adversary. Oz makes use of that concept to explain the tragic misunderstanding afflicting Israel and its Arab neighbors (1971c).

7. *Oz's works never offer the reader an unequivocal theme or a hard and fast message due to the nature of the world presented in them.* Several phenomena join together to repudiate an "official" indisputable interpretation. First, at the core his works present a conflict between diametrically opposed forces, but this struggle in itself is not unambiguous, for each of the rival forces includes within it its contradiction.[24]

---

24. Compare these arguments with the way Barbara Johnson characterizes the works examined in her book:
    Reading, here, proceeds by identifying and dismantling differences by means

Thus, for example, the struggle between Jews and Arabs in the novel *Elsewhere, Perhaps*, which at first appears to be a struggle between light and darkness, male and female, turns out to be a struggle between male-female and male-female (for a detailed discussion, see Chapter 5). From this double duality it appears that one's struggle with one's opponent is simultaneously one's struggle with oneself. Indeed, we have seen above that Dov Sirkin, who fights the jackals, is at the same time battling his own natural elements. This state of affairs leaves no place for division of the rival forces into "good" and "evil," and certainly not for hard and fast moral judgment. Moreover, this struggle cannot be concluded decisively with static balance achieved. Thus, the majority of Oz's works strive toward the finding of a fertile synthesis between the rivals, but this synthesis is never complete and whole.

Another significant point must be noted: the absence of an authoritative, objective point of view from which the world and the characters are evaluated and judged.[25] The narrator in Oz's stories is as clever as a chameleon. Combining his point of view with that of the various characters, he changes attitudes and points of view with the adroitness of a magician. One must never depend upon his explicit declarations: often he supports, implicitly, those characters he outwardly denounces. This characteristic complements the previous one: forces that the narrator repudiates and denounces in the name of accepted social values are revealed to be forces of great sagacity, vitality, and endless attraction. Thus, for example, Matityahu Damkov, the protagonist of "Where the Jackals Howl," is seemingly the representative of nature's dark forces on the kibbutz: he is compared to a jackal, an ape, and a horse in heat. Significantly, he is the kibbutz blacksmith. A close reading of the story reveals that Damkov is characterized as Hephaestus, the blacksmith of the Olympian Pantheon (see Chapter 3). Thus, this apelike creature has at one and the same time godlike features. Oz's short stories and novels constantly deconstruct themselves, thus

---

of other differences that cannot be fully identified or dismantled. The starting point is often a binary difference that is subsequently shown to be an illusion created by the workings of differences much harder to pin down. The difference *between* entities (prose and poetry, man and woman, literature and theory, guilt and innocence) are shown to be based on a repression of differences *within* entities, ways in which an entity differs from itself.... The "deconstruction" of a binary opposition is thus not an annihilation of all values or differences; it is an attempt to follow the subtle, powerful effects of differences already at work within the illusion of a binary opposition. (1980, x–xi)

25. This phenomenon is dealt with in depth by Gertz (1980).

creating a complete analogy between the text and the ever-changing existence it reflects. Needless to say, this narrative technique is inseparably connected to the double pyramid structure discussed above.

8. *The worldview expressed in "Before His Time" has far-reaching implications regarding language.* Oz's prose frequently deals with language, making it one of its main issues. In Oz's subsequent work one finds the following notions:

• Language is the legislator and police of society. Consciousness is constructed through words, and words determine to a great extent the way in which it records and interprets the world.[26] This topic is conveyed indirectly in "Before His Time" and shifts to the center of the picture in Oz's next short story, "The Trappist Monastery" (1962c, 1965a). In the climactic scene of the story, Nahum Hirsh explains to Itcheh, the protagonist, why the monks have to forswear words: " 'This is a monastery,' Nahum answered alertly. 'The Trappist monastery. Its monks have taken upon themselves eternal silence. Words are a source of pollution. Without words there are no lies. . . . They are silent there by the power of a vow.' 'Why is that?' asked the fatigued voice of the warrior. 'A dust of dead words is glued to you. In silence purify your soul,' Nahum quoted a saying of Tagore's" (89). Nahum Hirsh, whose weapons are his words, knows their power well. Words for him are not merely insulation that separate the human being from his world ("a dust of dead words"). Instead, they completely distort this relation. Words are a source of corruption, distancing people from their godly, pure origin. From Itcheh's response to these explanations, it becomes clear that he senses that the silence of the monastery is like an encounter with God, whereas words are like a Trojan horse of society in one's soul. The notion that silence is reality laid bare, authentic, uncorrupted, will appear time and again in Oz's stories and novels (*Where the Jackals Howl, Elsewhere, Perhaps, My Michael, A Perfect Peace*). The importance of this theme is manifested by the role it plays in Oz's latest novel to-date, *The Third Condition* (1991, 198, 232, and elsewhere).

The corrupting role of words appears in varying degrees in most of Oz's works and occupies a central role in *Touch the Water, Touch the Wind.* This novel conveys the limiting and distorting nature of lan-

---

26. This assumption is one of the foundations of the "linguistic turn." For an interesting discussion of the speaker-language-world triangle, and an analysis of the "linguistic turn," see Blackburn (1984). The societal nature of language is extensively discussed by modern philosophers of language. See, for example, Burge (1979) and Kripke (1980, 1982).

guage in an explicit and generalized manner by summarizing and dealing with Heidegger's theories (1973a, 157–58; 1974, 149).[27]

Oz's protagonists respond in two different ways to the power of language. Some of them adopt the world of the word, some seek to totally escape it. Many of Oz's characters believe in ideology, in "values." These figures use words as weapons, and through them they try to control human nature, or even nature itself. Words for them are a way to map the world, to command its chaos and wilderness (Reuven Harish in *Elsewhere, Perhaps*, the protagonist of "Late Love" [1972], all the main characters in *Touch the Water, Touch the Wind*). Yet, many other characters are attracted to primal experiences, and they feel that these experiences are beyond words. They desperately try to break the borders of words in order to reach beyond them (Hannah Gonen, the female protagonist of *My Michael*, is typical). Several characters equate existence within the framework of society to existence within the borders of words. Noga Harish, the protagonist of *Elsewhere, Perhaps*, tries on several occasions to explain to her father the discrepancy between words and reality. Attracted to the vital existence surpassing words, she rejects the world of words as barren and sterile. The same attraction motivates Yonatan Lifshitz, the main character of *A Perfect Peace*.

• Language, then, as the window through which one conceives the world, has tremendous power. Yet Oz's protagonists reveal time and again that in the encounter with reality itself, or with the primal experiences that enchant them, language is frustratingly limited and inadequate. That notion is conveyed in most of the stories of *Where the Jackals Howl*. The final story of this collection, "Strange Fire," strongly emphasizes the uselessness of words: "This is the nature of words, to betray us in crucial moments and to recede into darkness" (173). The protagonist of "Late Love" shares this bitter truth. Although he is a lecturer, well-versed in lectures and speeches, he opens his monologue emphasizing the ineptness of words: "I still have one or two things to say. Time is running out. What words can one use, though, that is the question?" (1971a, 9; 1975, 85). The entire story revolves around his attempt to find appropriate words but ends in his surrender: "Only, I ask, what words can be used? So I am back again where I began: words. Are there any possible words? Na! I have more or less miserably failed" (82; 166). This inadequacy of language is a subject of much of Oz's fiction.

---

27. A comprehensive examination of this novel is included in my *Toward Language and Beyond* (1988a).

- Words are a product of a society, a culture. The desire to map the primordial psychic powers or to reach a primal region beyond culture also implies an attempt to break through the limits of words and the patterns of thought and emotion that they carry along with them. How then is it possible to use words to describe an experience beyond words? One of Oz's solutions for this stylistic difficulty was the use of words as empty labels, as general outlines meant to portray the permanent elements. In his final moments Dov Sirkin tells his son that the founders of the kibbutz had tried to adhere to their lofty ideals "until things cried out that they were incorrigible" (74). The word "things" is a very general one, but it is a fitting choice to express the primal forces, those that have no name. Language in this case does not describe the phenomenon, but rather marks it out, drawing a circle around it like a sapper marking the position of a landmine with white cord. The word "things" appears repeatedly with the aforementioned connotation in most of the stories of *Where the Jackals Howl* and in Oz's subsequent novels.

That solution sheds light on other stylistic solutions: Oz refrains from the direct description of the primordial forces, contenting himself with suggestive, indirect language. One of his main devices is the frequent use of symbols (notably the symbols of the Great Mother) as interpreted by Jung. Analogy is another device Oz often employs. The story "Strange Fire," which concludes the first edition of *Where the Jackals Howl*, reaches its peak in a meeting between Lily and her would-be son-in-law, Yair. Lily tries to seduce Yair and when they arrive at a grove next to the Jerusalem Zoo and to the border between Israel and Jordan, they are about to make love. The location of the grove implies that Lily and Yair, breaking a severe societal taboo, have crossed the borders of culture and words (for an elaborate discussion of this story, see Chapter 5). Indeed, they had already stopped talking to each other, exchanging but "abrupt whispers, some of which are strange voices that are not joined into words" (172). Furthermore, at this point the narrator leaves his characters and dedicates the entire final chapter of the story to a highly suggestive description of the zoo at night. Doubtless, the wild animals serve here as an analogue for Lily and Yair, who have crossed the borders of society and words. The use of analogy, then, is not only an aesthetic device in Oz's fiction, but an inherent element of the experiential world he is trying to convey. Time and again he uses a direct descriptive language as an implicit representation of experiences that lie beyond the reach of direct words. The same technique is employed to delineate hidden, nameless psychic forces.[28] Words and various symbols in Oz's work serve not only as building blocks of a wall, but also as a window opening new vistas, which cannot be directly described in words. In many cases Oz does not try to draw in words the primordial realms that allure his protagonists but rather to open a window to them. If you wish—listen to the voices arising from there, if you wish—stand and observe. Your attempt to give this world a name goes against its very nature and the way it was revealed to you.

- The focus on the primeval world in which a reciprocal flow exists between opposing and conciliating forces gives rise in Oz's prose to a complete rejection of evaluative language that makes artificial distinctions between "good" and "evil." This approach is applied to language in general, and the language of the kibbutz and the Labor Movement in particular. In the stories of *Where the Jackals Howl*, *Elsewhere, Perhaps* and *A Perfect Peace*, Oz repeatedly employs the socialist vocabulary only to depict it as an empty tool.

This attitude toward evaluative language has paved the way for a deep suspicion toward any ideology (see also Chapter 1). First of all, several of Oz's characters feel that ideology corrupts the possible encounter with the world's many facets and leads to sterile, hypocritical life (as in "Where the Jackals Howl," "The Way of the Wind," "A Hollow Stone," *Elsewhere, Perhaps*, and *A Perfect Peace*). Second, ideology is depicted in these works as merely a disguise thrown over the primal psychic forces. Paradoxically, the more extreme a person's ideological positions become, the more evident their psychological nature. That matter is illustrated through many of the figures of the founding generation of the kibbutz in *Where the Jackals Howl* (the lonely protagonist of "Redeeming the World," Shimshon Sheinbaum, the main character of "The Way of the Wind," and others) and in figures like Mitia ("The Hill of Evil Counsel"), Frumma Romanov (*Elsewhere, Perhaps*), and others.

As expected from Oz's worldview, several of his protagonists realize that their ideological principles cannot protect them from their base drives. The protagonist of "Redeeming the World" falls prey to his sexual desires and the narrator sums up: "Even a person with solid ideology stands helpless in front of the night libertine voices" (1965a, 120). The "night voices" are mentioned in most of the stories of *Where the Jackals Howl*, representing time and again dark psychic forces.

---

28. In "Language and Reality in the Prose of Amos Oz" (1990), I examine some other tactics Oz uses to overcome the restrictions of language.

Reuven Harish shares the same painful experience in *Elsewhere, Perhaps*. The narrator describes the "night voices" that find their way to Harish's room, mentions his protagonist's rapacious dreams, and concludes: "Even a pure man of sound principles cannot control his dreams" (1966a, 20; 1973, 14).

It is not surprising, then, to find out that in several of his books Oz creates a clear connection between ideology and licentiousness. Abrasha Pinski, who volunteers to fight along the freedom fighters in Spain, mentions the name of the Spanish cities and "a tone of gay licentiousness breaks through the names" (1965a, 127). This point is further elaborated in the second version of the story: in his last photograph Abrasha "looked more as if he had been making love than fighting for the cause" (1976a, 184; 1981, 167). The ancient revolutionaries, who cluster into Stefa's bed in *Touch the Water, Touch the Wind*, are "schooled in lubricity," "so abandoned" (1973a, 52; 1974, 47); and even some of the kibbutz members are "shrivel-skulled like the ancient revolutionaries who ravished Stefa in Krasnoyarsk" (178; 169). Yolek, one of the main characters in *A Perfect Peace*, "looked more like an aging philanderer than a principled old socialist" (1982, 10; 1985, 7).

- The desire to pass beyond the limits of words, beyond consciousness, is also expressed in the desire to destroy common conceptual frameworks and routine ways of seeing. This wish is connected to Oz's conception of the author's task, as well as to his view of the function of education. In a conversation about *Soumchi* he said:

> Only in the field of electricity, perhaps in mathematics, am I prepared to bear the use of the terms positive and negative. In every other area those terms are emasculating. It's emasculation. There is no such thing as a positive man. Did you ever meet a positive man? There is no such thing as a negative person. There is no positive situation, or negative situation. There is no positive world or negative one. It's the kind of lie they tell to children about the stork. They tell them the world is divided up into positive and negative. The world has a thousand colors, a thousand odors, a thousand tastes, and a thousand bruises and burns. So what? Once we used to sing, "The world is large and open, let us go to it." (1978b)

He went on to relate that attitude toward the world with the nature and task of the writer:

> If there is one thing that the books I love do for me, the great books . . . what they did for me—and I really want the books

> I wrote to belong to the same club—they shattered those abstract patterns: floor and ceiling, window and door, negative and positive, good and evil. They opened the world up for me in all its infinite complexity, in all the bounty it can offer. (ibid.)

Indeed, in "Before His Time" all oppositions—life and death, voice and silence, Jews and Arabs, male and female—are blurred.

In order to understand Oz's caustic attack on evaluative language, one has to bear in mind the ambience Oz encountered upon coming to Kibbutz Hulda in the early 1950s. The kibbutz movement was motivated by sublime ideals and expectations. In order to live up to their ideals, kibbutz members were highly demanding of themselves and their comrades. Thus, passing a judgment on one's behavior or achievements had become a common practice (in *Elsewhere, Perhaps* Oz describes kibbutz public opinion as the kibbutz police). Expressions such as "a positive man" (meaning a good worker, or one who would volunteer to a project whenever he is needed), or "a negative man," are a typical mark of the kibbutz diction and rhetoric. From the very beginning of his literary career, Oz has implicitly criticized the simplicity of such divisions.

While one can understand the impetus behind Oz's rejection of evaluative language, complete denial of evaluative terms seems problematic. It does not seem too difficult a task to mention a whole list of people that Oz would not hesitate to define as "negative." In interviews and articles he has claimed more than once that the Palestine Liberation Organization is "one of the darkest nationalistic movements in history," a claim that has created a lasting split between Oz and some sections of the Israeli leftist intelligentsia. Even the above-mentioned citation, rejecting the use of terms such as "positive" or "negative" to describe humans or human activities, is concluded with Oz's preferred attitude toward life. Actually, Oz talks against one set of norms and suggests a new one instead: one has to experience the plentiful faces of reality, to meet one's world in an immediate, unmediated manner.

Oz's concepts of language are also expressed in his educational views:

> The temptation of many young people to specialize in a well-demarcated area and turn that specialization into a source of income, stifling their curiosity and interest in other areas, is a tendency to self-castration. If someone says to himself, "I don't have the strength to know everything, the world is too

> large for me, I'm going to mark off a little square for myself and live there," he loses contact with reality. Because, contrary to the impression created among their pupils by the schools, reality is not constructed according to academic disciplines, and it exists before one divides it up to its components.... I believe that one can come to know the world before it is broken up into little squares, before the artificial division between humanities and hard science. (1975)

It is not surprising to find that, as a direct concomitant of that view, Oz feels that the adult must preserve and develop the child within him. Moreover, he believes that the writer's task is to nurture this hidden child:

> I can divide all the people I know into two clans: those who drag a dead child along inside them, and those who carry a living one. Perhaps there are also people who carry within them children who are sleeping very deeply, hidden away. Only God can help the ones who are carrying a dead child. The ones carrying a living child don't need me or my stories. They have it already—the child within them. The ones whose child has long since fallen asleep and been buried under heaps of dust and earth, and maybe they are ashamed of it—those are the ones I have something to say to. What I want to arouse in them isn't a position for or against the evacuation of the Sinai. I want to arouse in them that astonishment and wonder before the most immediate things, the astonishment and wonder that a three-year-old child has when he grips a door and opens it, closes it, opens it, closes it. Deep philosophical or poetical wonderment spreads over his face, as he trembles from head to foot with an emotional and intellectual excitement. (1978b).

Indeed, many of Oz's characters are compared to children (e.g., Yonatan and Azariah in *A Perfect Peace*). *The Third Condition* opens with the protagonist's disillusioned realization that his childhood fathered his adult life like a butterfly fathering a cocoon (1991, 12). Yet, at one and the same time he feels that he has not lost his childhood. On the contrary, he imagines that from now on the child will always be hidden in the depth of this cocoonlike womb, "pure, immunized of degeneration" (ibid.).

"Before His Time" may not be one of Oz's best or best-known stories, but it is the first one in which he achieved artistic maturity. All his following works were influenced by that story, both structurally and stylistically. With "Before His Time" Oz's work steps out into the great wide world.

## A MEMORY
## First Encounter with "Where the Jackals Howl"

Near the spot where today the Main Office of Hulda stands, there once stood a small, square shack, covered with a green climbing vine. I don't really know who lived in that shack. Probably one of the kibbutz members' parents. We, the children of the nursery, loved to suck the sweet nectar of the deep blue flowers of the vine. For some reason we were convinced that the elderly inhabitant of that shack was mad, and we would scream at him. What was there in that shack and its inhabitant that left me with a memory of terror? I do not know. Over the years truth and childhood imagination utterly merge.

When I was in high school, junior year I suppose, Oz invited me to his room, which was then near the spot where the shack with the blue-flowered vine had once stood. I don't recall what prompted this invitation. Perhaps it was the conversation on poetry that Oz initiated following the publication of several of my poems. "Read this and give me your opinion," he said, shoving a bundle of tightly printed pages in my hands. This was how I first encountered his story "Where the Jackals Howl." The initial description of the protagonist of the story, Matityahu Damkov, conjured in my mind the image of the lonely, crazy, former inhabitant of the shack and the atmosphere of fear that surrounded him. The invitation that Damkov extended to Galila to visit his room aroused vague, muffled fear in me. (Had the old man invited us to his room? Had he truly threatened to imprison us for our brazen remarks?) From the very beginning with a feeling of deja vu, of being in a strange place where it seems one has already been, I sensed that Damkov meant to lie with his daughter. Yet I still hoped I was misled. As I approached the end of the story I shrunk into my chair, as one who stares at an exposed festering wound yet cannot avert his eyes. At that time I was a fervent socialist. In ideological courses in which I regularly participated we would discuss famine and the class system in India, or the role of the kibbutz movement in Israel. No one had spoken in our courses and group discussions on the world that unfolded before my eyes as I read "Where the Jackals Howl."

Exhausted, I finished reading. What did I think? I laid the pages on a chair, muttering confused, parting words. Along the dark path stretching from Oz's room to the brightly lit dining room I quickly raced.

# 3

## BETWEEN GOD AND BEAST
### Religious Aspects of Oz's Work

Oz describes the Jerusalem of his childhood as a highly religious city:

> The Jerusalem of my youth was a city of sleepwalkers, awash with contradictory dreams, a shaky federation of sects, nations, faiths, ideologies, and hopes. There were extremely orthodox Jews who sat and waited in prayer for the coming of the Messiah, there were energetic, revolutionary Jews who intended to play the role of the Messiah themselves, and there were oriental Jews who had lived in Jerusalem for generations, in their easy-going Mediterranean fashion, and there were fanatical Christians of strange and various sects who came to Jerusalem to be "reborn." (1979a, 209)

Oz himself partook of that religious atmosphere: "My parents chose to send me to a Hebrew elementary school with strong religious and national tendencies, where they taught us to long for the glory of the ancient kingdoms of Israel and to aspire to restore them in blood and fire" (ibid.). He subscribed fervently to these religious-national ideals, composing "Biblical poems about reinstating the kingdom of David in blood and fire and about dreadful revenge against all of Israel's enemies" (207). At fourteen Oz turned his back on Jerusalem and its atmosphere of waking dreams, and went to live, study, and work at

Kibbutz Hulda. Kibbutz socialism was avowedly anti-religious; however, for Oz there was no essential difference in these ideologies except in surface appearances:

> When our forefathers said: "There in the land beloved of our fathers / all our hopes would be fulfilled, / there we would live, and there we would create / a life of purity and a life of freedom"—they put their souls into that song. I know a number of pioneers, those who came to the land to build it and be built by it, in whom that melody resounded all their lives, the song of their souls, stronger than all others. If we were to ask ourselves, "Where is that land, where is that sun? Where is the place where all our hopes were fulfilled?" we would have to reach a strange and fascinating conclusion: those veteran pioneers, in their enthusiasm and desperate devotion, gave religious status to secular acts. (1967)[1]

Amos Oz declared himself a secular Jew (1979a, 76), but religious mythos, the belief in dynamic forces that are conceived of as spirits, demons, and gods, is a central element of his world.[2] The cosmos as described in his stories is imbued with mighty vitality, threatening and enchanting, and Oz's protagonists seek to touch it and be touched by it. The forces of nature—the sea, the mountains, the winds, and the stars—driven by desires and appetites, are strong and active characters in his works. Wonderment over the connection between people and the forces of nature, the question of destiny and free will, repeatedly appear in his works as key questions.

Rudolf Otto's description of religious experience (1958) can assist us in illuminating the implicit essence of Oz's works.[3] In Otto's view, the common use of the word "holy" is inexact and misleading, for the original sense of the term (he uses the Hebrew word *kadosh*) did not emphasize the moral aspect of religious experience but rather elements beyond morality. Moreover, the holy originally referred only to that which surpassed the rational and moral (5). Otto termed this

---

1. In a lecture given at Brandeis University on the occasion of the publication of the American edition of *In the Land of Israel* (1983), Oz emphasized the religious character of the Gordonia youth movement, despite its secular and socialist vision. The members of Gordonia established several of the kibbutzim in the *Ihud Hakibbutzim* movement, including Hulda.

2. On the "religious function," see Jung (1958, 8).

3. Otto's book, first published in 1917, is today thought to be a landmark in the study of religious phenomena.

primary existential root of the holy as "numinous" and he devoted his research to defining it. The encounter with the numinous includes elements of faith, trust, and love, but beyond them, and separate from them, one is exposed to a power that is difficult to bear (12). Only one term can describe that experience: "mysterium tremendum." This description implies fear and trembling, enchantment, swooning with astonishment and wonder (26, 31). Otto attributes two more characteristics to that experience. First, the holy object has energy or urgency, which is given various symbolic expressions: vitality, desire, will, power, movement, activity, drive, and others (23). Those traits appear most clearly in the form of divine "wrath," which is the second characteristic of religious experience. Divine wrath is " 'like a hidden force of nature,' like stored-up electricity, discharging itself upon anyone who comes too near. It is 'incalculable' and 'arbitrary.' " (18).[4] Those who are accustomed to thinking about the divinity in terms of its rational traits, says Otto, view divine wrath as malicious caprice and lust. In fact, that wrath is an essential aspect of religious awe itself.

Rudolf Otto's description is a precise account of the religious feelings contained in Amos Oz's stories. The world described in his works is permeated with an "energy" endowed with will and impulses. His protagonists, who seek union with that energy, experience dread and fascination. On the other hand, many of his protagonists, who were brought up on the "ethical" view of God, condemn the way in which He rules the world as arbitrary, capricious, and malicious (Nahum in "The Trappist Monastery," Yosef Yarden in "Strange Fire," Jephthah the Gileadite in "Upon This Evil Earth," Srulik in *A Perfect Peace*, and others). The protagonist of *The Third Condition* blames God several times for amusing Himself with human misery (1991, 73, 102, 197).

As a youth at Kibbutz Hulda, Oz avidly read the works of Spinoza (cf. the character of Azariah Gitlin in *A Perfect Peace*, who quotes Spinoza all day long, thus receiving the nickname of "Chimpanoza").[5] The avowedly secular world of the kibbutz did not do away with Oz's

---

4. A similar image was proposed by Oz himself. In a conversation with him in the summer of 1985 I compared the bond between a human being and his world to a person heating his house with an open fire blazing in the middle of the living room: if he puts it out, he will freeze, if he fans it up, it will burn down the house. Oz preferred a sharper simile: "No," he said, "getting close to the forces of nature is like touching a five thousand watt electric current."

5. Azariah Gitlin is one of Oz's most autobiographical characters. Years before I decided to write this study Oz told me that in his high school years he was an avid reader of Spinoza.

basic urge to see a structure of significance in reality, every part and parcel of which has meaning and purpose. That urge, expressed in many of his stories, is decidedly religious, leading a person to seek dialogue—complaint and accusation, the expectation of a sign—with the higher power that is responsible for everything that happens.[6] Spinozan pantheism fascinates him in that it describes the holiness that penetrates a deterministic world (the issue of free will appears frequently in many of his works). However, Spinoza's religious schema did not satisfy him completely. The inclusive harmony that characterizes God lacks the drama and struggle that mark Oz's experiential world. Because Spinoza's God lacks human traits and will, He could not be the partner in dialogue whom Oz sought. From Spinozan pantheism his course led to two different theories: one philosophical, the panentheism of Schelling, and the other psychological, Jungian analytical psychology; at the center of both lies the divine duality that includes evil as an essential aspect of divinity.[7]

Schelling, one of the first modern philosophers to grasp the importance of Spinoza's work, began as a pantheist, and in his early philosophy of nature, God and the world are one. An important turning point in Schelling's philosophy is found in *Philosophical Inquiries Into the Nature of Human Freedom* (1936), in which he turns his back on the optimistic idealism of his youth and emphasizes the evil in God and the world He created.[8] The ideas presented here are typical of panentheism: a combination of pantheism (holding that God and the universe are identical) and theism (the doctrine that God created the world and is separate from it).[9] To explain the sources and essence of evil,

---

6. Expectation of a sign is found not only among Oz's protagonists (e.g., "Upon This Evil Earth," *The Third Condition*), but also in autobiographical writings such as "Questions and Answers" (in 1977b). The piece raises metaphysical questions about the conduct of the world, and central to it is the search for a bond with the forces of nature and the quest for the proper place of the writer among them. At the end he expresses hope for an answer, for a sign that will one time be given to him. In his interviews Oz has mentioned more than once this expectation (see, for example, 1989b).

7. The developmental itinerary described here is hypothetical, inferred from Oz's fiction and other writings. As noted, in his youth Oz was highly interested in Spinoza. Following an introductory essay on his work which I published in *Ah'shav* (1984), in personal conversations and in personal letters, Oz confirmed his deep affinity with Jung's psychological theories and with Schelling's panentheism.

8. On the development of Schelling's views and the place of Jakob Boehme in that process, see Bergman (1977) and Tillich (1974).

9. The term "panentheism" was coined by the German philosopher Karl Krause, a follower of Schelling's. His system was meant to bridge pantheism and theism: God, or absolute existence, is one with the world, but the world does not exhaust Him.

Schelling distinguishes two strata within God: that is, God and nature within God (32). In contrast to Spinoza, who minimized the importance of evil (1982, 155, 197), Schelling emphasizes the enormous power of evil in the world. The world is not created from God, light, and holiness, but from the nature that is within God, a dark, chaotic stratum ruled by blind desire (32–33). Law, order, and form extend over the threatening abyss; they have not been victorious and probably never will be (ibid.). The dark, primal stratum has an extremely vital task: God was revealed in it, and from it the world was created. Moreover, the bright, pure stratum of divinity rests upon it, and without the constant contention between the strata, life would be impossible (34–37). Life is a prolonged struggle in which opposing forces need each other.[10] Thus, existence has two faces—merciful and threatening, creative and destructive. The correct balance between the two strata making up God must be set by "measure": the wrong dosage of a curative medicine could become a fatal poison.

Schelling's deity does not possess the "infinite intelligence" of Spinoza's God (1982, 46, 59). His dark "nature" does not allow the qualities of purity and indifference, making him more personal. The world is not run, as Spinoza held, according to general, serenely indifferent laws of nature, but controlled by a divine personality (see Schelling's remarks on Spinoza's pantheism in the introduction to his work). Because of the duality of that personality, it arouses both enchantment and fear. Indeed, certain commentators on Schelling compare that duality with the ambivalence characteristic of the encounter with the numinous object as described by Rudolf Otto.[11]

Panentheism offered Oz a religious structure with two principal components: first, the whole world is a revelation of God who penetrates the mineral, vegetable, and animal kingdoms. Second, that revelation is a product of the deity's greatly merciful and dreadful personality, not the result of mechanistic and indifferent natural laws. In addition, we find other characteristic features of Schelling's philosophy in Oz's work. For example, suffering and sadness constitute the basic foundation of divine and human experiences, implied by the duality within them; longing is a basic element of experience (the longing to give birth to the world that lay within the darkness brought

---

10. Here lies one of the critical differences between the divine sphere and human existence. Within the divine sphere those two elements grasp each other inseparably. In the human sphere the two components are likely to be separate: thus one can either dedicate himself to darkness or strive toward the light (39–40).

11. See Bergman (1977, 192).

about the creation [34–38]),[12] as well as the principle of proper measure (cf., for example, the character of Ezra Berger in *Elsewhere, Perhaps*).

Oz found a complement to Schelling's panentheism in Jung's psychological theories. Schelling's dark, basic stratum is similar in most of its important features to Jung's collective unconscious (the blind, chaotic source of life containing vitality and destructiveness; the unity of opposites existing between that source and the illuminated stratum above it). Even Schelling's descriptions of the Biblical God, angry and selfish, are very close to Jung's conception of the Biblical "Yahweh" (see principally his "Answer to Job" in 1958). Jung repeatedly emphasizes the duality in religious experience and the necessary unity of opposites that characterizes it, while noting that the original Christian conception of the image of God embodied by Jesus was a comprehensive, all-inclusive view, including the animal side of man (1959b, 41). The first symbols of Jesus were, in great part, those of the devil (ibid., 72), and only an ambivalent image of God is truly monotheistic, with its contradictory moral opposites existing side by side (1964, 447–48).[13]

An important aspect of Jung's theory is the process of the discovery of the self, a process through which one can go back and relive the image of God. In fact, Oz's first story, "A Crack Open to the Wind," describes that process, which is also a primary concern of subsequent stories and novels. Jung emphasizes the heavy price human beings must pay for the process of adapting to society, a process which demands that they develop but one side of themselves, consciousness and the persona, while restraining and suppressing their natural instincts, the wild and vital forces stored in their unconscious. The first period of a person's life is characterized by the development and

---

12. Yearning is a powerful element in most of Oz's works, early and late. Srulik (*A Perfect Peace*) gives it an explicitly religious significance: "And this leads me to another, in a certain sense, theological observation. Does not this inner urge to give our all for what we can never have bear a mysterious resemblance to the inner workings of the universe itself, to the orbits of the stars, the procession of the seasons, the migrations of the birds that I have been reading about in Griffin? Perhaps the correct word is not urge but yearning" (311–12; 302).

13. A German theologian and a contemporary of Jung's, Paul Tillich emphasizes the duality of religious experience in his writings: "In its original sense the Holy denoted both the heavenly and the demonic. But as soon as the dichotomy of religious consciousness characterizes the demonic as demonic, the idea of the Holy is equated with the divine. The Holy immediately becomes the right thing, the thing that must be done" (1962, 76; translation mine). It is no coincidence that Tillich's doctoral dissertation deals with Schelling's religious outlook (1974).

the stabilizing of the ego as the center of consciousness, which causes feelings of limitation, truncation, and alienation.[14] The only way to achieve a feeling of fullness and unity in the second part of one's life is through a return, simultaneously involving both conciliation and struggle, to the repressed forces of the soul:

> Conscious and unconscious do not make a whole when one of them is suppressed and injured by the other. If they must contend, let it at least be a fair fight with equal rights on both sides. Both are aspects of life. Consciousness should defend its reason and protect itself, and the chaotic life of the unconscious should be given the chance of having its way too—as much of it as we can stand. This means open conflict and open collaboration at once. That, evidently, is the way human life should be. It is the old game of the hammer and anvil: between them the patient iron is forged into an indestructible whole, an "individual." This, roughly, is what I mean by the individuation process. (1959a, 288)

While the ego is merely the center of consciousness, the self is the center of the whole personality, including both consciousness and primordial urges and instincts. A person who achieves wholeness reaches a state beyond emotional confusion and violent shock, consciousness at a remove from the world (1968, 46).[15] Because of the unity it attains, which includes the primordial, eternal elements of the psyche, the archetype of the self is identical to the image of God. Hence, the discovery of the self is tantamount to the discovery of God within oneself (1959b, 22). Individuation, then, becomes a spiritual voyage wherein the traveler who has no recognizable creed sets out on a religious journey. One of the characteristic forms taken by that journey is the dangerous quest for a treasure (the captive princess, the precious pearl, the living waters, the golden flower that gives

---

14. Jung discusses that process in many of his books. See, for example, "The Relations Between the Ego and the Unconscious" (1953a). An interesting discussion of the cost incurred by the construction of the ego is found in the books of Shoham (1980, 1982).

15. Cf, the description of Rimona in *A Perfect Peace*: "Drawn inward and quiet, drawn up within herself and concentrated in deep and tranquil heedfulness, as if from a distance she were being told what would happen tomorrow and what would happen in the coming days, and as if there were neither sadness nor joy nor surprise in that information" (107). The process of discovering the self overlaps in its major stages with the hero myth as described by Campbell (1973).

eternal life). A person who has achieved selfhood enjoys the unity within it, a divine unity bringing together both the lowest and the most exalted qualities. The search for the treasure appears in the final story of *Where the Jackals Howl*, "Strange Fire" (see Chapter 5), and with a close reading of Oz's subsequent work, we find that the journey for the treasure is the foremost model for most of his novels and novellas (*Elsewhere, Perhaps, My Michael*, "Crusade," *A Perfect Peace*, and *Black Box*). Some of Oz's characters have already gone through the process of achieving the unity of the opposites (Segal in *Elsewhere, Perhaps*, Srulik in *A Perfect Peace*). Other works depict characters in the course of their journey for the treasure (Yonatan in *A Perfect Peace* and others).[16]

It is likely that Jung's view appealed to Oz in two significant ways: first, the ambivalent character of the religious experience as it is presented by Jung fit in with Oz's own divided and contradictory world of experience; and second, according to Jung's view, religious fulfillment is not achieved by means of a struggle against the body, one's instincts, and the primordial heritage that whispers within one's heart, but, on the contrary, by explicitly acknowledging and accepting that heritage and its vitality. The Dionysian element of Oz's world is extremely powerful, as all his books indicate. Jung offered him a way in which he could avoid waging a desperate war against his own roots, but could lay them bare and nurture them; this would provide a solution that would bring about coexistence between the various forces within him, yet still involve constant drama. One might also postulate that Jung's view of the revelation of the "God within you" taught Oz how to bring his religious yearnings and his secular, kibbutz reality into harmony.

The examination of Oz's religious outlook calls for a detailed discussion of most of his works, since that outlook is apparent in a majority of his literary motifs. Due to the limitations of the present chapter, however, I cannot fully discuss his religious views in all of their manifestations and contexts. To convey the essence and importance of these views in Oz's world, I shall first describe at length several of the stories in *Where the Jackals Howl* ("The Trappist Monastery," "Where the Jackals Howl," "Strange Fire," and "Upon This Evil Earth"). Then, to show the continued presence of that element in Oz's works, I shall discuss three novels, *Elsewhere, Perhaps* (1966a), *A Perfect Peace* (1982), and *The Third Condition* (1991).

---

16. I elaborate on this issue in Chapter 5. Other aspects of this theme are discussed in my *Toward Language and Beyond* (1988a).

Oz's first story, "A Crack Open to the Wind" (1961b), shows his great interest in religious experience. In Chapter 2 we saw how the "city father," the mayor, is portrayed as though he were God. The protagonist asks who the father of the city is and whether he exists; these questions lack all meaning unless we interpret them metaphysically: Is there any direction to the world? Does God exist? The story offers no unequivocal answer to these questions. At any rate, the main protagonist decides to act as though the mayor's office were empty.[17]

Oz's following stories indicate a change in his view. God is not only described as a high power who is supposed to direct the world and its creatures from above, but also as an entity revealed within the world itself. The nature of God is the nature of the world. Thus, God is presented as both a destroyer and a creator, all-merciful yet malicious.

In "Before His Time," the earliest of the stories in *Where the Jackals Howl*, silence represents the voice of primal, holy reality, which is beyond words and culture. The degree to which Oz was immersed in that subject is shown by the central place given to silence in the following story, "The Trappist Monastery" (1962c). In fact, the Hebrew title of that story stresses the vow of silence taken by the Trappists.

## "The Trappist Monastery": Confronting the Silence of God

"The Trappist Monastery" describes the reprisal raid of an IDF battalion against a Jordanian village in response to provocation. The

---

17. Oz expresses himself on that issue in his articles, too. In his comments on Berdyczewski's story, "The Hidden One," Oz points out the ambiguity that characterizes the story:

> The problem presented in this story is a religious problem, the metaphysical problem of providence and reward and punishment. If the world is in fact guided and corrected, then Dov Eliahu was a hidden saint. And even if it is like a faded copy, the copy is still legitimate: the house of study is the Temple, and the village idiot is the chorus of Levites. But, if there is no God, then everything is vanity, and everything is only as it seems. The idiot is an idiot, and the story ends with "vanity of vanities, everything is vanity." (1976c)

On Agnon Oz comments:

> Man is a guilty creature. All the protagonists of Agnon's stories are guilty souls. But Agnon is not a theological preacher or some kind of literary Rabbi Grunem May-the-Redeemer-Come [a character from *Just Yesterday*]: there is guilt, but there is no way of knowing where the accusing finger comes from. Who is the judge and who is the punisher, and perhaps, there is no ruler in the capital, and there is nothing at all, and then everything is an ugly joke on everything else, and purposeless shaking and trembling. (1974, 43)

main characters of the story are Itcheh, an officer of the battalion, and Nahum Hirsch, a medical orderly. While Itcheh is on his way across the enemy lines, Nahum Hirsch stays behind and pursues Bruria, Itcheh's girlfriend, finally persuading her to sleep with him. When Itcheh returns to the camp, Nahum convinces him that Bruria has gone to Jerusalem with the operations officer and urges him to follow her. Nahum Hirsch joins in the pursuit, hoping the jeep will go off the road and into a chasm, so that he could then rescue the "national hero" and win some heroic glory of his own. The jeep carrying the two men breaks down on the way to Jerusalem not far from the Trappist monastery. Nahum finds that an appropriate moment to explain about the Trappist's vow of silence and Itcheh is filled with awe and wonder before the monastery. At the end of the story the jeep is still out of commission, and the soldiers prepare to walk to a nearby kibbutz.

This short summary of the plot points out the main difficulty in understanding it: there is no apparent connection between the body of the story and its conclusion. What is the function of the Trappist monastery in the story? What is its relation to the plot involving fighting and sex that preceded it? Why does the monastery arouse such strong feelings in Itcheh? And why does the author emphasize those feelings in the conclusion and in the title "The Trappist Monastery"?

Of course one could argue that we are dealing with an artistic failure here, that the end of the story is unconnected with its body. In fact that is Nurit Gertz's opinion: "That ending is a kind of 'deus ex machina' in the story and does not follow from the processes that precede it. It is not likely that the sight of the Trappist monastery would bring about such a sudden and drastic change in the characters" (1980, 104). However, the ending is not merely superfluous; it provides a climax for which the story has prepared us. The ending is the very heart of the story, and to call it a "deus ex machina" is to miss the entire point.

In order to understand what happens at the end of the story, let us first examine the figure of Itcheh. In many ways Itcheh is an extension of the characters presented in Oz's earlier stories, "Purple Coast" and "Before His Time." Like the mythic figures who populate "Purple Coast," and like Dov Sirkin in "Before His Time," Itcheh does not have the qualities of a regular human being. Even though he is not the battalion commander, the soldiers call him "king" (78), and "lord" (84), and everyone around him is his "obedient subject" (79). His mythic stature is also evident in the reference to his jeep as a "cyclops" (88). According to one tradition, the Cyclopses, members of the first generation of Greek gods, along with the Titans and the hundred-armed monsters, were Zeus's helpers, while another tradition has them as Hephaestus's assistants (the great interest Oz took in the figure of Hephaestus is shown by the fact that the protagonist of his next story, "Where the Jackals Howl," is an avatar of Hephaestus).[18] Thus in Itcheh, called "king" and "lord," we find elements linking him to the Olympian pantheon. That mythic figure contains the primal forces of nature: like Dov Sirkin in "Before His Time," Itcheh is called a "bear" (79) and a "savage" (78, 86).

Also like Dov Sirkin, who tried to channel the primal forces within him toward the ideological structure of the kibbutz, Itcheh apparently finds his place as a soldier, and his heroism is famous throughout the army:

> After every reprisal operation Itcheh's name was heard in high military circles. In one action he leaped into a trench full of armed enemies all by himself. His savage shouts froze their blood, and he cast dark dread upon them. His giant body passed among the stricken foes like lightning. Their bodies, petrified in horror, give themselves over submissively to the volleys erupting from his weapon. Alone he had leapt into that trench, and alone he emerged from the other side, a drunken cry of exultation bursting from his hoarse throat. (78–79)

However, Itcheh's integration into the army appears complete only if viewed from the outside. His heart is not with his many friends and admirers. Like one of the Biblical Nephilim, a man within whom primal forces churn, he feels isolation that human society cannot dispel. Nahum Hirsch, sitting beside him on the jeep, tries to "crack Itcheh's tired solitude" (87). Can Itcheh, constantly surrounded by admirers, be in solitude? Yet the verb "to crack" shows the magnitude of his isolation, which encloses him like a fortified rampart. Nahum Hirsch is completely mistaken in his assessment of Itcheh's character. He is convinced of Itcheh's absolute identification with the military, an identification behind which lies Itcheh's belligerent spirit: " 'You'll be a professional soldier,' said Nahum with certainty. 'People like you lust for war' " (87). Itcheh is astounded at such utter misunderstanding and tells Nahum that he wants to be demobilized and become a

---

18. As a "king" and a "lord" Itcheh has something of the figure of Zeus; as a refugee he partakes of Hephaestus.

member of the *Egged* bus cooperative, making a career for himself as a professional soccer player.

To prepare the ground for the encounter with the Trappist monastery, Oz introduces a religious element into the story at the end of section six, a short time before the jeep motor dies. On their way to Jerusalem the two men meet a "pale yeshiva student with long earlocks," but they cannot understand what he says and continue on their way. The only explanation for the presence of that figure, it seems to me, is the hymn that Itcheh sings as they drive on:

> The sound of a faint and muffled hymn stole into Nahum's ears. Evidently Itcheh was thinking about the cross-eyed yeshiva boy who had accosted them as they left the coastal plain, because he was singing to himself in pleasant and threadbare melancholy:
>
> Our Father, our King, be merciful and answer us,
> Though we have no merits.
> Deal with us in charity and kindness,
> And save us.
>
> "Amen," whispered Nahum with enthusiastic devotion. (88)

Strangely, Itcheh, who has just returned from a reprisal raid, asks God to be merciful to him and answer him, "though we have no merits." Of course one might argue that the words of the hymn are unimportant, but Nahum's response, which is indisputably religious, refutes that argument. In addition, the jeep motor dies in the following scene, and the two find themselves next to the Trappist monastery, an incident that clarifies the importance of those lines. Without thinking, Itcheh addresses the only power that can dispel his great, metaphysical isolation. It is noteworthy that in the second version of the story the author enhances the religious background of his protagonist. In that version it turns out that upon his arrival in Palestine Itcheh had been sent to a religious agricultural village (1976a, 100; 1981, 109). Nahum's unexpected response lays the ground for his address to God at the end of the story. As noted, immediately after Nahum says "Amen," the jeep motor dies, and the pair find themselves not far from the "obscure silhouette of the Trappist monastery to the northwest, in enemy territory" (89). Now the story reaches its main point.

What transpires between Nahum and Itcheh? What happens in Itcheh's heart as he faces the Trappist monastery? Nahum finds relief from the two urges that have driven him all evening long. First, as a medical orderly behind the lines, his position in the battalion is abject and humiliating, and he desperately seeks a modicum of heroism. He covers his lack of real heroism with endless chatter containing elements of delusion and madness. That chatter ultimately brings him, in his relations with Bruria, to "tired, heroic pride" (81). Now, too, words and the knowledge he demonstrates give him a feeling of superiority and masculinity (89, 90). Paradoxically, Nahum's remarks about human language are entirely trustworthy here, particularly because his verbal maneuvers illustrate his view. In contrast to Itcheh, who is now filled with a feeling of "reconciliation," Nahum becomes prolific. First he tells Itcheh what the building is and who lives in it:

> "This is a monastery," Nahum answered alertly. "The trappist monastery. Its monks have taken upon themselves eternal silence. Words are a source of pollution. Without words there are no lies. For years and years they live together and never open their mouths. Imagine the depth of that clear silence. They are silent there by the power of a vow. . . . 'A dust of dead words is glued to you. In silence purify your soul,'" Nahum quoted a saying of Tagore's. (89)

"Before His Time" describes silence as an existing and active element in the world. Similarly, "The Trappist Monastery" refers to silence even before the men's arrival at the monastery: "Volleys of the final convulsion continued to rebel obstinately. In the end they lost heart and gradually died down and fell silent. Silence came and pieced together its fragments with gentle, merciful patience" (83). The religious nature of that silence is only hinted at in this story (the adjective "merciful" that modifies it also modifies God in Nahum's address to Him, 91). The second version of the story explicitly refers to silence as divine: "They live there cheek by jowl and never exchange a word among themselves. Imagine what a divine silence that must be" (104; 113).

Nahum, for whom words are a weapon, knows very well how much falsehood and pollution they contain. Words, with the habits of thought and the moral and social norms they carry with them, distance men from primal, natural reality. "Dead" words act as a kind of insulation, cutting one off from one's world.

Nahum, proud of his knowledge, unknowingly touches upon the hidden, vulnerable strain of Itcheh's world. A chatterer like Nahum, whose entire world is words, is unlikely to grasp the import of Tagore's saying. Itcheh, in contrast, has lived like Gulliver, bound up by

Lilliputian words, and for the first time in his life he sees the possibility of a different kind of life, vital and liberated. Vis-à-vis Nahum, who maliciously exploits his momentary superiority, Itcheh keeps asking the same question: Why are they silent? Unlike Nahum he understands that the significance of silence is immediate contact with the world, with God, and he is filled with awe: "That's absolutely dreadful, to be quiet that way. It scares me" (90). The experience of life embodied by the monastery inspires both dread and fascination within him: "He sought repose. He was tired to death. His body was weak and stunned, and his glance was riveted to the tall monastery as though under an enchantment" (ibid.). At the end of the story, we find the protagonist compared to an animal trapped in a beam of light (91). Their shared fear and shock hint at the affinity between Itcheh and the jackal (Itcheh is "stunned," the jackal is "stricken"). The jackal's filthy fur also recalls Itcheh's furry hair. In the second version of the story, Oz emphasizes that similarity by describing Itcheh as "tired to death," just as the animal twitches "with deathly fear" (106, 115). Thus, Itcheh's gaze, riveted to the monastery as though under an enchantment, proves to be similar to that of the animal, petrified and stricken as it is trapped by the light. In the primal world beyond words, an enormous force exists to which the heart is unaccustomed and unlikely to withstand. The powerful fascination and dread that accompanies that encounter causes one to flee to the safe haven on the other side of the barrier of words, like the jackal running away from the light. Itcheh's experience is the same feeling of holiness described by Rudolf Otto, an experience characterized by attraction, fascination, and infinite dread. Moreover, the image of the jackal illustrates not only the power of human experience, but also Itcheh's "jackal" nature. As with Dov Sirkin, Itcheh has primal savagery which alone fully permits him to feel the powers latent in the world. That connection between the holy and the impure is clarified in Chapter 2, and I shall return to it in the present chapter.[19] Here it should be added that the second version of the story further emphasizes Itcheh's silence. First, Itcheh stops talking and starts to "croak faintly," speaking "with what was left of his voice" (103–4; 112–13). Finally, he falls completely silent as noted four times by the narrator. As if adopting the vow of silence taken by the monks, he stops answering Nahum's questions. In the second

---

19. The unity of sin and sanctity is also indicated in the story by the name Latrun, which commemorates the "faithful thief who was crucified with the Nazarene" (90). Latrun is the name given to a prominent ridge near the valley of Aijalon. The Trappist monastery is located in this area.

version Nahum himself comes to the conclusion, "I need silence" (106; 115). Beyond their differences, a certain fraternity is forged between Nahum and Itcheh—the fraternity of silence.[20]

While Itcheh stares in fascination at the monastery, Nahum silently addresses God:

> If you managed your affairs sensibly, if your acts had some degree of responsibility, you would have sent Yonich a different way. You could have let Yonich reach the Trappist monastery and sip years of muffled silence behind thick stone walls, in the midst of calm pine groves. You should have ordered the German whip to horrify Itcheh's face and not Yonich's, to carve some dread and pain into Itcheh, a human visage. You should have accorded me a pinch of tranquil force, O merciful God, a pinch of tranquil force. (91)

Nahum's religious views are beyond Itcheh's primal, existential grasp. He addresses a "merciful God" with words of reproach and advice. God, the ruler of the world, lacks good sense and responsibility. In this respect Nahum becomes the forerunner of a number of Oz's characters who believe in God but find the way He manages His affairs questionable. At the same time, Nahum misinterprets what is happening around him. He mistakenly assumes, for example, that Itcheh wants to make a career of the army, and he consistently ignores Itcheh's dread that renders superfluous his request that God "carve some dread and pain into Itcheh." Previously, he has misinterpreted Itcheh's fears and suggested, as a solution, that they go to one of the kibbutzim in the vicinity. Further, he also misconstrues existence within the monastery: unlike Itcheh, who knows that life beyond words has enormous power, Nahum believes that life offers peace and tranquillity. Therefore, Nahum is trustworthy only when speaking of himself: torn between conflicting drives, he asks that God give him a bit of tranquillity before a "wave of shame" and "crushing nausea" overcome him. In this light, Nurit Gertz's claim, that Nahum's words sum up the meaning of the work, that "they contain the truth that the

---

20. That unity, which is created between the very characters who were supposed to desperately hate each other, will continue to occupy Oz in his work. Examples of that fraternity is the bond between Yonatan and Azariah in *A Perfect Peace*, and between the main characters in *Black Box*. That bond is another aspect of the ideological and experiential synthesis to which many of Oz's works aspire. An extensive discussion of that topic appears in the last chapter of this study.

author is interested in transmitting to the reader" (1980, 102), appears questionable.

"The Trappist Monastery" typifies a very interesting trend among the younger Hebrew writers. We can find the same plot in a typical story of the "Palmach generation," but unlike these writers Oz does not emphasize the elements of the plot involving war, politics, and society. The emphasis of this story moves from the social and political stratum to the metaphysical level, the experience of an encounter with the numinous object. Thus the story demonstrates one of the central tendencies of fiction by younger Hebrew writers.[21] Oz does not "make conspicuous use of the plot and thematic structure of the previous generation as a model for criticism and parody," as Gertz claims (100). Oz took the figure of the hero of the Palmach generation and altered it to fit his own needs. First, Itcheh, the pride of the battalion, is not a "mythical Sabra" but a refugee who came to the country as a child and discovers that army life and heroic adventures are not the center of his world. Moreover, he suddenly discovers another threatening yet fascinating realm to which his soul reaches as he is stricken with dread and enchantment.

Itcheh's character, since it is deeply rooted in Oz's world, renders baseless Gertz's claim that he is a parody of the hero. If this story contains criticism of the Palmach generation, it is not directed at the hero, but rather at the Palmach philosophy of life, which viewed social and national goals as a universal vision, and asserted that human society had answers for all possible questions. "The Trappist Monastery" transfers emphasis from the national and social plane, from life centered on speeches and orders, assemblies and parades, to the opposite realm of existence, that which is beyond words. Regarding the Palmach generation the story seems to say: "Words aren't everything, carrying out orders and listening to speeches isn't everything, social and ideological theories aren't the main point. On the contrary, real life takes place somewhere completely different." In this sense we find a certain similarity between this story and one of A. B. Yehoshua's early stories, "The Slumber of the Day," which expresses utter fatigue with "building," with life consisting only of diligent labor (in the service of the Zionist enterprise?).[22] The story transposes a "religious" approach to work with a "religious" approach to sleep.

---

21. I discussed that topic in my articles, "Secularism and Religiousness in Modern Hebrew Prose" (1988b) and "Elections and Literature in Israel" (1989).

22. The story was first published in *Lamerhav*, Aug. 8, 1959, and later included in Yehoshua's first collection of stories (1963).

## "Where the Jackals Howl": What Is the Hidden Thread?

Oz's following story, "Where the Jackals Howl," contains no explicit reference to the religious sphere. Nevertheless, we can find a latent religious element that is of great importance for understanding the story.[23] "Where the Jackals Howl" returns to the kibbutz landscape, surrounded by jackals, where "Before His Time" takes place. The central encounter is between Matityahu Damkov, a refugee who arrived at the kibbutz in the midst of the Second World War, and Galila, a sixteen-year-old girl native to the kibbutz. Damkov invites Galila to his room to tell her that he is actually her true father, and thereby to strike out at the social order of the kibbutz and shatter it. Galila does not believe Damkov, though she is willing to sleep with him. At the last minute she is persuaded that he really is her father, and she heeds the ancient prohibition against incest. Parallel to that plot, the story also describes a jackal cub caught in a trap in the kibbutz fields.

The religious element here is a significant part of the story's worldview, which is a direct extension of the one expressed in "Before His Time" and "The Trappist Monastery." A key for understanding that world appears in the description of a trapped cub in Chapter 2:

> A wall of old and dusty cypress trees surrounds the plantation. What is the hidden thread that joins the lifeless to the living? We look for the end of this thread in despair, in rage, doubtful, quivering, screaming, clenching jaws, gnashing teeth, biting our lips till they bleed, squinting madly. The jackals know that thread. Sensuous, pulsating currents are alive in it, flowing from body to body, from being to being, vibration to vibration. (15)

If I had to point to a single passage that contained, like a crystal, the essence of Oz's world, I would without hesitation choose this one. Within nature a "mystic union" occurs wherein a free, mutual flow is shared by various beings. The world, including the animal, vegetable, and mineral kingdoms, is a pantheistic All. The development of consciousness and culture has cut human beings off from that all-embrac-

---

23. For a detailed analysis of the story from different points of departure, see Gertz (1980) and Ben-Baruch (1982). See the following chapter for the meaning of water in the story.

ing realm of experience, and they struggle bitterly in order to go back and rejoin it. The dogs, domesticated wolves and jackals, are like their owners: "How much lightness, how much tender springiness is there in the gait of the jackals. The dogs of the kibbutz, they alone can understand this enchanted motion. That is why they shout in rage and envy and dread. That is why they paw at the ground, straining at their chains till their necks are on the point of breaking" (14). The motion of the jackals has something "enchanted" about it, and the dogs, like the members of the kibbutz who seek the end of the thread in "rage," shout out before it in "rage." The flow that characterizes the "hidden thread" ("tender currents bubble in it") emerges again later in the story and is also mentioned in the opening lines: "At last the heat wave abated. A blast of wind from the sea pierced the massive density, opening up cracks to let in the cold. First came light, hesitant breezes, and the tops of the cypresses shuddered lasciviously, as if a current of vitality had passed through them, rising from the roots and shaking the trunk, anointing them with a quiet caress" (9). Thus, the cypress trees partake in the mystic union of the natural world.

The feeling that the natural world has a soul of its own emerges in the frequent use of personification. Even inanimate objects (Heb.: *domemim*), mentioned about half a dozen times, have a life of their own. What is the character of that soul? As in his earlier stories, Oz makes use of water metaphors here, too, to depict the ancient foundations of nature:

> At this twilight hour our world is made of circles within circles. On the outside is the circle of the abstract, distant darkness: a dim lake murmuring with tremors and hums. Sealed and enclosed within it is the circle of the night lands, dotted with vineyards and orchards. Our lands betray us in the night. Now they are not brittle and submissive and familiar. Now our fields have gone over to the enemy's kingdom. Like a quiet and turbid threat they send us waves of vague, strange scents. At night we see them bristling, turning into a dark being, hostile and wicked. The circle of light keeps guard over our little houses. That wall is invaded by the odors of the enemy and his whimpering and triumphant cries. And inside, in the innermost circle of all, in the heart of our little world, is Sashka's writing desk. A tiny circle of brightness pours out of the desk lamp onto his papers. (15–16)

The description is clearly one of a Jungian ocean ("a dim lake"), the collective unconscious, on the surface of which grows both the personal unconscious (parallel to the fields surrounding the kibbutz in this description) and consciousness (the light). The weakness of consciousness is hinted at, among other things, by the indirect comparison between the "lake" of darkness and the "puddles" of the old light of the kibbutz (14). The world's soul is like the ocean, the rapacious Great Mother. The world's primal impulse opposes human consciousness and the culture it has built, manifesting hostility and malice toward it. The second version of the story expands the descriptions attributing the characteristics of a beast of prey to the dark land (1976, 16; 1981, 9). The development of culture is like the conquest of nature, and nature, in turn, seeks revenge.

The opposition between darkness and light appears throughout the story, placing the illuminated, the bright, the dry, and the warm in confrontation with the dark, the shadowed, the wet, and the cold. As one might expect from Oz's philosophy, which emphasizes the vitality of the world of nature, light is not the stronger side in that confrontation, nor is it the side yearned for. The opening description of the heat wave is connected with light and warmth, and it shows the pinching, sterile character of conscious life within the orderly reaches of human society. In contrast, the world of Galila and Damkov is connected to water and rain (cf. the first description of Galila and the description of her realization of her father's identity in the second version of the story: " 'Father,' said Galila in surprise, as if waking on the first morning of winter at the end of a long summer, looking outside and saying, rain" [24; 19]).

One of the most essential conflicts of Oz's work grows out of the bestial, malicious character of the world: how is it possible to unite with the world? Only those similar in character can return to their origin and enjoy its pantheistic bounty; only the jackals "know the thread."

## *Between God and Beast*

In "Where the Jackals Howl" the jackals represent the dark and base side of nature, unrestrained drives and evil urges. However, the jackals are not merely an instinctive, evil element. They possess a kind of knowledge that human beings struggle "in despair and rage" to acquire: they know "the hidden thread that joins the lifeless to the living." Indeed, the story's religious view implies that an essential closeness exists between primal holiness, which is the closest of all to the world's soul, and pollution and sin. To be united with God, a person must go back to his bestial sources. This notion constitutes one of Oz's central themes. In earlier chapters we saw that Dov Sirkin ("Before His Time") and Itcheh possess both holiness and jackalness. The same unity of opposites shapes the figure of Damkov in the present story, that of Jephthah the Gileadite ("Upon This Evil Earth," 1976a), those of Siegfried Berger (*Elsewhere, Perhaps*, 1966a) and the Christian pilgrims ("Crusade," 1971a). That unity of opposites explains why Oz's protagonists who are the strongest believers are frequently also the basest. In this light it might be interesting to add that an important god in Egyptian mythology is the jackal god, Anubis.[24]

It is worth noting that in his articles Oz uses the words "god" and "beast" as though they were synonymous. He describes Berdyczewski in this way, for example:

> Berdyczewski sought to create a kind of antithesis to the anthology of rabbinic Jewish legends, to bring out a kind of opposing myth, not Jewish but primordially Hebraic. Versus the "lineage" of rabbis, Geonim, teachers of halakha, and saints, he wished to lay bare a kind of "lineage of the descendants of Cain," of the accursed, a lineage that would shed another kind of light—perhaps one ought to say, would cast a shadow—upon the chronicle of the Jewish people. They are the rejected heroes, with their drives, ostracized and banned. Thus he wished to break the religious infrastructure in order to descend to a more ancient infrastructure, savage and instinctive, of flesh and blood. (1979a, 34)

Later in this article Oz points out that the power that animates Berdyczewski's protagonists is the desire to "break the boundaries of culture and to be a beast or god or a god-beast" (35). He repeats that identification in his article on Agnon (ibid., 48), as well as in his remarks on Brenner (ibid., 40).

"Where the Jackals Howl" suggests two courses through which one

---

24. Oz is very familiar with the heroes of Egyptian mythology. In a letter of June 12, 1984, in response to the second chapter of this book, published in *Ah'shav* (1984), he wrote to me: "Yesterday I got back from a short trip to Egypt with the members of Hulda, where I finally became closely acquainted with some of the heroes of my youth (the cow-goddess Hathor, the gods Isis and Osiris, Set who killed his brother and Horus avenging his father's blood, and the jackal-god Anubis, the god of mummification)—and now I find your introductory essay on my table." On the Egyptian animal-gods, see Bonwick (1956), Lurker (1980), and Schwaller de Lubicz (1978).

may once again become part of the all-encompassing inclusiveness of the world. The first is through forgetfulness: "In the past, forty years ago, our veterans entrenched themselves into this land. . . . During the long, burning hours of the day they used to curse the scorching earth in despair and rage, but in the hours of the night they used to sing to it songs of devotion, forgetful of their place and time. Oblivion gave taste to life. At night it would embrace them like a mother" (20). The bond between the pioneers and the earth of the kibbutz is characterized, like the search for "the hidden thread that joins the lifeless to the living," by "despair and rage." Forgetfulness bound the veteran members of the kibbutz to that hidden thread. In company, together, the boundaries of the singers' egos were dissipated, and despair and rage made way for devotion (a word with a decidedly religious connotation). "Forgetful of their place and time," the pioneers experienced the mystic union that typifies the natural world, and the feeling of belonging and harmony that characterizes it. Galila is graced with a similar experience in Damkov's room: "In forgetfulness and dedication the girl grasped the delicate brush. She ripped the caps off the tubes and painted enthusiastically. The warmth flowed from her body to his, and his body responded with waves of desire" (21). The flow "from being to being, vibration to vibration" that characterizes the lost harmony for which the kibbutz members are longing, now occurs between Galila and Damkov, while Galila paints in an ecstasy that partakes of forgetfulness and dedication.

Another possibility for unification with the world is embodied in the figure of Damkov. He would appear to represent the sinister, base forces of nature, everything opposed to the humane and human. The story compares him to an ape (his body is apelike, 11), he sets out for the kibbutz dining hall from his "lair" (11) like a jackal, and he is indirectly compared to a lustful stallion (a comparison strengthened in the second version, see 19, 24; 13, 19). Nevertheless, his character is developed along different lines. Not coincidentally, he is a blacksmith by profession: a profession reminiscent of that of Hephaestus, the blacksmith of the Olympian pantheon. Like Hephaestus, Damkov is muscular and hardworking, capable of repairing anything. Both figures are gloomy, isolated from society, and amazingly ugly. The description of Damkov as someone who "fell upon us" in the midst of the war (11) is reminiscent of Hephaestus' being thrown to the earth from Olympus. Like the blacksmith god, generally depicted in statues and paintings with one shoulder bare, Damkov works with his upper body exposed. Thus Damkov, despicably similar to the jackal and the ape, is also an avatar of an Olympian god. Further, his profession links him with the fire below and the lava of creation.

Fate plays an important part in the religious conception of "Where the Jackals Howl." Before the narrator wonders "what is the hidden thread," he poses another rhetorical question: "Was it really a matter of chance? It is commonly said that chance is blind; we say that chance peers out at us with a thousand eyes. The jackal was young and tender, and if he also felt the thousand eyes fixed upon him, he could not understand their language" (15). The proximity of those two subjects is not coincidental. Here we see a clear indication of Oz's affinity with Spinoza: the world's divine nature prevents the possibility of change, development, or chance. The world operates cyclically, and to suggest that events occur by chance indicates misunderstanding or shortsightedness. The story devotes the concluding lines to this notion. This Spinozan outlook is expressed repeatedly in *Where the Jackals Howl* ("The Way of the Wind," "All the Rivers," "Strange Fire," and others) and in Oz's later works. The most recent representatives to-date of the view that no chance exists in the world are Azariah Gitlin and Rimona in *A Perfect Peace*. Azariah believes in the "God of the philosopher Spinoza," frequently stating that in the opinion of his mentor, there is no chance in the world, only necessity and natural law.

The religious view expressed in the earliest stories of *Where the Jackals Howl*—"Before His Time," "The Trappist Monastery," and "Where the Jackals Howl"—persists in the other stories in that collection along with the conception of the cyclical nature of destiny that rules the world ("The Way of the Wind," "All the Rivers"). "Strange Fire," which concludes the volume (in the first Hebrew version) and unifies its various motifs, also sums up the religious outlook of the book.[25]

## "Strange Fire" as a Metaphysical Story

The subject of this story is a "treasure hunt," the discovery of the mutual affinities between the world's diverse oppositions (Chapter 5

---

25. Chronologically this is the fifth of the stories of *Where the Jackals Howl* (1963c). Nevertheless, the subject of the story made it a natural conclusion of the book. In the Am Oved edition of *Where the Jackals Howl* (1976a), "Upon This Evil Earth," a story not included in the original edition, is placed at the end of the book. This new story also summarizes, from a different point of departure, the various motifs appearing in the other stories of the collection.

deals extensively with this story). That affinity, a kind of "union of opposites," also finds expression in the story's religious outlook. An argument breaks out between two of the main characters, Dr. Elhanan Kleinberger and Yosef Yarden, on the nature of the metaphysics of the author H. Giladi:

> "It's simple, Yosef. I shall phrase it simplistically. H. Giladi is a metaphysical author, and his metaphysics have had their day. He repeats himself over and over again, and therefore..."
> "And therefore what? A narrow range is typical of many great authors."
> "Thus H. Giladi is a great author. He is a great author who completely fulfilled himself. His metaphysics have been milked dry. Over and over again he places man before God in a monotonous confrontation. And over and over again he avoids decision. A metaphysical author must achieve the union of opposites, formulate a stance with regard to God." (165–66)

Here, Oz indirectly proclaims himself to be a metaphysical author, for the whole story deals with the opposites existing within the world (opposites within nature itself, within human nature, and in his relations to the world) and with the hidden unity that binds them together. It is not that he "avoids decision" but rather that he "formulate[s] a stance with regard to God."

As in "The Trappist Monastery," the two characters represent two different religious experiences. Yosef Yarden continues the approach taken by Nahum Hirsch: "Yes, I believe in His existence, but I don't feel much sympathy for Him. In my eyes he is antipathetic.... That is, he does things which either lack logic or are unfair, or else they are both illogical and unfair at the same time. He has a sense of humor, but it's the kind of humor you would certainly call vulgar" (166). Dr. Kleinberger, in contrast, does not grasp God merely through moral judgment, claiming that an author must decide to "achieve the union of opposites, formulate a stance with regard to God," a demand that he fulfills in his own life. He does not say explicitly what the union of opposites might be, but it is hinted at in the course of the story. In his writing he tries to achieve a "marvelous unity of opposites" (173), in the course of which "a kind of sanctity hovers over the dark room" (ibid.). The creative process (in the second version of the story, the scholar writes poetry in that scene) is not one of organized, rational thought. Music brings a decidedly Dionysian element into the room, and the "strange fire" kindled in the man's eyes shows that his consciousness attempts to unite with elements that are entirely opposite to it, elements drawn from the primary source of his being. The substance of these elements, which Dr. Kleinberger is unable to formulate, is hinted at in a description occurring earlier in the story: "Muffled and distant the cry of the jackals is heard. Words flee from him. Something that is not words seeks to be uttered but cannot be. True, the jackals don't belong to the body of the story. . . . But how could we dispossess them from the story. They stand in its basement and turn its wheels" (168). Here, too, as in the earlier situation, words fail to express something primal and powerful. The relationship between this passage and Dr. Kleinberger's process of creation suggests that culture does not entirely oppose the jackals' nature. Culture, words, and creativity are nourished by primordial, primitive experience whose qualities are that of the jackal. Moreover, the source of holiness lies in the unity attained by joining with that primal experience.

The story presents the duality of holiness in three other characters: Lily Dannenberg, the gigantic taxi driver Abbu, and the crazy old woman who accosts Lily and Yair. Like the olive trees of "noble" mien, acquired thanks to their roots, which penetrate "to the moisture with passionate powers" (158), Lily Dannenberg exemplifies nobility (152) and unbridled primality. Her name expresses that unity of opposites with mathematical precision. It not only echoes the name Lilith, but like her namesake, Lily seduces men and seeks to harm the young couple. The chilling question she asks Yair, "You won't wait long before you make me a grandmother?" reminds us of Lilith, who is particularly notorious for tormenting mothers giving birth as well as tender infants. Yet, the lily is a symbol of purity, and it is one of the most common symbols of the Virgin Mary in Christian mythos. It is no coincidence that Lily and Abbu, the bearlike taxi driver, immediately come to mutual understanding. Abbu, a vital, animal-like figure (169–70), never speaks without naming the Creator. He demonstrates his absolute faith by never uttering God's name but rather by using a substitute for it (170–71).

The old woman provides a kind of summation of the story's religious conception:

> There is an inner connection between everything in the world. God is angry, and people don't see it. One meaning to all deeds, fine deeds and ugly deeds. Those women who walk in darkness saw a great light, not tomorrow and not yesterday,

but today, all the time, all at once, the whole world has a single meaning. . . . The blessing of the sky above, and the blessing of the water beneath, from Frankfurt to Jerusalem. One meaning to all deeds, to those that build and those that destroy" (162–63).

In the power of her madness the old woman penetrates realms that are seldom attained, an idea fully corroborated by the story. Her words refer to God's "wrath," which appears to Yosef Yarden as illogical and unfair arbitrariness, and also to the duality and the "marvelous" union of opposites that characterize Dr. Kleinberger, Lily, and Abbu. The old woman's litany proclaims the existence of God as revealed within man as it is revealed within the jackal, in good deeds and coarse ones, in construction and destruction. God embodies not only grace and mercy, but also malice and destruction. All the manifestations of the world emerge from a single entity, and are connected by an inner bond.[26]

Oz's first collection of stories, then, concludes with the author's awareness that he is a metaphysical author, who views his task as the formulation of an attitude toward God. His religious view derives from Schelling and Jung: duality exists both in God and in the world He created. Holiness cannot be attained by isolating light from darkness and separating it from the world, but must be attained through the unification of light and darkness. Darkness is not the absolute opposite of light, but its source. As a significant part of the world's order, the jackals cannot be left outside the fence, outside the divine world, nor can Lilith, the queen of the realm of evil, one of the mothers of the spirits. The believer must perforce vacillate between bitter complaints about divine "wrath" and full acceptance of the world, the ability to experience the inner unity that conjoins the opposite and contradictory manifestations of God.

## *Jephthah the Gileadite: God-Bear*

Oz added "Upon This Evil Earth," written shortly after the other stories of *Where the Jackals Howl*, to the revised edition of the

---

26. A similar notion is expressed by Tova, the main character of "All the Rivers": "And God collects us too and pastes us in the album and enjoys the harmony hidden behind the visible pains" (1965a, 108).

collection (1976a; 1981). The story is a fictional account of Jephthah the Gileadite's life: his birth, his flight from home, his appointment as a Judge, and his death. The story's Biblical background would appear to be far from the world of the other stories of that collection, which are set in contemporary Israel. Nevertheless, the distance is merely a surface one. Rather than describing contemporary protagonists rooted in archaic, ancient times, Oz forwent the modern facade, creating an archaic figure who renders the metaphor a reality. A wealth of motifs connect this story to the nine earlier ones and establish its strong affinity with them (e.g., confronting silence and "the voices of the night," the blazing sun in the daytime and the dew that moderates its burning during the night, the desire for a connection with the forces of nature, and many others). Undoubtedly, this story utilizes and summarizes the forces active in the world of the protagonists of *Where the Jackals Howl*, in particular the force motivating the search for a nexus with God.

Jephthah, the son of a concubine, represents an extreme version of exile and human alienation. His narrow eyes are described repeatedly as though "they were turned inward" (200, 209; 185, 186).[27] He is a "stranger" in love, in the desert, and in society (200, 205, 209; 185, 181, 215, and elsewhere). In his reply to the King of Ammon he says: "Gatel, I am not your brother or your father's son. You know that I am a stranger. I do not fight for the Israelites, I fight for one you do not know. In his honor I shall put you to the sword and your enemies, too, for I have been a stranger all the days of my life" (235; 228). Jephthah's only directive comes not from those who sent him, the children of Israel (a subject developed in the concluding passage of the story), but rather from the Lord God, whose love he seeks. All his life Jephthah aspires to return to the ancient entity of the world, to the Great Mother, to the "Sea" (216, 219, 222; 205, 209, 213, and elsewhere). God is the bestial, savage, and threatening side of the Great Mother; He is a bear (212, 216; 200, 205).[28] Jephthah does not know God's illuminated side, only "nature in God," to use Schelling's terms. His God is the God of the desert, the God of wild animals:

> O Lord of the asp in the desert, do not hide yourself from me. Call me, call me, gather me to you. . . . You are the lord of the

---

27. Thus Jephthah is similar to Noga in *Elsewhere, Perhaps*: "Her big eyes seem constricted as if they are looking not outward but inward, into her own mind" (1966a, 35; 1973, 28).

28. The bear as a negative, ferocious aspect of the Great Mother is discussed at length in Neumann (1973).

> fox and the vulture and I love your wrath and I do not ask you to lift up the brightness of your countenance toward me. Your wrath and barren sorrow are all I want. Surely anger and sadness are a sign to me that I am made in your image, I am your son, I am yours, and you will take me to you by night, for in the image of your hatred I am made, O lord of the wolves at night in the desert. (223–24; 214)

The inner plot of the story connects only indirectly with the flight from home, the great ascent, and battle. The core of that plot revolves around Jephthah's desperate effort to join with God, to merit a "sign" from him. As a child Jephthah "weighed the love of God against the love of Milcom" (212; 200), preferring the love of God with its dark severity. Hearing from his father "that God must be approached not in the way that a butterfly approaches a flower but as it approaches the fire" (213; 201), he tries to fulfill that directive. He conceives of the encounter with God as one that requires a personal trial, involving the risk of self-sacrifice: "He even pitted himself against a wolf. One night he went out alone and unarmed to find the wolf and fight it at the mouth of its lair, and with his bare hands he broke the beast's back, and returned home from the test merely bitten and scratched. He was trying to court God's favor, and in the autumn he even trained himself to pass his hand through the fire without crying out" (213; 201).

That expectation of a sign relates to another motif in the story: to prove to God the power of his faith in him, Jephthah asks to be put to a more extreme test, the test of the Binding of Isaac (233; 238). That request, the focus of Jephthah's relationship with his daughter, comes immediately after Pitdah reminds Jephthah of his promise to take her to the sea (232; 225). The expectation of a sign, the Binding of Isaac, and the sea are indissolubly bound together as the story proceeds. As the head of the Israelite armies Jephthah waits for a "sign" that will tell him when to start the war (238; 232). Pitdah's dream about her bridegroom, who "came in darkness and said to her in a still small voice: come, my bride, arise, for the time has come" (238; 233), is taken as the hoped-for sign for Jephthah. He sets forth to do battle, swearing: "O God, if you will surely deliver the children of Ammon into my hands, then it shall be that whatever comes forth from the doors of my house to meet me when I return in peace from the children of Ammon shall surely belong to God, and I will offer it up as a burnt offering" (239; 233). Jephthah, who loves his daughter "with a savage love" and cannot bear the thought that a stranger will take her (230; 223), will become his daughter's groom in an act of simultaneous betrothal and sacrifice: "In later times the wandering tribesmen would speak around their campfires at night of the great joy they had both shown, she a bride on her marriage couch and he a youthful lover stretching out his fingers to the first touch. And they were both laughing as wild beasts laugh in the dark of night, and they did not speak, only Jephthah said to her, Sea, sea" (242; 238). Jephthah returns his daughter to the sea as he had promised, and at the same time he subjects himself to the supreme test of the Binding of Isaac: "You have chosen me out of all my brothers and dedicated me to your service. You shall have no other servant before me. Here is the dark beauty under my knife; I have not withheld my only daughter from you. Grant me a sign, for surely you are tempting your servant" (243; 238).

From the physical trials to which Jephthah subjected himself as a youth, he takes on a much more difficult trial when he attempts to force God to reveal himself and to send him a sign that will save his daughter and redeem him from eternal exile. As necessitated by Jephthah's worldview, according to which God is the God of the wolf and the asp, God does nothing in the spirit of grace or mercy. You can unite with the bear-god by adopting his predatory ways, but you cannot force the bear to become human or moral.

## *Elsewhere, Perhaps:* Why Should We Accept the Good and Not Accept the Evil?

With regard to its religious elements, as in many other respects, Oz's first novel, *Elsewhere, Perhaps*, develops and expands the stories of *Where the Jackals Howl*. The religious element in the novel is principally expressed in the figures of the three Berger brothers. Their father, Rabbi Naftali Hirsch Berger, was "a Jewish man, the cantor in a synagogue of peddlers and wagoners" (1966, 125; 1973, 100). He is described as an authentically religious figure whose dealings do not distract him from the main point, from the next world (126; 100–101). His countenance suggests the spark that was buried within the shells, to use Kabbalistic terminology: his bull-like head had "two small slits in a dense net of deep wrinkles, but both sparkling an amazing blue" (125; 100). Those blue eyes are later called "tiny blue sparkles" (126; 101).

Each son, in his own way, carries on his father's tradition. Dr. Nehemiah, the eldest and the intellectual among them, researches "the sources of Jewish socialism from the times of those great reformers, the prophets, up to the establishment of kibbutzim in the revived Israel" (21; 15), linking the world of the Bible, his childhood environment, with modern Israel. Nehemiah's life has not turned out so well, however. When he attempts to join a kibbutz he fails, and in Jerusalem, where he settled, he remains unmarried. Truly, all of Nehemiah's "ways are enveloped in dessication" (128). While Nehemiah is entirely cut off from the "ocean," Zechariah is up to his neck in it (cf. his swimming in the kibbutz pool, his explanations about the water, "Warm and caressing like a woman" [272; 212], and his remarks about the "ocean" [352; 274]).

Like Oz's earlier protagonists, who are connected to the primal, animal world by a continual inner flow, Zechariah is characterized by the movement around his mustache: "On his upper lip there was a tiny, shapeless mustache, around which a curious movement could be detected, as if his nose and its surrounds were forever twitching with some mysterious life" (256–57; 198). That hidden life is the first thing that Ezra Berger, the kibbutznik among the trio, notices in his younger brother (264; 205).

Further, Zechariah often quotes the Bible and uses religious expressions (268, 271, 351, 365; 211). As one might expect, he, the animal-like, primal man, is the absolute believer. In his conversation with the dying Reuven Harish he declares himself to be a believing man ("By the way, there's a slight inaccuracy: I believe. I'm no heretic. He exists" [389]), but he voices harsh complaints: "He isn't logical. He's hysterical. He's tyrannical. He's hypocritical and self-righteous. A foolish king. A corrupt ruler" (ibid.). Zechariah believes that God exists, but as a "dreadful father," a tyrannical and arbitrary ruler. Like Jephthah the Gileadite, Zechariah tries to force God to reveal Himself to him: "I intend to compete with Him. Let Him get out of there. Let Him talk with me. Let Him hear me out" (389). His other alternative is to imitate God, to behave like Him (ibid.).

Thus, Zechariah's religious view is an extreme version of the religious conception expressed in *Where the Jackals Howl*, a conception in which the divine and the bestial cling to each other inseparably. Like Jephthah, Zechariah knows only the dark, cruel side of divinity. The "sparkle" in Rabbi Naftali Hirsch Berger's eyes became "dark lightning" in those of his youngest son (127; 102).[29]

---

29. It is noteworthy that Zechariah expresses some of Oz's own ideas, as they are formulated in his articles and interviews. Thus, for example, Zechariah insists on the Darwinistic principle that was at work among the founding generation of the kibbutz, an idea that Oz has repeated in many places (1965b, 1965c, and elsewhere).

Ezra Berger, the middle son and a kibbutz member, is a synthesis of his older and younger brothers. He has earthiness and ebullient vitality, yet at the same time "there is something noble about his restraint, if you can call moderation and self-control noble" (27; 19). That combination, without the dryness characterizing Nehemiah and the openly jackal-like nature of Zechariah, wins the narrator's praise: "We respect him as a man of action, and for his rough good humor, which always, however, retains a serious element and never degenerates into cheap buffoonery. We are almost tempted to detect a noble quality in his roughness—as indeed there is, if, once again, you can call moderation and self-control noble" (70; 61). The narrator has already mentioned that nobility in his first description of Ezra (27; 19). Indeed, the synthesis achieved in the character of Ezra makes him one of the key figures in the novel.

It is Ezra who truly follows in the footsteps of his father, Naftali Hirsch Berger. He resembles him physically: "It is a thick-set body, hirsute, and somewhat pot-bellied, with thick, heavy limbs. His muscular shoulders support without the intervention of a neck a dark head with thinning hair" (26; 19; cf. the description of the father: "short, stout legs, a pot belly, and no neck to intervene between his strong, bulging shoulders and his huge dark bull head" [125; 100]). He is also closed to those around him, "a withdrawn man. His affected gravity is a barrier between him and us" (27; 19). The similarity between him and his father suggests that in closing himself up, he pays heed to another realm of experience, beyond time and place. Ezra often reads the Bible (26, 316, 395; 19, 250, 308), and he frequently uses Biblical verses when he speaks. His philosophy is that of Ecclesiastes (122, 202; 97), but his great vitality protects him from the dark pessimism of the Preacher. One's origins lie in a "drop of stinking fluid," and he is heading toward "a pit full of worms," but in the interval between those two points Ezra tries to live his life to the fullest. He does not dedicate himself to research like Nehemiah, nor to the fight against the gentiles, like Zechariah, but lives his life in praise and gratitude: "But I'm not Nehemiah Berger; I don't work with premises and conclusions. And I'm also not Zechariah Berger either; I don't make war on the whole human race because the Jewish worm has been trampled underfoot. I am just an ordinary mortal, thank the good Lord" (69–70; 60). Whereas Zechariah wallows in a death cult, Ezra clings to life (69; 59–60), with its enchantments and its flaws. His bond with God gives him his power, the talent for moderation and self-control. Even in a crisis, when Noga goes with him to Tiberias and he hears that she is pregnant, he preaches to his fellow fishermen:

"His life abhors bread and his soul dainty meat, his flesh is consumed so that it cannot be seen, yea, his soul draws near unto the grave, and his life to the destroyers"; that's what it says in the Book of Job [a slight misquotation of Job 33:20–22], and there is a great moral. Listen, Kabilio, you listen too. It says that a man mustn't complain. Why should we accept the good and not accept the bad? I say this not as a religious man, Saragosti, but quite simply; you have to take the rough with the smooth. One day you're licking honey, the next you're chewing onions, as they say. (250; 191)

Zechariah Berger holds a similar point of view ("True Judaism has one meaning, complete submission to the will of the Most High"; "Can we take the good from Him and not accept the bad?" [328]). However, he does not act in accordance with it. He defies God and tests Him, while Ezra, in contrast, practices what he preaches with submission that is not resignation but rather recognition of necessity.

Noga Harish illustrates the duality of experience in another way. Ruled by urges and "dark forces," her ties with Ezra Berger conspicuously violate the taboo of kibbutz society. Noga's indifference to the social pressure to leave her middle-aged lover and part with the embryo in her womb arises from her natural, harmonious nature, and having lived away from the kibbutz society. The unity embodied within her gives rise to her sanctity, which is referred to in several instances. First, her nickname, "Stella Maris," repeated a dozen times in the course of the novel, is one of the common appellations of the Virgin Mary (Hall 1979, 330). The pomegranate associated with her (31, 160; 24, 128) also contributes to that meaning: the fruit is one of the symbols of the church, and in Christian art it represents Mary's modesty and innocence (Hall 1979, 249, 328). In fact, after her pregnancy is discovered, Noga leaves Ezra Berger, and, later on, "she hardly associated her fetus with Ezra Berger. . . . It was not that she has forgotten the facts, but the connections between the facts had ceased to exist" (316; 249). At the same time she has Christ-like qualities. Zechariah declares that she has overcome suffering and thinks only of her fellow man: "You're a saint, my child, you're choosing to sacrifice yourself for people who don't love you. You're a real saint" (365; 283). The vine and grapes with which she is identified (58, 94, 149; 40, 70, and elsewhere) symbolize the blood of Christ, just as the fish ("I'll be a goldfish" [202; 158]) commonly symbolizes Jesus. The narrator emphasizes the saintliness of his young, much-desired lover when describing her fine eyebrows "as in old pictures of Madonna" (29;

22), the "halo" of her hair (ibid.) and of her hands clasped over her head (149).

Describing the three Berger brothers at the beginning of the novel the narrator sums up:

> All three, however, have experienced hardships and sufferings. Those who believe in an ultimate justice hold that even suffering is a sign of divine Providence, since without suffering there is no happiness and without hardships there is no redemption or joy. We, on the other hand, who yearn for a reformed world, do not believe in this kind of justice. Our aim is to eradicate suffering from the world and to fill it instead with love and brotherhood. (21–22; 15)

The book sustains a tension between the socialistic, optimistic outlook and the view that the flawed world cannot be set right until the idealistic, socialist view is completely rejected. In the course of the novel the narrator learns that one cannot uproot from the world suffering, pain, and the urges of the heart. Suffering is not desirable, as Noga claims ("If you don't suffer, you don't live" [280; 219]), nor is it an appendix that can be removed from the body with a successful operation. While the narrator advocates the values of the kibbutz, the implied author rejects the Marxist view according to which alienation and human distress have a social and political source. The novel shows this view that regards society—social justice, economic equality—as a vision to be shared by all, to be simplistic and inadequate. Ezra Berger's religious worldview ultimately emerges in the novel view: God's world includes suffering and affliction, love and brotherhood perpetually mingling, and one must learn to accept both in tranquillity. Ideological principles will not lead to a reform of the world. On the contrary, they are likely to increase pain and suffering. One must live by participating in the flowing, living current of existence, with its happiness and painfulness, and not under the cover of "premises and conclusions" or of social ideas. This attitude is reflected in all of Oz's following works. In *A Perfect Peace* it receives extensive illustration in the figure of Azariah Gitlin and in "the God of Spinoza" to which he is devoted.

## *A Perfect Peace: Religious Malefactors and the Rural Righteous*

As in the stories of *Where the Jackals Howl*, in Oz's novel *A Perfect Peace* we find a reciprocal bond between the primordial existence of the world and the religious sphere, between the forces of nature and holiness. Several of the main characters experience an open, exposed encounter with the world, which has religious significance. That mutual bond is expressed in the figure of Azariah Gitlin, who has something both animal-like and holy about him, as well as in the figure of Alexander Tlallim, the surveyor of desert lands, a figure with a primal, native element ("skin dark as an Arab's" [280; 268]) and a holy element too. Similarly, Yonatan returns to his kibbutz "brown and lean as a Bedouin" (376; 369), and with his beard and ravaged face he is like "a young scholar of proud old rabbinical stock who was studying to become a rabbi" (377; 369–70).

Rimona, Yonatan's wife, also embodies these contradictions. Rimona represents the sea in the novel, the primordial forces of nature that live their lives in undisturbed harmony, but she is also "like a baby, like a divine angel in colorful kitsch pictures" and when she suckles her daughter "a thin light like the halo around the full moon" radiates around her face (379). Upon first meeting her, Azariah reflects on her Christian beauty (106; 95), and as a "symbol," he gives her a cyclamen, a flower sacred to the Virgin Mary in the Christian tradition. Later on, he describes her to Yonatan as "a saint with a kind of Christian beauty," and Yonatan answers him in the same manner: "She, how should I say it, really should be yours. That blessed saintliness" (212). Moreover, Rimona indirectly fulfills the way of life dictated by the Spinozan pantheism of which Azariah is such an enthusiastic proponent. Influenced by his mentor and teacher, Azariah argues: "All things should be accepted calmly and with a light heart, because fate in its many disguises always stems from the same eternal decree.... If you were to think about this fact for a minute, Yonatan, you would be surprised to realize that not only is it true, it can also give us the most wonderful peace of mind. To accept all things, to understand all things, and to respond to all things with perfect inner tranquillity" (91, 82). Rimona possesses such tranquillity. Intuitively understanding everything that goes on around her and knowing what is going to happen, she sits "near the radio, the pocketbook on her knees, without opening it. Drawn inward and quiet, drawn up within herself and concentrated in deep and tranquil heedfulness, as if from a distance she were being told what would happen tomorrow and what would happen in the coming days, and as if there were neither sadness nor joy nor surprise in that information" (107).

Although Biblical references are plentiful in the book, my focus here is on the existential religious perspective that characterized the founding generation of the kibbutz in this novel, and, surprisingly, the younger generation too. Let us first look at the characters of Yolek and Srulik, who are among the founders of the kibbutz and involved in its activities.

Apparently, Yolek had a religious education: he incorporates verses from the Bible and the liturgy into his speech (58, 130, 201, 205; 49), and in his letter to Eshkol he begs forgiveness "for there is neither foolishness nor levity before Him" (168; 156); he distinguishes between the one who has a "spark" in his heart (Azariah) and the one who lacks it (Yonatan), and he even curses vehemently in the name of God (202–3; 190, 192). He describes his life in Israel, which was dedicated to the kibbutz and to the labor movement, in "religious" terms: "I won't deny that I'm a wicked man, as wicked as they come, yes, wicked to the very marrow of my old bones. In fact, I may even be one of the thirty-six perfectly wicked men on whom our world depends. I mean one of those wicked enough to have sold their own souls on behalf of the cause we held sacred from the very time we were young, one of those whose wickedness alone enabled them to preach and practice the faith and all its many commandments" (164; 151). Later on in his letter to Eshkol, Yolek repeats that idea again and again: "And yet, in the last analysis, our wickedness, if you will, was almost religiously selfless" (164; 152); we were "mystical Jewish cutthroats" (168; 155). But Yolek's "religious" experience finds expression beyond his relations with the kibbutz and the building of the land. Walking in the kibbutz yard at night, he experiences renewed contact with the world:

> Three or four stars peered coldly through racks of tattered clouds. Twinkling. For a moment, Yolek thought of them as no more than pinpricks, little moth holes in a heaven velvet curtain, beyond which shone a vast, terrible illumination, a blinding incandescence. And the stars themselves, it seems to him, were but the faintest of allusions to the great storm of light raging behind that veil. As though the vats of heaven had sprung a few tiny leaks and several drops of bright liquid clung glistening to their black underside. Yolek found comfort. (203–4; 192–93)

Religious connotations abound in this account, explaining the consolation that Yolek suddenly finds, the feeling of "caress" that accompanies him, after his wife's harsh reproaches and the vigorous soul-searching he had just gone through. The religious nature of his experience finds expression in these lines: "Nature itself, as it were, cares for all the soul and gives a certain number of mother years even to a bad-hearted intellectual" (204). The expression "all the soul" stands out in its unusual diction (in this context one would expect to find "every soul" or "all souls"), and in the consciousness of a man with a religious foundation such as Yolek there can be no doubt that it refers to the familiar last verse in the book of Psalms: "Let all the soul [usually rendered, "everything that has breath"] praise the Lord." Through this all-inclusive experience Yolek now sees the relativity and limitations of all the principles to which he had clung all his life, and he now wishes to become a grandfather and to act "despite all my principles" with the child, as he had not done with his two sons "for which those principles are to blame" (205). Thus, he stands in place "entirely drained of the old passions and the high principles that had guided him all his life. As though the answer had been obvious from the start, he had suddenly made up his mind. Frosty, hushed, and desolate the night, pinioned against the sky and earth. Yolek waited until he saw a falling star. And begged for mercy" (205; 194). Responding to the encounter with that bounteous essence of the world, Yolek decides to refuse his wife's request to help remove Azariah from the kibbutz. Azariah had, in fact, deviated from the collective morality, in breaking the family taboo, but that morality is not all-inclusive. Behavior dictated by the expectations of society and its tenets leads to remorse, and one must beg for mercy from the flowing being of the world, a being free of prohibitions and principles.

While Yolek has clung his whole life to the principles of the kibbutz, failing to discover their offenses and flaws, Srulik has lived his whole life in deep awareness of the primal powers of the universe, and in knowledge of the hopelessness of any attempt to reshape human nature. The arena of his struggle is far broader than the kibbutz courtyard:

> "Solve." How odd this verb sounds to me. We have spent our entire lives in this place, coming up with one solution after another. To the youth problem, to the Arab problem, the Diaspora problem, the elderly problem, the soil and water problem. . . . It's as if all these years we've been painstakingly seeking to inscribe a few ingenious formulae on the waves of the sea or to make the stars line up in the sky by three in drill formation. . . . I have lived my life here to the music of a marching band. As if there were no sea or mountains or stars in the sky. And as if death had already been abolished, old age eradicated, suffering and loneliness ridden out on a rail, and the whole universe nothing but a giant arena for political and ideological quarrels. (233, 236; 223, 226)

Srulik lives constantly heeding the silence "hovering over the darkness—in the valleys, in the mountains, on the sea—mutely but insistently demanding some answer or explanation from us all, man, dog, bird" (234; 224). He attempts to find that answer in his diary (233; 226), which explains why many of the reflections and remarks contained in it are presented by Srulik as "theological." He defines "a theological observation" as the need of every creature to give an account of his actions (233; 224). One such observation is that every father is "trying to make of himself a fulminating Jehovah. Complete with thunder and lightning. Hailing fire and brimstone" (252; 241); and when he notes that the "inner urge to give our all for what we can never have" bears a mysterious resemblance to "the inner workings of the universe itself, to the orbits of the stars, the procession of the seasons," he again calls it a "theological observation" (311; 302). Srulik also views his task on the kibbutz in religious terms. He knows the unchanging urges of the heart very well, and the disharmony and pain that accompany them; his single goal in life, as a kibbutz member and later as the secretary of the kibbutz, is "to mitigate the pain" (373; 365). In another "theological observation" he writes that of all the Ten Commandments and of all the modern, national, and movement commandments, he has been left with but a single one: "Thou shalt not cause pain" (237; 227).

Srulik, the "hidden saint" (287; 276), "the village priest" (326, 372; 316, 363), is aware of the eternal forces of nature and the nullity of the human spirit as it faces them. Again and again he repeats the verse "as the waters cover the sea," as a kind of contrary to Isaiah's vision of the end of days. In Isaiah's vision, water is compared to the knowledge of God that covers the earth ("They shall not hurt nor destroy, in all my holy mountain: for the earth shall be full of the knowledge of the Lord, as the waters cover the sea" [Isaiah 11:9]). In Srulik's reflections the sea symbolizes the primordial existence of the world that effaces all human endeavors (372, 374; 364). Srulik's recognition of the hopelessness of the human spirit, along with the pain and suffering that permeates life, makes him another Amos Oz protagonist who protests the way God rules the world:

> If there really is a Higher Being, he mused, God or Whatever, I personally beg to differ from Him, or that Being, on several issues, some of them quite fundamental. He could have done everything in a far better way. But what I most dislike about Him, if I may say so, is His cheap, vulgar sense of humor.

What He finds amusing is unbearably painful to us. If He gets such pleasure from our suffering, then He and I are in deep disagreement. (358; 349)

Nevertheless Srulik does not see the life he has led at the kibbutz as having been wasted. He does not renounce the possibility of reducing human pain. Toward the end of the novel he once more complains about God's coarse sense of humor, asking, "how can we mitigate the pain?" and adding: "At this point I refuse to give up. I will continue to wait for an answer" (374). While he acknowledges the power of the forces of nature, "as the waters cover the sea," Srulik discovers that human beings are not completely without hope of redemption, not completely deprived of the possibility of choice: "But a thing or two we can do, and since we can, we must. As for the rest, who knows? Let's wait and see. Instead of continuing this entry, I think I'll play my flute tonight. Certainly there is a place for that too. What's the point? I don't know" (381; 374). These words, which conclude the novel, have an "in spite of everything" quality, both desperate and optimistic. The forces of nature stand firm, as always, and man's ancient, murderous urges still dwell in his heart. Neither can be dominated, but one can strive, with patience and endurance, for a change, even if only a small, slow one: "a thing or two we can do." With these words Srulik seems to justify the religious appellations that have stuck to him, achieving an awareness similar to Azariah Gitlin's understanding that the universe runs according to a great, divine plan, which includes a place for all creatures and their actions.

In a certain sense Srulik is an extension of the figure of Zechariah Berger (*Elsewhere, Perhaps*). He lives in deep awareness of the life that throbs in the cosmos and of the ancient urges lurking within the soul. Every day he lives out the ill-matched relationships between man and the universe, the contradictions within the human soul, and the questions of existence that society is powerless to confront (old age, death, solitude). For him God cannot, therefore, be a God of grace, but must be one of hostility. At the same time, he does not reach Zechariah Berger's conclusion, but rather that of his brother Ezra: one must cling to life, learn to accept it in tranquillity, with its blessings and curses.[30]

---

30. In *Touch the Water, Touch the Wind* (1973a), the secretary of the kibbutz also has a bond with the religious sphere (169–70; 160–61).

## *Azariah: Filth, Reptile, Jesus*

The novel extends and develops Srulik's views through the figure of Azariah Gitlin. Like Srulik, Azariah heeds the forces of nature, sensing that they demand something of people (139, 234), but unlike him, he acknowledges the religious quality of that bond with nature. Whereas Srulik is aware of the primordial power of natural forces but does not know how a person can live with them, Azariah has a clear point of view, in the spirit of Spinozan pantheism: in his view God penetrates the entire world, and humanity must learn to approach Him, imitate Him, and understand His lesson. To his new friends, the kibbutz members, Azariah preaches: "To be close to nature. Close, so to speak, to the rhythms of the cosmos. We should learn from those olives. We should learn from everything, the hills, the fields, the mountains, the sea, the wadis, the stars above. That's not my own idea. It's Spinoza's. In a word, we should relax" (154; 139). Here and in other places in the novel, Azariah follows in Spinoza's footsteps: the way to happiness, to peace, lies in the recognition of human nature and the understanding of humanity's place in the universe.[31] At the start of the excursion where Azariah made the remarks cited above, he reflects, "Indeed the miracle already happened when I was quiet and calmed down and said, 'God, what am I after all? Why did you keep me alive? What am I needed for at a moment like this?' A simple answer arose from the silence and the light and the soil and the mountains and the wind. And the answer is the question, which is silence: don't be afraid, boy, don't be afraid" (138). Typical of his religious feelings, Azariah receives the answer to the question that he addressed to God from the forces of nature, the light, the soil, and the wind. It is no surprise, then, that at the sight of Eshkol and Yolek, who are impervious to the odors of the sea, to the stars above, to the silence of the earth and the desert stillnesses, Azariah states: "There is no God in their hearts" (292).

Azariah's God is the "God of the philosopher Spinoza" (114), whose pantheism taught him that chance events do not occur but everything is eternally decreed: "I myself do not believe in chance, in coincidences.

---

31. Cf. those words to Oz's advice to former Knesset member Yitzhak Refa'el, in his article, "Good Advice to a Member of the Knesset" (1979d): "To raise our eyes to the mountains to learn perfect peace from them. To be as similar to the mountains as flesh and blood can be. And when we are tired, we shall rest. And after resting we shall once more raise our eyes to the mountains, and everything will be in its place. Nothing new. Nothing to fear."

Behind every event stand fixed forces that are unknown to us" (103; 93; see also 90, 91, 100, 359; 81, 82, 90, 350, and elsewhere). He reads Yonatan some passages from Spinoza and explains that they imply "that there is a necessary and predetermined order to the world" (210; 199). The implied author supports this view as seen in the description of Azariah's arrival at the kibbutz: Yolek rejects his request to be accepted on the kibbutz, but "a peculiar coincidence"—the kibbutz's need for someone to work in the garage, the fact that Azariah had been a technical sergeant in the army—changes his mind. Chance, as it were, has a determining role here: that very week Yolek had published a "help wanted" ad for a garage worker; Azariah had just finished his military service and decided that he would live on a kibbutz. He came to Kibbutz Granot without having read Yolek's want ad, choosing Granot by planting his finger on a list of kibbutzim (50; 61). Yolek finds it hard to believe in that "peculiar coincidence," but to his wife he presents Azariah as "a young volunteer, a gift from heaven, who may save our tractor shed in the nick of time" (58; 49).

Upon his arrival at the kibbutz Azariah has a clear and well-established religious outlook. Yet he is quite far from the peace and reconciliation that he preaches when he tells Yonatan that in Spinoza's opinion "we're free to recognize Necessity and to learn to accept calmly, even lovingly, the powerful, unspoken laws underlying the inevitable" (211; 200). In his nervous loquacity, in his desperate attempts to make everyone like him, and in his fears, he represents the polar opposite of his sought-after reconciliation. At the end of the novel he continues to quote Spinoza, but his behavior no longer contradicts his words. Influenced by the members of the kibbutz, as well as by Rimona, the principles of his mentor cease being merely pretty words, for now he acts upon them (359; 350 and elsewhere).

Indirectly, Azariah illustrates another aspect of Spinoza's doctrine. Spinoza distinguished among three levels of consciousness, the highest of which was "intuition" (1982, 90). That level of consciousness exists in unmediated unity with the thing itself, which is God or nature. That unity gives birth to intuitive vision, beyond rational consciousness. Azariah, like Rimona, has intuitions that prove to be correct time and time again: like an echo of Yonatan's thoughts Azariah knows that "something seems to have gone out in his soul" (246; 235), and that Yonatan has set out "on a journey" (263; 249), to save "the bright first principles of his soul" (292; 281). During their excursion to the abandoned Arab village, he senses that "someone is in the vicinity and watching us" (144; 131), and he suspects that the Bolognesi has a connection with that presence. The rest of the novel confirms those intuitive premonitions.

The novel illustrates this aspect of Azariah's character in another way. Azariah, no military hero, goes by the nickname "little stinker" (212; 201) in the army, yet descriptions of him suggest that he will play the role of the hero and redeemer, the bearer of a message. His name means "Helper of God," and in his youth he believed that "he had a mission" (370; 361). During the excursion to the Arab village next to his kibbutz he thinks about "the special voice" he occasionally hears (138), and also that "the time to reveal myself has not yet come. I have to suffer and keep silence for many years yet" (137). On his first night at the kibbutz he thinks about the original ideas that "he had suffered so hard to arrive at during his long years of isolation," and about "the severity of his ascetic solitude," which gave birth here and there to "the word of good tidings" (84–86; 75–77). Not incidentally, half the verses of the Bible recited by his neighbor that night come from Isaiah 53, describing the servant of God who bears the sins of the multitude in silence until the day of redemption (88; 79).[32] The appellation "Jesus" which Yonatan uses for him (213; 202) relates to this side of his character. Like Srulik, Azariah is also something of a hidden saint.[33] At the same time, as one might expect given Oz's religious outlook, Azariah has other characteristics. Connection with the forces of nature implies the union of opposites and not one-dimensional fulfillment. Azariah emerges from the darkness like an animal, and he is often compared to an "animal," a "reptile," and to

---

32. These misquotations of the Bible and others spoken by the Bolognesi that night and on other occasions mostly refer to two principal subjects: the mistreatment of the Jewish people at the hands of the Gentiles and the people's divine redemption (Psalms 2, 124), and also total faith in God, who, sooner or later, will extend His grace to His believers (Psalms 23, 55, 135). The verses he quotes support Azariah's words about "the miracle that happened to the Jews after their afflictions and persecutions" (212), as well as his religious outlook.

33. Srulik is in fact called "the hidden saint" and Yolek frequently refers to the thirty-six righteous men upon whom the world rests, according to legend. Oz began his discussion of Berdyczewski's story, "The Hidden One," with a reference to that motif (1976c).

The indirect comparison of Azariah to King David contributes to the aforementioned aspect of his character. Azariah quotes David's lament for Jonathan (129, 157; 118) and plays before Yolek as David played before Saul. Yolek himself, alarmed by an "evil spirit" (163), writes to Eshkol that he hesitated as to whether to accept Azariah on the kibbutz: "Am I lacking in eccentrics?" (171; 159), repeating, with a slight change, the words of Achish, king of Gath, when David comes to him (1 Samuel 21:16). Yosef Oren (1983) noted the parallel between the trios of Yolek-Yonatan-Azariah and King Saul-Jonathan-David from a different point of departure.

various animals (dog, cat, grasshopper, and others). He comes as the redeemer with a religious message but also represents Mephisto (240), the messenger of the underworld.[34] The author conveys this idea even through the novel's minor details. Thus, for example, during the Six Day War, Azariah works "like a demon" day and night, and his officer calls him "our angel" (380–81).

That union of opposites is carried through into the descriptions of Azariah as a boy (180, 187, 366; 171, 176, 357) and as a fetus (180, 217; 170, 205). As a fetus Azariah has something both animal-like (he sleeps as though in a "cave") and angelic. The child is, among other things, a symbol of unity, symbol of the spiritual perfection in which all the psyche's forces coexist and nurture each other (Jung, 1953b, 1954, 1956).

## *Yonatan: To the Underworld and Back*

The younger generation of the kibbutz does not use Biblical and liturgical verses, having distanced itself from the sphere of religion. When Yonatan asks his friend Udi what he thinks is the most despicable hoax, Udi answers: "I guess it's religion. Or communism. Or both" (15; 11). Yet the members of the kibbutz have a strange longing for the world of the Bible and its relics, apparently hidden in the abandoned Arab village, Sheikh-Dahar. The Arab village exhibits, among other things, a primal autochthonous essence, which umbilically binds them to the earth, uniting them with the primary, Biblical world.[35] Yonatan embodies the vital need for that bond.

---

34. Indeed, many motives connect *A Perfect Peace* with Goethe's *Faust* (mentioned in *Elsewhere, Perhaps*, 292).

35. Oz wrote on that topic in *In the Land of Israel*:

>And then I study the elusive cunning of the Biblical charm of this landscape: and isn't all of this charm Arab, through and through? The lodge and the cucumber garden, the watchman's hut and the cisterns, the shade of the fig tree and pale silver of the olive, the grape arbors and the flocks of sheep—these picturesque slopes that bewitched from afar the early Zionists like Yehuda Halevi and Abraham Mapu; these primeval glades that reduced the poet Bialik to tears and fired Tchernichowsky's imagination; the hypnotic shepherds who, from the very beginning of the return to Zion, captured the heart of Moshe Smilansky, who even called himself Hawaja Musa; the tinkle of the goats' bells which entwined, like magic webs, the hearts of the early Zionist Settlers, who came from Russia thirsty to don Arab garb and to speed their horses toward this Arabic Biblicality, the play *Allah Karim* by Orloff

A loyal product of kibbutz society, Yonatan discovers the cost of the principles to which his parents and their comrades had been loyal. The price of socialization was particularly high on the kibbutz, given the character of its founders and the severity with which they maintained their principles: "All the time, all my life, I've been giving in and giving in, even when I was a little kid the first thing they taught me was to give in, and in school, to give in, and in our games, to give in, to be considerate, to take the first step, and in the army and on the kibbutz and in my house and on the playing field" (13). The constant need to concede is repeated frequently in Yonatan's reflections during the novel, as is the feeling that he was never treated as a free human being, but as a "human factor or manpower or a phenomenon" (184), "a means for implementing a fervent plan" (21), "a little flag on their war map" (267). Yonatan's process of acculturation succeeded much like the proverbial operation during which the patient died. With increasing intensity he feels that his life is like a desert waste (65), and that he is withering away. Understandably, his father complains that his son lacks a "spark," for Yonatan himself frequently feels that something within him has "gone out" (14, 89, 186; 10 and elsewhere). His condition resembles that of the tractor halted by a blocked gas line which Oz describes at length (93–95; 83–84).

The beginning of the novel foreshadows the process Yonatan will undergo: "One evening, on the radio news, a certain Rabbi Nachtigall talked about religious revival. He used the phrase 'a desert wasteland and a wilderness.' For the rest of that night, through the next day, Yonatan absentmindedly recited these words as if they were a mantra: The magic of wilderness" (19; 15). As noted, Yonatan felt that his life was like "a desert waste"; indeed, the "magic of wilderness" will bring about his religious regeneration. When he responds to the voice that calls him, he takes the first step in that regeneration. Frequently, he imagines he is being called (14, 30, 271; 24, 258, and elsewhere), though he does not know where he is being called or who is calling him.[36] There are suggestions that Yonatan is a "hero" setting out on a

---

and the "Silence of the Villages" of Yizhar, the tales told around the campfire of the Palmach, the enchanted groves of Amos Kenan and the longed-for cisterns of Naomi Shemer, yearning for the bare-faced stony mountain, for merger into the bosom of these gentle, sleepy scapes so very far removed from Shtetl alleyways. (1983, 98; 1983, 121–22).

36. The call as the call of conscience encouraging the individual to break his meaningless existence plays an important role in the theories of Heidegger (1962) and Buber (1958, 1967). Neumann, following Jung, sums up:

"The inner voice" is stifled by the growth of a superego, of conscience, the representative of collective values. The voice, the individual experience of the

journey to find the lost treasure, the "water of life." He wants "to get up right away and go look for some sign of life in the wasteland" (30; 24); he "is looking for life" (225; 214). In fact he succeeds in finding the treasure, but only by exposing himself to the horrors of the world of the dead.

As noted, Yonatan is uncertain of his destination. He envisions a journey beyond the sea, exotic lands, studies, wealth, but those imaginings are nothing but faltering attempts to formulate what "life" is for him (65, 225; 214 and elsewhere). Only upon leaving the kibbutz, when he gets into a car headed south, does he suddenly discover his destination, Petra, the red rock: "Just then, as swiftly as a flame, a flash of piercing joy shot through him such as he had not felt since he was wounded in the raid on Hirbet Tawfik—a wild, exquisite joy that percolated through every cell of his body to its very nerve endings. . . . [F]or at that exact moment he understood at last where he was going, and what it was that was waiting for him, and why he had taken his gun and was heading south to that place beyond the mountains from which legend had it no one had ever come back alive" (228; 217). What does the trip to Petra represent? For Yonatan it is an encounter with a world which is the complete opposite of his familiar one, but it is also an encounter with the depths of his soul, with the "shadow side" of consciousness. When he understands that Petra is his destination, Yonatan reflects on "that necessary journey calling to him from the depths of his soul" (228; 217). Now it is clear why he could not formulate the goal of his trip before this: Who is calling him? Where will he find life? In "the depths of his soul," in the primal world hidden within him, which the life of the kibbutz has repressed, sealed up, and buried. Indeed, the trip to Petra represents the polar opposite of Yonatan's life up to now. It puts an end to his concessions and he

---

transpersonal, which is particularly strong in childhood, is renounced in favor of conscience. When paradise is abandoned, the voice of God that spoke in the garden is abandoned too, and the values of the collective, of the fathers, of law and conscience, of the current morality, etc., must be accepted in order to make social adaptation possible. (1973, 403)

In contrast to most adults, whose individuality has been taken over by social values and restrictions, the extraordinary individual, the "hero," continues to hear the inner voice calling to him. That voice expresses the instinctive foundation within him, and it is opposed to the father, to society, and to the conscience (379). The inner voice is an expression of the self, and it has the urgency of a command.

The feeling that he is called upon to carry out some task, and the effort to understand "what is wanted from you now, right now, in this very moment" are expressed in Oz's article, "Questions and Answers" (in 1977b), and later on in *The Third Condition* (1991).

experiences liberation, abandoning all cultural frameworks (family, kibbutz, state).

Yonatan's existential experience parallels, in all of its stages, motifs, and symbols, the process of finding the self described by Jung. Yonatan sets out on a journey that will connect him with the dark side of life, with the "depths of the soul" that has been blocked off from him up to now. In the course of that trip he has religious experiences, and after withstanding the trial of the descent into the underworld he finds the life he has sought. Upon his return from the underworld he contains elements of primordiality and holiness like those that characterize his wife Rimona and Alexander Tlallim, his spiritual mentor. Let us discuss that matter in detail.

When he gets up in the morning after his first night in the desert, Yonatan experiences a sense of fervor and thanksgiving: "The dawn chill was sharp and bracing. Yonatan put on his jacket, wrapped himself in the blanket with the solemnity of a Jew donning a prayer shawl, and stood with his face to the mountains in the east" (285; 273–74). That Yonatan should wrap himself as if in a prayer shawl, face eastward—normally the direction of Jerusalem toward which all Jews pray—and lift his eyes to the mountains is curious. It evokes the Psalmist who seeks the help of his God: "I shall raise my eyes to the mountains whence shall come my help. My help comes from the Lord, the Creator of heaven and earth" (Psalms 121:1–2). Standing before the open expanses, Yonatan is filled with a feeling of belonging ("Here, praise be, I've come home at last. Here I'm no more theirs") and gratitude ("Thank you for all this beauty. For Michal. Thank you for every breath. For the very sunrise"), along with a desire to kneel "or make a deep bow." The description of the sunrise that follows also has religious connotations. The similarity between Yonatan's religious experience and that of his father as he walks at night in the courtyard of the kibbutz is indicated by their physical actions. Both men withdraw within themselves, feeling tranquil: "Yolek Lifshitz raised his coat collar, pulled down his cap against the cold, and stood looking at them" (205; 194); "Yonatan squinted into the wind, pulled down his wooled cap, and lifted his jacket collar" (285; 274). Like an echo of his father, who thinks of "all the soul" (Heb.: *kol haneshama*), Yonatan wants to give thanks for "every breath" (*kol neshima*).[37]

---

37. There are additional similarities between them. Yolek wants "to get up and go west before the time is up" (125; 113), just like his son. In the description of the clouds, through Yolek's eyes, and the description of the kite, through Yonatan's eyes, the same mythological beasts appear. Their fear of death is also similar (148, 161; 146).

In another example, the narrator describes Yonatan's religious experience: when he stays in the desert alone, before leaving on his journey, "a wind blew from the north. The desert grew darker. At long last he was truly alone. And he heard the still soft voice" (342; 335). The description recalls God's revelation to Elijah at Mount Horev (I Kings 19:12). The flask of water offered to Yonatan by the old surveyor is also connected to the story of Elijah (ibid., 19:6).

Beyond these momentary experiences the entire trip has a religious motive. Yonatan is captivated by the Sabra myth of the trip to Petra before his own motivations are entirely clear to him. Further, the narrator gives the trip unexpected significance: the trip to the depths of his soul becomes one to the depths of the world, to the underworld. Yonatan's guidebook describes Petra as a city of the dead, where there are "red palaces of the dead." It is also full of fire: among the ruins "blaze" oleandar bushes, "and the sculptured rocks flared upward in tongues red, purple, and vermilion flame" (332; 323–24). Yonatan thinks of Petra as a place where the souls of the dead are gathered (345), and Sasha Tlallim defines Petra as "the bottom pit of hell" (337; 329). Oz reinforces that myth in his description of the smoke that Yonatan smells when he starts walking (343, 344; 336), and of the soft earth: "as if he were walking on light ash left after a fire" (344). If that is insufficient, Sasha Tlallim, who takes Yonatan to the beginning of his path in his jeep, named "Burlak" (in Russian: to sail rafts on a river), plays the role of Charon (from Greek mythology) and of the "ferryman" (in Egyptian mythology), who help the dead soul cross the river on his way to the world of the dead. This illusory world reveals itself in the "illusory shadows" cast by Yonatan's body, illusions that freeze his blood and prepare him for a vision of the underworld (in Greek mythology the dead reaching Hades are described as shadows).

When the moon begins to shine, the trip reaches its climax. The silvery light of the moon cloaks the whole desert in a mask of death, and Yonatan imagines that he is surrounded by dead spirits, among them the Syrians and Jordanians whom he and his brother have killed, and also his parents and wife (348; 339).[38] Yonatan's journey, which

---

38. The abandoned Arab village near the kibbutz becomes a kind of extension or parallel of Petra in his mind: "The ruins of Sheikh-Dahar, in the claws of the wild vegetation, the light of the moon is also pouring out there, and not a single living soul is left, only corpses turned over, lying here and there on the sparkling dirt" (348) (cf. the description of Petra [332; 323]). Throughout the novel the ruins of that village serve as a projection of the shadow world, the unconscious of the members of the kibbutz. The connection between Petra and those ruins implies, among other things, that life and death are inseparably interwoven with each other. Every settlement has, like a shadow,

began under the sign of the search for "life," reaches its end and bedrock here. Fearing death, Yonatan fires all his ammunition at the rocks of the desert and at the moon, and flees back to the Israeli border in panic.[39]

What is the meaning of this voyage to the world of the dead? The reader familiar with Jung's interpretation of alchemical writings could infer what was going to take place in Yonatan's spirit, even before his return to the Israeli border. Let us look at the light of the rising moon again: "Red, enflamed, huge, the moon emerged from behind the Edomite range. In an instant the world was transformed. Bright swaths of moonlight streaked the swarthy mountainsides. Ripples of pale light eddied in the plain. Lifeless silver flowed silently over the lifeless earth" (348; 340). The passage describes moonlight as a leaping, trembling liquid, a metaphorical language further developed in the following passage: "[T]he moonsilver poured on its naked body, its corpse. . . . In the splendor of gloomy thoughts the dead sit, bathed in the glory of that silver baptism. The ruins of Sheikh-Dahar, in the claws of wild vegetation, the moonlight pours out there too" (348; 341). What is the purpose of that metaphorical language, repeatedly indicating the "liquid" nature of the moon's silvery light, describing it as shimmering, leaping quicksilver? Understanding the meaning of mercury, a central symbol here, will enhance our understanding of this passage. Quicksilver (the philosophical mercury) played a decisive part in the experiments and writings of the alchemists. Because of its contrasting characteristics the meanings of mercury were radically opposed to each other: it is water and fire, matter and spirit; on the one hand it is the ancient matter, a demon or monster (and it is no coincidence that the silvery light in Oz's description comes from the moon, the symbol of the Great Mother), and on the other hand it is soul and spirit, the world's soul (Anima Mundi). It has a divine element and also a cloacal element at the same time, a structure of higher powers in the lower ones. Jung summarizes that duality as follows:

---

its own Gehenna. Paradoxically, this Gehenna, as the unconscious, is a source of creative renewal.

39. Indirectly, Yonatan takes the part of the hero fighting with the dragon of the Great Mother here. It is no coincidence that he aims his rifle at the moon, one of the main symbols of the Great Mother, and it is not a coincidence that the moonlight slows him down as he flees back to Israel: "All the time a web of moonbeams surrounded him, wrapped him up, made him stumble, until he collapsed on the earth, his burning face immersed in the silver sands" (350; 341). The struggle with the dragon is hinted at even earlier. One of the common symbols of the dragon is the whale, and Rimona thinks: "Yoni's game will be to pretend he's a brave sailor hunting for whales or for desert islands in the South Seas" (180; 170).

- Mercurius consists of all conceivable opposites. . . .
- He is both material and spiritual.
- He is the process by which the lower and material is transformed into the higher and spiritual, and vice versa.
- He is the devil, a redeeming psychopomp, an evasive trickster, and God's reflection in physical nature. . . .
- . . . [H]e represents on the one hand the self and on the other hand the individuation process, and because of the limitless number of his names, also the collective unconscious. (Jung 1968, 237).

With this insight we can understand why Oz took such pains to describe the light of the moon as liquid silver, as mercury, in a half dozen metaphors which give shape to that meaning in the short climactic scene of the novel. Yonatan finds the "primordial material" within himself, the bedrock of his soul, as he experiences the process of individuation. In that process he lays bare his dark side, which, until then, had been concealed from him, as well as the image-God within him. Mercury, which represents among other things the devil or underworld, once again illuminates Yonatan's journey, showing it to be a trip to the world of the dead. At the same time it reflects his religious conversion. Further, we find a reference to alchemical transformation in the sentence, "For everything changes for the better" (350), as well as the phrase "my Zolotoy" (Russian: my gold), which the old land surveyor uses to call Yonatan (337, 341). It is worth noting that one of the common symbols of mercury is the unicorn. Like mercury, it partakes of the devil and the monstrous, and at the same time, of the holy spirit (Jung 1953b, 436, 438, 440). When Yonatan sets out, deciding he is not seeking "any justice" but rather life itself, he is described as a unicorn: "The face that stared at him from the mirror gave him a start. . . . above his eyes a wild shock of hair springing forward like the horn of a charging animal" (219; 207). Moreover, Jung identifies the unicorn with the "re'em" (oryx) of the Talmud (1953b, 460), and Rimona calls Yonatan "re'em" (180).

As predicted by the old land surveyor, a kind of benevolent demon who has preached to Yonatan that life is more important than anything, Yonatan turns back that very night, letting out his agony with a great wail (350; 347). But the Yonatan who returns to the surveyor is not the same Yonatan who had parted from him. Amos Oz leaves no room for doubt: Yonatan has gone through something like a religious conversion, expressed in several different ways in the half page that describes Yonatan's life as the "armor bearer" of the "king" of the desert. Thus, for example, throughout the novel Yonatan repeats the verse, "But their hearts were not true," after the poem by Benyamin Trotsky (8, 27, 142, 344; 5, 21, 130, and elsewhere). The verse derives from Psalm 78, where the poet describes people who pretend to believe in God ("Nevertheless they did flatter him with their mouth, and they lied unto him with their tongues. For their heart was not true with him, neither were they steadfast in his covenant" [vv. 36–37]). Now Yonatan reflects: "I'm beginning to understand. And my heart is getting true because everything changes for the better" (350; 342).[40] The change that takes place within him finds its full expression in the new similarity he is surprised to discover between himself and his wife: "One day, Yonatan happened to see that smile reflected in a broken mirror in a corner of the trailer, and he was struck dumb. It was an exact replica of Rimona's, the woman who had been his wife" (ibid.). As noted, in the novel Rimona stands for the holy, primal elements of the world. After his conversion, Yonatan feels the harmony and the sense of belonging that his wife knows. Unknowingly, he even repeats her words. The line "because everything changes for the better" is one that she has already spoken ("No need to be sad, because everything changes for the better" [232; 222]). After reaching the bedrock of his soul and connecting up with the roots hidden there, Yonatan becomes a boy ("Malchik," as his spiritual master tells him), a symbol of unity, a symbol of fulfillment that cannot be obtained by banishing the primal forces of the soul, but only by coexisting with them.[41] In this way he is also like his wife Rimona, who is compared to a little girl several times during the novel.

---

40. Yonatan thinks about his "true heart" for the first time after his first night in the desert and the religious experiences he has undergone (286; 275). At this point the "true heart" is still the heart that craves for "the enchantments of death." Only upon his return from the journey to Petra, when he serves as his spiritual mentor's armor bearer, does Yonatan learn that a "true heart" does not mean complete liberation from the restraints of culture and consciousness, but the acceptance of life in its full reality.

In reaction to my interpretation of *A Perfect Peace*, Amos Oz wrote to me saying that in fact the first working title of the book had been "The True Heart" (Heb.: *haLev haNakhon*).

41. The appellation "boy" and the invitation to "the royal palace" to sleep like a king "on sheets of royal purple, of byssus and lace" (334; 326) recall the image of the child dressed in royal garments that had symbolized, for the alchemists, the philosophers' stone, the symbol of fullness, of unity, the symbol of the mystic identification with the god within man and with the eternal.

The spiritual course Yonatan traverses during the novel, at the end of which he is a "boy," also recalls the three metamorphoses of which Zarathustra hears from the wise man (Nietzsche 1966, 26–27). Indeed, Yonatan does go through the path of the metamorphoses of the soul, the start of which is a camel hurrying to the desert overburdened with life and knowledge, followed by the lion who aspires to freedom, fighting the

It is not only Rimona that Yonatan is similar to now. First, in finding the child within him he also identifies with Azariah, who is also a "child" and a "fetus" (on further similarities between them, see Chapter 5). Second, because of the nocturnal experience he underwent on the way to Petra, and through his life with the old surveyor, Yonatan begins to resemble his spiritual guide. Alexander Tlallim, an exceptional figure, does not adapt himself to the restraints of society. He possesses an archaic, autochthonous element ("skin dark as an Arab's" [280; 268], "pouring out a lament like an Arab" [337]), as well as a holy element ("I'm sort of a, nu, a holy man to them, a dervish, a yurodivy. And that's what I am around here too. You just ask about Sasha, how he rode to Petra on a camel like Father Abraham" [341; 333]). He lives in the desert, in nature, and lives in peace with the nature within him. He knows there is no life without pain and there is no pain without life (on the surveyor as a demon, see Chapter 5). After his conversion Yonatan clings to Sasha Tlallim and pours water on his hands. Upon his return to the kibbutz, he also has something indigenous about him ("He had grown a beard, turned brown and lean as a Bedouin" [376; 369]) and also something holy ("resembled a young scholar . . . who was studying to become a rabbi" [377; 369–70]).[42]

Yonatan returns to the kibbutz, not to continually have to give up what is his, not "to be all right and not to be selfish and not to make a fuss and not to bother and not to be stubborn, but to pay attention, be thoughtful, and give to the other guy, to contribute to society" (13). After his night of adventure in the desert he now knows that hell exists not only in one's fellow man, but in total liberation from him. Life must be found between those two poles. He has come to understand that life cannot be divided into the positive, the illuminated, and that which is enclosed in the fence, versus the negative, the dark, that which must be silenced at any price. The life he had sought must be led according to the dictates of his "true heart," even at the cost of breaking a social taboo, even at the cost of ignoring the expectations and the tasks imposed upon him by society. He now lives on the

---

dragon while seeking the absolute. The final stage is the boy, naive, who starts afresh, simultaneously denying reality and affirming its holiness.

42. Contrary to the gods of growth and fertility (e.g., Adonis, Osiris), who die during the harvest season and return to life during the winter and spring, Yonatan disappears from his kibbutz in the winter and returns to it at the peak of the harvest season. His descent to the underworld is not a cyclical experience that he must go through again. It is a unique journey, putting the hero to the test, so he can find the treasure he seeks and merit life. Yonatan's "death" in the winter is meant, among other things, to indicate the vitality and fertility that accompany his encounter with the underworld.

kibbutz in peaceful silence. Completely contrary to the accepted social norm, he returns to his "happy triangle," to life together with Rimona and Azariah.

Mercury and the image of the unicorn prepare for Yonatan's return to the kibbutz as a figure who represents both the Arab and the rabbi. It is noteworthy that during the Middle Ages both mercury and the unicorn were symbols of Christ (Jung 1953b, 438). Apparently the association here is no coincidence. Surprisingly, it turns out that Azariah is not the only one in whom there is the archetype of the holy hero. Unlike Azariah, as a child Yonatan did not dream that he had an exalted mission. When he leaves the kibbutz he does not recognize that he has a task to fulfill, but gradually discovers that he too has a purpose in life: "And please excuse me, Professor Spinoza, for being a little slow to get what you meant when you so wisely said that everyone has a role in this life and that the only choice we have is to understand what our role is and to accept it gracefully" (279; 267). Moreover, this role demands his death: "But what I'm afraid I'll have to do after that, sir, once I've given you my all, is to go tonight or tomorrow night to Petra and die there for the good of the cause" (ibid.). Like the scapegoat bearing "all the sins of the children of Israel" and sent to Azazel as a symbol of repentance for those sins (Leviticus 16:8, 21, 26), Yonatan goes off to Azazel (228, 335, 347; 327, 340). In retrospect the reader might recall that his wife had earlier compared him to the crucified Bach (180; 170), and that the adjective "good," often applied to him during the novel, commonly describes Christ's character. His lengthy period of "monasticism" in the desert also contributes to his holiness.

Yonatan responds to the voice summoning him and leaves his kibbutz to undergo the test of descent into the underworld, of contact with the primordial flames. He spares the other members of his kibbutz the need to withstand that horrifying experience. (The desire to get up and go, to start a new life in solitude with the forces of nature, is expressed by both Yolek and Srulik, among others [125, 253; 113, 241].) Thus the figure of the holy hero who bears the sins of the multitude and atones for them is not only a symbol of Azariah, but also of his "brother," Yonatan. In different fashions both of them undergo the pains bound up with achieving the unity of opposites, with finding spiritual fulfillment. Both of them will, on the one hand, offer an outlet for evil tongues, for the cravings of the other members of the kibbutz, and on the other hand they will spread their immunity, the source of which is reconciliation with the various strata of their soul, upon their surroundings.

Like *Elsewhere, Perhaps, A Perfect Peace* rejects the social solutions of the founders of the kibbutz as feasible or satisfactory. Yolek, Hava, and their comrades want to develop their characters according to the social theories they hold, and in the end they become divided, unbalanced people. The novel suggests that docile acceptance of kibbutz society might arouse outbursts of madness, on the one hand, and lead to spiritual death, on the other. Yonatan and Azariah find a different kind of existence. Instead of warring against nature (both external and internal), they propose a ceasefire, a coexistence that would not close off the channels leading to the bedrock of one's being. For on the contrary, these channels must be maintained so that sustenance can be received from the mighty forces hidden there, and so that their destructiveness can be dismantled. In this coexistence the "true heart" of the individual is no less important than society, its needs, its expectations, and its regulations, and the ear gives heed to the forces of nature no less than it hearkens to the radio or the voice of the secretary of the kibbutz. In Azariah and Yonatan's world, the jackal is no longer the sworn enemy of the dog, but its father. Unlike Srulik, who quarrels with God, the two younger men have learned that God is in the whole world, its upper and its lower parts, and that the former cannot exist without the latter.

In *A Perfect Peace* we find the key to Oz's religious outlook as it was expressed in his first stories. Nevertheless, the novel depicts the unity of the divine and the bestial in a less dramatic way than in *Where the Jackals Howl*. Some of the traits of the devouring mother and the dreadful father do not appear in this novel. Whereas in the earlier works emphasis was given to "the nature within God" (Schelling), in the present work that concept has been balanced with "the God of Spinoza." This development is also evident in the moral element that accompanies the religious experience, an idea presented for the first time in Oz's work. Several of the characters feel that the correct way of life can be found by approaching the rhythm of the cosmos, and they feel that some kind of presence, which is embodied in the cosmos, teaches them a lesson or demands an explanation or a response from them. Azariah teaches the young people of the kibbutz that one has "to be close to nature. Close, so to speak, to the rhythms of the cosmos" (154; 139), and Srulik reflects: "The silence is hovering over the darkness—in the valleys, in the mountains, on the sea—mutely but insistently demanding some answer or explanation from us" (234; 224). Rimona also thinks about that silence and what it demands: "And that up above the clouds, up above the air, all is quiet too, the quiet between the stars. And that beyond the last star is the last quiet of all. What do they want from us? Not to disturb, not to make noise because nothing untoward will happen if we keep still" (181; 171–72). Yolek too changes his ways because of the window into the cosmos that has opened up before him. In this novel Oz has, undoubtedly, reached the threshold of perfect peace for the first time.

## The Third Condition: More Light, More Light

Oz's panentheistic notion remained unchanged in his latest novels. The importance of the religious theme in *Black Box* (1987; 1988) is enhanced by the confrontation between Dr. Gideon's defiant attitude toward God and His believers, on the one hand, and Michel Sommo's orthodox standpoint, on the other. One can clearly discern the author's panentheistic concept in his latest novel to-date, *The Third Condition* (1991); yet here it is presented from a completely new angle. The name of the protagonist's father, Barukh Nomberg, should remind the reader of Oz's first story, "A Crack Open to the Wind," in which the protagonist travels to Tel Aviv to see his influential relative Barukh Makhtesh. The shared name is not incidental, nor is the fact that both characters are described as divine figures. Importantly, in "A Crack Open to the Wind" the way to reunite with the divine world goes via the jackal, the dark night. Oz's latest novel is his first work that mainly relies on the Kabbala, its worldview and symbols. The connection between the author's familiar panentheistic notion and the Kabbala (which also has a strong panentheistic element) has brought about an important change in Oz's world: now holiness is achieved not through uniting with the jackal and darkness but rather through mingling with the light in which a "spark" finds its lost origin.

The protagonist, Ephrayim, is a fifty-four-year-old divorcé, who spends most of his time bothering his friends with his leftist peace plans, arguing with them at the most inconvenient hours while exposing the shortcomings of both left and right political attitudes. His friends put up with his behavior because, among other things, they appreciate his brilliant mind: several of his predictions have turned out to be very accurate. The novel pictures, on one level, the impotence of Israeli leftist intelligentsia. Yet the present Israeli political scene, though overtly discussed throughout the novel, is overshadowed by the protagonist's principal quest for the meaning of his existence.

The novel's point of departure is similar to that of *A Perfect Peace*: Ephrayim feels that his soul has died (163, 171, 174, and elsewhere), just like Yonatan in *A Perfect Peace*. Both characters find themselves lacking a "spark" and, despairingly, they search for "life" and for "home" ("life" is described in both novels as a treasure that has to be found). Both Yonatan and Ephrayim imagine that they are being called to go somewhere and that only by responding to this call might they find their lost life. This existential condition is illuminated by Ephrayim's frequent description as a "golem" (12, 48, 56, 94, 131, 149, 152, and elsewhere), as well as by his constant fatigue and inability to concentrate. Another facet of this situation is Ephrayim's feeling that he is far away from his "true," authentic self (187 and elsewhere). Indeed, at the very beginning of the novel, he "once again realized that he is here by mistake and actually he should have been in a completely different place" (10).

Where should he be? Here is the problem, for Ephrayim does not have an answer to that question. Still, he feels that in ancient times he had already lived in Jerusalem and that at that time he had strong ties with the cosmos and its elements (189 and elsewhere). In his present life he experienced this affinity with the cosmos only when he stayed with three young women in Greece. In those days his complete mingling with the world was expressed, among other things, by "the sharp powers of sight" that awakened in him and enabled him "to watch the sunrise behind the olive orchard and to see the creation of the world" (21). At the time he palpably realized that all the different manifestations of the world were but different embodiments of one and the same entity. He knew, then, that his present life was not his first life. Furthermore, with the "enlightenment of the inner holiday that engulfed him" he sensed that all the women he had met, including his mother and his lovers, "have almost turned into one woman" (ibid.).

Far from this experience in time and place, Ephrayim cannot but feel that "the essence" of his life is missing (72, 198, 225, and elsewhere), and time and again he looks for a "loss" whose nature he cannot define (72, 190, 198). Thus, like previous works of the author, *The Third Condition* confronts two realms of existence: on the one hand, a total blending with the cosmos that is accompanied by a feeling of strong vitality, and on the other hand, an existence characterized by separation and alienation. Importantly, the dream that opens the novel is concluded by the saying, "we need to separate" (8), and this need recurs throughout the novel on different psychological, familial, and societal levels. Other expressions of the separation theme are "the death of the soul" (163, 171, 174), the deadening daily routine, and the many lies permeating the protagonist's life. Moreover, Ephrayim imagines that only when he was one with the cosmos was he able to intuitively understand his life and his place in the world (21, 189), whereas, in the separation situation, the bond with the world is severed. He is left, then, without any answers, unable to quench the urgent need to comprehend the meaning of his life (17, 51, 72, 107, 181, 189, and elsewhere). The protagonist's religious quest stems from this need.

Ephrayim sees himself as being part of the Israeli left-wing intelligentsia and declares that he is "a one hundred percent secular Jew" (228). But this leftist secular person is charged with deep religious yearnings. He envisages "the Creator of the worlds" as a sixty-year-old Sephardi merchant in Jerusalem (72), and he maintains a constant dialogue with Him. He argues with Him, brings facts that negate His grace and charity (the Holocaust, the killing of Arab children by Israeli soldiers); he surveys the different theological attempts to prove the existence of God and the different efforts to demonstrate His nonexistence. Like Oz's previous characters, Ephrayim blames "the Creator of the worlds" for being apathetic to human suffering, or even worse, for laughing at and enjoying human troubles (73, 102, 197, 201). Ephrayim harshly blames the Creator and His silence, yet he recognizes that even when he turns his back on Him he is "like an escaping man who knows that he is escaping and knows that his escape is doomed" (73). Thus, he lives waiting for a sign. Addressing the elements he urges them: "Say a word. Give only a small road sign, a hint, a clue, a wink, and at this very moment I stand up and go. Won't stop even to change a shirt. Stand up and go. Right now. Or lie to your feet. Falling down but having my eyes uncovered" (189). These are not the words of a secular left-winger. These are words of a deeply religious person. The allusion to Balaam's words ("The oracle of the man whose eye is opened, the oracle of him who hears the words of God, who sees the vision of the Almighty, falling down, but having his eyes uncovered"; Numbers 24:4, 16) is not coincidental. In Chapter 1 I argued that Oz is a "double agent." Nowhere before in his writings was this spiritual situation so crucial as it is in *The Third Condition*. The "one hundred percent secular Jew," who ostensibly takes active part in the struggles of the left-wing intelligentsia, all of a sudden depicts these secular struggles as marginal, not to say redundant, in comparison to his main concerns.

Kabbalistic terms are frequently used in Oz's previous works (*Elsewhere, Perhaps, To Know a Woman*, and elsewhere). Yet *The Third Condition* is the author's first novel in which the Kabbala plays such a pivotal role. The protagonist's expectations for some divine sign are carefully prepared by the author. A receptionist in a women's clinic,

Ephrayim calls the clients' register "the lineage of Kabbala" (Oz puns here on the word *kabbala*, meaning both reception, tradition, and mysticism), and he mentions the Kabbala on several occasions (71 and elsewhere). His vocabulary is full of typical Kabbalistic terms, such as *tikkun* (improvement, correction), *pgimah* (flaw, defect), *gilgul* (metamorphosis, metempsychosis), *nitzotz* (spark), *galut* (exile), and many others. The narrator adds to this vein by frequently using the term "golem" (shapeless lump, robot), a term also charged with Kabbalistic meanings, and by describing the sapphire ring of his protagonist's mother. The term *sefirah*, one of the Kabbala's pivotal terms, originated from the Hebrew word for sapphire, *sapir*. The ancient Aramaic expressions that he recalls—arousing in him awe and shudder (98, 124, 133, 160, 188, 197, 198)—are an important aspect of the protagonist's vocabulary. All these ancient expressions hint at a hidden world that sends its signs to this world.

Furthermore, the protagonist time and again describes his situation in terms that call to mind one of the major concepts of the Lurianic Kabbala.[43] According to the Lurianic Kabbala, the vessels that were meant to hold the divine light were broken, hence the sparks of this divine light were dispersed and buried inside the *klipa* (husks) of reality. Ephrayim uses similar metaphors. Regretting his inability to communicate with a taxi driver who drove him home, he thinks that his obligation was to change the driver's heart with calm and effective arguments: "Deep under many poisonous layers of cruelty and fear a spark of wisdom is certainly flickering. One has to believe that it is possible to dig down and rescue the good that was covered under the ruins" (128). He employs the same metaphors in an imaginary attempt to change Prime Minister Shamir's mind (181). Ephrayim depicts his own life as "buried" under layers of lies and dust and routine chores (198, 225, and elsewhere), and he sees all human beings as losing their way in darkness "without even a distant spark of *nehora me'alya* [Aramaic: prime, great light]" (160). Undoubtedly, the "one hundred percent secular Jew" protagonist constantly seeks the divine light from which he was severed. This is the background for the epiphany he calls "the third condition."

Indeed, "the third condition" implies a fusion with the primordial light. Watching the winter morning through his window, Ephrayim sees it as a "noble matter" covering the summits and the slopes: "The light kissed the ridges, glided in the valleys, awakened in every tree and every stone their sleeping, shining essence, the essence that was

---

43. On this late and influential branch of Kabbala, see Scholem (1965).

buried long ago beneath layers of the greyish routine of inanimate objects" (197). *Mahut* (essence, being) was one of the names of the hidden God the Kabbalists tried to discover, and Ephrayim himself showed interest in examining "the hiding God" (23). This essence restores to the world, at least for a moment, its "primary nature that went out ages and ages ago" (197), and Ephrayim discovers one of the main truths of the Kabbala: the world's different objects and phenomena "are but different expressions of the very same entity. An entity that was ordained to separate into endless flawed, ephemeral embodiments, though by itself it remains complete and eternal and one" (198). Only on such a winter morning does the light remove from the earth "the constant turbid veil, a veil of desolation and lies," and everything is seen "as in the day it was created" (ibid.). Unable to define this light Ephrayim calls it "the third condition." And he feels "that it is not only the clear mountain light but a light that, as a matter of fact, flows forth from the mountains and from him simultaneously, and only the copulation of the beams brings about the third condition." The "third condition" is, thus, a situation in which the primal nature of creation is unearthed, and the spark, usually buried under layers of lies and mundane chores, is reunited with its original light.

Interestingly, the protagonist is not overwhelmed by the encounter with the primal light. He enjoys this unique bond with the cosmos and observes it at one and the same time. The nature of this experience is dictated by his panentheistic concept. He does not want just to meet the light, to be utterly inundated by it, but also to understand his Creator and the way He rules His creation. Lo and behold, right when he discovers the light that gives its primal nature back to the world, the protagonist addresses God: "Will Your Honor grant me with a flick of His chin if I kneel and say 'I render thanks to thee?' Is there a certain, specific thing Your Honor asks me to do? Is Your Honor interested in us? Why did He throw us here? Why did He choose us? Why did He choose Jerusalem? Is Your Honor still listening? Is Your Honor giggling?" (ibid.). The verb "giggle" has appeared in previous descriptions of God's indifference to the human plight (72, 102). The mystic experience has, then, a decidedly cognitive facet. The protagonist does not give up his wish to obtain a sign from God, to have a dialogue with Him, to comprehend His conduct and the meaning of his own life.

It is worth noting that, embraced by Annette, after making love with her, the protagonist feels himself "empty and light like light" (153). Later on he portrays his semen, moving toward Annette's womb, as "completely similar to his father, who yearns only to curl up once and for all in the depth of femininity's mucosity, and to be enraptured and pampered and to fall asleep" (182). The novel creates a clear analogy between the protagonist's yearning to curl up in the womb (see also 55, 137) and his mystic reunion with the cosmos.

This analogy, amply dealt with by Neumann (1973) and Shoham (1980, 1982), clearly manifests the change in Oz's fiction. For many of his previous characters (Yonatan in *A Perfect Peace* is typical), the way to return to the womb was via the dark night, the underworld. Yonatan has to resist this temptation because its only meaning is death. In *The Third Condition*, on the other hand, this reunion is achieved through light. Still, there is an interesting similarity between Yonatan's experience and Ephrayim's epiphany. The light is not deadening like darkness, but it lacks any features of selfhood: "The third condition is grace that can be won only if you leave behind every will: to stand under the night sky, a son without age, a son without sex, a son without time, a son without a nation, a son without anything" (246). In fact, this notion is implied in Oz's work from its inception. Many of his characters realize that they can join the living world only by ignoring their ego, either through forgetfulness ("Where the Jackals Howl") or through shattering the borders of their consciousness (*Elsewhere, Perhaps, My Michael, A Perfect Peace*). Earlier Ephrayim had claimed that daily routine implies desolation and death. Now he realizes that "life" means naught, lack of any individuality. Paradoxically, the sought-after "life" turns out to be lack of life, a return to the womb or fusion with the primordial essence of creation. Ephrayim's behavior after his father's death implies that his solution follows the path of the righteous Kabbalist: taking part in the world of actions in order to increase the light in the world and to diminish "evil" and "suffering."

The Kabbalistic experience is hinted at throughout the novel by dozens of descriptions of lights and sparks of light, on the one hand, and sheer darkness, on the other hand.[44] The most striking phenomenon is the fact that in this novel Oz has accepted the Lurian concept of the soul. According to this concept an intimate affinity can be established only between souls that belong to the same "root"; parents and their children usually do not originate from the same root. This concept explains the nonbiological dynasty that ties Barukh Nomberg, his son Ephrayim, and Dimi, Yael's son. Yael is Ephrayim's divorced wife, and although she makes it clear that she aborted the fetus of

---

44. Some aspects of the Kabbalistic component of the novel are discussed by Zilberman (1991).

Ephrayim's child, his father still imagines that Dimi is his own grandson. Dimi's relationship with his parents, Yael and Ted, is characterized by complete alienation. Both parents feel that he is just a burden and Dimi wonders why they brought him into the world in the first place (120). Yet there is a deep closeness between Dimi and both Barukh and Ephrayim, and he calls the two of them "grandfather" (27). Ephrayim himself loves Dimi "as his own soul" (166), and this love is stronger than the love he felt for any woman in his life, including his mother and his ex-wife (250). Yael's uncertainty about her love for Ephrayim, though they are not family relatives at all (215), hints at the same Kabbalistic concept.

There should be no doubt that *The Third Condition* is a religious novel. The protagonist recalls that when he was three or four years old, he woke up during the night and saw in the window an angelic figure. Hearing his cry his mother came and tried to calm him down, reassuring him that it was just a nightmare, not a real figure. As an adult Ephrayim is convinced that his mother lied to him. Moreover, this figure and his mother's lie have decided his fate "to be all these years here and yet not here" (190). His constant expectation for a sign (189 and elsewhere) stems from, among other things, this formative experience. The "one hundred percent secular" protagonist turns out to be a believer who dwells among us all these years, living "here and yet not here."

*The Third Condition* is thus far the most explicit expression of Oz's religious worldview. With its recognizable Kabbalistic elements, it changes some of Oz's pivotal premises, yet it leaves his panentheistic concept intact. The religious impulse that typified Oz's first protagonist, in "A Crack Open to the Wind," has lost none of its power in *The Third Condition*. The religious quest has remained one of the main motivations of Oz's protagonists and one of Oz's central themes. In this sense Oz reflects an important phenomenon in Israeli culture: Zionism as a secular movement has failed to produce a satisfying spiritual and intellectual worldview. The schism in Israeli culture between secular and religious Jews is a known fact. Yet this schism does not begin with the confrontation between the secular intelligentsia and the religious quarters of the Israeli population. It is anchored in the very heart of the secular component of Israeli society whose most eloquent mouthpieces are not content with the secular platform and its culture and seek solace on the other side of the fence.[45]

---

45. I dealt with this issue in "Elections and Literature in Israel" (1989).

# A MEMORY
## A Desire to Belong

I do not recall if it was Israel's eighth or ninth Independence Day celebration, but I clearly recall the happiness that engulfed the kibbutz dining room where the celebration was held. The state was still young, and there was a momentum in the air, a certainty, a heartwarming brotherhood: kibbutz, labor movement, state. Undoubtedly, the archetypes had not yet died. After speeches and the reading, the tables and chairs were moved aside and the dining room finally cleared to serve its true function—that of dance floor.

The dining room was too narrow to hold the circle of dancers and an additional circle began to form within the larger one. In a few minutes three or four joyful *hora*-dancing circles had formed. All the happiness of the day flowed into the dance floor. Ozer Hulda'yi (one of the key members of the kibbutz and principal of the school) charged the air with his cries: "Who are we?" —"ISRAEL!" the crowd roared. —"Who are we all?" —"ISRAEL!" —"Who is our Father?" —"ISRAEL!"

Sitting to relax for a moment, I discovered Amos Oz among the dancers. All his classmates were wearing their own colorful clothes. Oz was the only one in khaki, the color that in the early days of the kibbutz symbolized the ideals of its members (equality, simplicity, modesty). I was then twelve or thirteen, and there was no special relationship between us. But something in his appearance caught my eye, and amazed me: he did not dance the *hora* as others did, with abandonment and gusto, or with sweat pouring from his brow. How to express it? He did not dance, did not perspire, but rather seemed to try to dance with all his heart, and tried to perspire, with all his soul. I recall the amazement which seized me at that moment: why did he have to so exert himself to achieve what others did effortlessly? For years I recalled that picture as the embodiment of the desire to belong, an attempt to break through the circle of alienation. And also, a desire to become one with the body, to throw aside the yoke of the intellect, the conscious. When was it that I realized this? Had the khaki-dressed Oz perspired that evening, had he danced as his comrades did, one of the principal impulses behind his writing would have been extinguished.

# 4

## WATER AND SKY
## Water Images and Female Characters

From its inception Oz's work has grappled with primal forces that hiss like embers beneath the thin surface of consciousness. His books illustrate, through sea and water images, the destructiveness and violence of those forces, as well as their vitality and creativity. The worldview conveyed in these works is decidedly Jungian: human consciousness and the ego grow out of the sea of the collective unconscious (that topic is treated extensively in Chapter 2). They depict the sea as both source and destination, as the beneficient mother and as the devouring mother, one who enchants in her attractions and kills her lovers. The sea is a reservoir of all the primal urges, sex and violence, and yet contains all the vitality and wisdom of the natural world. Among the main sea symbols we find the snake with its tail in its mouth (the uroboros) and the ring. Both symbolize primal wholeness in which all opposites (good and evil, spirit and body, life and death, man and woman, sanctity and sin) cling to each other. At the start of his discussion of the snake devouring its own tail, Neumann writes of the circle: "It is also the perfect state in which opposites are united—the perfect beginning because the opposites have not yet flown apart and the world has not yet begun, the perfect end because in it the opposites have come together again in a synthesis and the world is once more at rest" (1973, 8). The nascent ego is part of that all-encompassing state of existence, and later it will recall it as a lost paradise (ibid., 12, 227).

Not surprisingly, Oz's female figures are linked to the sea and the circle. For example, "Purple Coast" (1962a) models Dita after Aphrodite who, born of the sea, has a close affinity with the ring and the circle (see Chapter 2). As a character, Noga Harish also conveys the identification of woman with the sea and the circle (*Elsewhere, Perhaps*), as does Rimona Lifshitz (*A Perfect Peace*) and Ilana (*Black Box*). All four of them embody some of the contraries that characterize Oz's religious conception. Hannah Gonen (*My Michael*) is exceptional in this regard. She yearns for the sea as though it were a lost paradise to which the way has been blocked.

As a realistic element in Oz's works, the sea appears as one of the eternal, unchanging forces of nature. The stories emphasize, first of all, the might and primordiality of the sea, and, second, they assert that man can neither shape it as he desires nor overcome it. Zechariah Berger, attempting to define the nature of power to Tomer Berger, finds it best expressed in the ocean and the cosmos: "Force is something very powerful. An Ocean. A universe. A Law" (*Elsewhere, Perhaps*, 1966a, 352; 1973, 274). Ernest Cohen, the Secretary of the kibbutz in *Touch the Water, Touch the Wind*, reflects on his last day: "And then this will-o'-the-wisp had appeared at the last moment, the peace of the mighty silent elements, the stars, the sea, the wind, the sands, darkness, music" (1973a, 173; 1974, 164). Dov Sirkin, in despair after his effort to change human nature, realizes before he dies that "the imprint of our fingers doesn't last on a watery surface" ("Before His Time," 74). Srulik's reflections echo the same certainty; he compares the various solutions proposed by the kibbutz in response to the problems of the human condition and society to writing down "a few ingenious formulae on the waves of the sea" (*A Perfect Peace*, 233; 223). In other places in his notebook the sea appears as one of the forces of nature along with the mountains and the stars (236, 372; 364 and elsewhere).

In many cases Oz's plots take place near the sea. The kibbutz described in *Where the Jackals Howl* is in the north, near the sea. The stories introduce water and sea images in various ways: a character's dreams ("The Way of the Wind"), an aquarium with tropical fish ("A Hollow Stone"), and a trip to Tel Aviv ("All the Rivers"). The only story in that volume which takes place in Jerusalem, "Strange Fire," mentions the myth of the sun's nightly journey to the sea (154). In *A Perfect Peace* the kibbutz adjoins the sea, as does Tel Aviv (*To Know a Woman*). In *Elsewhere, Perhaps* the swimming pool, along with the

Jordan River and the Sea of Galilee, replaces the sea. When Hannah Gonen, the Jerusalemite, travels to Holon and goes to the sea, she experiences a few days of tranquillity (*My Michael*, 100, 102; 144, 127). The plot of *To Know a Woman* begins with the protagonist's decision to move from Jerusalem to Tel Aviv, and the Tel Aviv beach is mentioned throughout the novel. Water is also introduced in the novel through the light in Annemarie's room, a "vague green underwater light" (1989, 142; 1991, 186). Led to her bed by her brother, Yoel gazes "at the face of the pretty baby in the faint watery light" (142; 187), before he starts making love to her. It is worth noting that the novel contraposes the "feminine," moisty, tropical climate, seducing the protagonist and threatening his life (98; 126), and the snowy climate of Helsinki. Throughout the novel Yoel tries to decipher the meaning of the crippled man he saw in Helsinki, hoping that he represents a solution to the existential puzzles that baffle him.[1] As we shall see below, the tropical climate is a central image of *Black Box* as well.

## *The Point of Departure: Dita-Aphrodite*

The ocean appears as a central symbol in Oz's early story, "Purple Coast,"[2] in which a group of passengers cruise endlessly on the ocean with no destination. In Chapter 2 I pointed out that the story juxtaposes two principles of existence: the feminine principle, symbolized by the ocean, the ring, darkness, and the unconscious; and, opposed to it, the masculine principle, symbolized by dry land, the straight line, light, and consciousness. The ring signifies, among other things, that the ocean is the source and end of life. The protagonist's sea-burial also implies this notion, as well as his reflections as he floats in the water: "The waters within my body are holding traitorous conversations with the waters about my body" (210). The water within the body becomes an independent element here, potentially collaborating with the threatening ocean. From time immemorial it has known the language of the sea, and now it wishes to unite with it, to be reconciled ("I beg my body to not reconcile itself with the water"). Water as an

---

1. In this novel Oz follows the alchemists' quest for the philosophers' stone. The crippled man the protagonist had seen in Helsinki is implicitly described as the Antropos, one of the main symbols of the philosophers' stone in alchemy. I offered this interpretation in a book review on *Kol Israel* (Israel Broadcasting Co.).

2. In his first published story, "A Crack Open to the Wind" (1961), water represented the forces of nature threatening the integrity of the protagonist's house.

element conserving the primal urges of nature has already been characterized at the beginning of the story by its desire: "At night the ship rushed like a caress across the warm ocean surface. The talons of the ship's propellors scratched the water, and the water replied with a wavy whisper. The desire of the water seeped into the ship and hovered over the decks like a thin vapor" (202). Further on, the water caresses the loins of the ship, and while the narrator and Dita make love, it disturbs them, crying out and roiling. Dita, the female protagonist who was born of the sea like Aphrodite, embodies the desires of the water and the story compares her to the sea by means of sea imagery. Like Aphrodite, Dita's love needs no arousal, and she lavishes her favors on gods and mortals alike.

The connection between water and sexual desires appears frequently throughout Oz's works. *Touch the Water, Touch the Wind* compares sexual intercourse to the movement of a dinghy across the water (66); the same simile appears in *A Perfect Peace*: "And when he took her this time it was not in an iron drive like a plow breaking earth but with a wistful yearning, like a small craft upon a smooth sea" (284; 273). Before that, at the start of the night, "his bride began to move beneath him like the sea" (283; 272). When she sleeps with Ezra Berger for the first time, Noga Harish feels that her body floats "on spreading ripples," wave after wave breaks over her, and the "boiling water battered her body" (160; 127). Hannah Gonen envisions how the man lying in ambush will destroy her body, and how she will celebrate his arrival: "I will scream burn and suck his blood like a vampire a madly whirling drunken ship in the night will I be when he comes at me, singing and seething and floating I will be flooded" (148; 214–15). Nonetheless, it should be noted that "Purple Coast" depicts water as more than a dark, instinctual, and chaotic element. As the primordial, eternal matter of the world it also contains the divine. Dita represents the drives contained in water, but as an avatar of Aphrodite she also demonstrates the divine spark within it. Before their separation, the sky and the water were a single entity. The combination of the primal and the holy expresses Oz's religious conception (see earlier chapters), and it characterizes his water images as well.

Dita's figure serves as a model for many of Oz's female protagonists. A key issue regarding these figures is the question of their link with the sea and the world of the depths—to what degree the horn of plenty is open or closed for them. In this chapter I will examine, among other things, the characters of Galila ("Where the Jackals Howl"), Noga

Harish (*Elsewhere, Perhaps*), Rimona (*A Perfect Peace*), Ilana (*Black Box*), and Hannah Gonen (*My Michael*).[3]

## *Galila: Between Heatwave and Rain*

"Where the Jackals Howl" focuses on the encounter between Matityahu Damkov, a refugee who reached the kibbutz toward the end of World War II, and Galila, a sixteen-year-old kibbutz girl, the daughter of two kibbutz founders. Damkov, having revealed to Galila that he is her real father, tries to seduce her, but at the last moment the two recoil from the deed. The story lays bare the lands of the jackals, which extend both beyond the kibbutz fence and into its inhabitants' hearts. Along with the symbols of light and darkness, water serves as a central symbol reinforcing this theme.

At the beginning of section 5, the narrator describes the circular structure of the kibbutz world: "In this twilight hour our world is made of circles within circles. On the outside is the circle of the abstract, distant, darkness: a dim lake murmuring with tremors and hums" (15). He goes on to delineate that structure of circles within circles, describing the circle of the nocturnal lands and the circle of the lights in the center of Sashka's illuminated writing table. We have here a structure typical of Jung's concept of the human soul, beginning with the lake of darkness, the collective unconscious, and ending in the circle of light and the writing table in the central ring, consciousness with the ego in the middle. The size and power of the world of darkness are

---

3. Some of these female figures are discussed by Esther Fuchs (1987). Fuchs's book is an attempt to apply feminist criticism to contemporary Hebrew fiction. Some of her arguments are valid and deserve further examination. Yet her reading in the fiction of Oz and his contemporaries relies on the overt level of the works, ignoring the complexities and nuances of modern literary texts. Her characterizations of many of Oz's female characters are, then, highly questionable. Thus, for example, she depicts Rimona, one of the main characters in *A Perfect Peace*, as a "slow-witted" woman (20), whereas a close reading of the novel reveals that Rimona is one of Oz's most complicated characters, a divine figure endowed with unmistaken intuition and wisdom. The description of Eva (*Elsewhere, Perhaps*) as "driven by materialism" (22) is another example in which Fuchs misses the main motives of the character; the same is true of her description of Hannah Gonen (*My Michael*) as a "political enemy" (75).

Nehama Aschkenasy's book (1986) is yet another attempt to read Hebraic literary tradition in light of feminist theories. Her interpretations of some of Oz's work (notably *My Michael* and some stories of *Where the Jackals Howl*) go beneath the surface level of the text and offer a much more balanced and persuasive picture than Fuchs's reading.

expressed, among other things, by the implied contrast between the dark lake and the old, dim "puddles of light" of the kibbutz (14). A similar confrontation exists between the masses of black men who appear in Damkov's visions of the deluge and the kibbutz inhabitants. Damkov views the masses of people as a torrent flowing "in great cascades" down to the coastal plain, inundating it with "roiling eddies" (22). The kibbutz members, in contrast, make their way to the dining room "in slow streams" (11). Sashka's writing also expresses that confrontation. Describing his writing table as the heart of the structure of rings, the narrator dwells on his style: "How biting are Sashka's formulations. The words flow out of him in dependable, orderly jets. Do they really feel their ridiculous isolation?" (16). The metaphors describing this process (flowing and surging) juxtapose writing with the previous descriptions of flow. The surges explain the ridiculous and dreadful isolation. A "dependable, orderly jet" is one that has lost its primal impetus, and its link with its origins has been weakened. Moreover, the water's major characteristic, as a material, is its wholeness, its indivisible unity that can never be shaped. Water embodies the *unio mystica* characterized by flow and reciprocal bonds between its component parts. Words are the contrary of that unity: language acts as a filter that separates and sorts out that primal wholeness. Words are the fragments of that archaic unity, and thence we have their dreadful isolation. Another reason for that isolation is the weakness of words in opposition to the primal, prelinguistic experience represented by Damkov and the jackals in this story.

The story introduces Galila's character while she is taking a shower, refreshing herself with cold water. Since she has no mirror she cannot look at her body, splattered with water, and therefore she finds herself lacking tranquillity and unable "to take part in that tired, bluish softness raised up by the sea breeze and surrounding the place and its people" (10). In this version Galila does not dry herself off: she shakes her skin like an animal getting out of the water, stretching as she puts on her evening clothing. Hurried and tense, Galila thinks about Matityahu Damkov and decides to accept his invitation. At the beginning of the evening Galila discovers the world of the depths, the existence of which had been unknown to her: "A man walking about a room in his undershirt is not a strange sight, but the black, hairy, apelike body of Matityahu Damkov stirred things up in her depths" (17). Vacillating between dread and fascination, she stays in the room, finding the tranquillity she had previously been denied ("It was a peaceful time between them, somewhat heartwarming" [21]). While she paints obliviously and with devotion, she becomes part of the flow that characterizes the world of nature (see the discussion of this story in the previous chapter). The somnolence that falls upon her and Damkov might seem surprising. When Damkov calls Galila to tell her his dark secret, he means to shatter the tranquillity of life on the kibbutz (17). Galila, visiting a strange man's room, finds Damkov both threatening and attractive, which arouses dread within her. Why do these characters experience somnolence in a scene so permeated with tension? The somnolence is not the result of fatigue but an extension of oblivion, of being part of nature's flowing existence. In other words, somnolence occurs as consciousness regresses. Thus Damkov envisions masses of black people sliding into the sea like a cascade, and Galila "slowly wakes up, as though floating on the surface of a mighty flood. A soft embrace was in her voice" (22). Doubtless the mighty flood is an extension of the dark lake, the world of the depths of which Galila first becomes aware that evening. Also the "soft embrace" indicates that Galila has now taken on part of the natural existence of the world, linking her to the "silent, soft embrace" of the cypress trees (9).

At this point Galila remains entirely in Damkov's power, despite the shreds of opposition still audible in her voice. Her association with water explains the far-reaching change that she experiences, at the peak of which she wishes to have intercourse with Damkov. It is also noteworthy that the story's second version links Galila's recognition of her father to the water: " 'Father,' said Galila in surprise, as if waking on the first morning of winter at the end of a long summer, looking outside and saying, rain" (1976a, 24; 1981, 19). Galila's behavior that evening demonstrates the powerful element missing in the conscious, orderly life that society has carved out. When she acknowledges Damkov as her true father, Galila passes from the long summer to the dark, damp life of winter.

In earlier chapters we saw that Oz's stories show human consciousness emerging from the ocean of the unconscious and of nature. Descriptions of water in the present story express that view. While on the one hand, water symbolizes the primal, unrestrained world of nature, on the other hand society has harnessed it for its needs: the narrator often mentions the kibbutz swimming pool and the network of irrigation pipes spread out over the fields.

To summarize this point: the water in "Where the Jackals Howl" is inseparably bound up with darkness ("the dark lake"), with the immutable night sounds, with the world of the depths lying in the human psyche. Water, the opposite of light, of the heatwave, of consciousness, embodies destructive and violent urges, hostility and wickedness, but also fertility and plenty. For its needs, society can exploit the water's fertility. The heatwave is the scourge of the kibbutz fields; the rain and the water from the sprinklers will make them bloom afresh.

"Nomad and Viper," the following story, develops metaphors of water and flowing that contribute to the connection between the two stories.[4] Water and the sea appear in other stories in the volume, and in two of them, "All the Rivers" and "A Hollow Stone," they are a pivotal symbol. In addition, "Upon This Evil Earth," a revised version of which was included in the Am Oved edition of *Where the Jackals Howl* (1976a; 1981), also uses the sea as a pivotal symbol.

## *Water—Germany—Elsewhere, Perhaps*

In *Elsewhere, Perhaps*, Oz's first novel, he extends the themes of *Where the Jackals Howl*. Dozens of motifs link the two works, beginning with the thematic elements, the characters, and the geographical setting and landscape, and extending to the use of phrases, similes, and symbols. The novel focuses on the same tension expressed in *Where the Jackals Howl*, the struggle between the "good order" the kibbutz tries to impose on its surroundings and its members, and the external and internal forces which disrupt that order, forces repeatedly linked to water. The novel extends and develops not only the stories of *Where the Jackals Howl*, but Oz's earlier story, "Purple Coast." Noga Harish, the main protagonist, is known as Stella Maris, "The Star of the Sea," and her name (Hebrew *Noga* = the planet Venus) associates her with Venus-Aphrodite. As with Dita's figure, she expresses divine, primordial unity, both creative and instinctual, which explains the recurring presence of the circle and the ring in the symbolic structure of the novel.

The novel represents water in a variety of ways. In the realistic world, it is found in the swimming pool, in rain, in the Jordan River, and in the Sea of Galilee. We also find it in descriptions of nature's forces—mountains and the night noises—and in various ways it expresses each of the major figures.

In Reuven Harish's poetry a stream's turbulent waters represent the primal, blind element of nature that stands in contrast to light:

---

4. On that subject see the appendix, "On the Structure of *Where the Jackals Howl*."

> Opposite the loss-river of turbid nature. . . .
> In our heart-blood let us light a spark here.
> (11)
>
> The turbid river rushes into gloom:
> Can man, so stunted, pitiful and weak
> Reach up to snatch a firebrand from the sun. . . .
> Has he the strength to build a mighty dam
> To stem the torrent and to tame the flood?
> (19; 12)

The narrator himself adopts that symbol, and in his words the river represents nature, "selfish, blind, biological instinct, denied freedom of choice" (16; 9). The "holy Jordan," next to which dwells Kibbutz Metsudat Ram, is apparently the contrary of that raging river which carries away everything. However, the opposition is only partial. The Jordan's bed lies in the Syrian-African rift, presented in the novel as "the primeval crack" (40; 32), the world's pudendum. In fact, Jacobi mentions that in mythological periods the snake symbolized both the ocean and the Jordan Valley (1974, 149). Before the Jewish pioneers reached the place, the valley where they settled had been flooded with "savage waters" (82). That explains why many matters in the kibbutz cannot be managed calmly (the idiom in Hebrew is literally "on calm waters" [110]), why "dark forces" repeatedly break out on the kibbutz without any visible explanation (150) in the character of Oren Geva (150, 290, 358; 227 and elsewhere), as well as in that of Noga Harish (159). Paradoxically, when Reuven Harish tells his pupils about the savage waters that had spread out through the valley, and about the pioneers who came to build up their land imposing culture upon mutinous nature, he arouses ancient memories in the children—that of their woods tribe heritage: "His words cast a kind of fear upon them, the echo of the children of the tribe at a secret swearing-in ceremony" (83).

The story depicts the blind, archaic nature of water as it shows the natural world threatening to uproot the enlightened settlement. The night noises, "changing every minute but never changing at all," are like the dark ocean that seeks "to wash away our frail houses with its breakers" (56; 48). The mountains, representing enemy territory, "intend to bury us alive under torrents of heavy shadows" (47; 39), and at night, against the background of the fields and the stars, they represent "a defined pool of black" (195; 155). The novel emphasizes the rain's arbitrary nature rather than its importance to the fields' prosperity. The rain suddenly pelts down in the middle of a May Day assembly, and the kibbutz cultural director decrees: "Force majeure" (100; 75). Oz weaves several of the major motifs around that rainfall. First, when describing the sky before the rain begins to fall, it is "as if the sea had risen to hang upside down in the air over our tiny roofs" (96; 72). Later, he describes the sky as "an upper sea," and thus rain becomes an outpouring of that sea. The speaker at the May Day assembly points out that organized society has not yet resolved the greatest questions, the questions of existence. The passage that follows illustrates this notion, which Oz has referred to in many of his interviews. It describes the scene in which young Ido sits next to Hassia, tortured with desire for the woman at his side. The remainder of the passage creates a sophisticated counterpoint between Hassia's and Ido's conversation and the speaker's words, which are reaffirmed by the cloudburst. The participants of the holiday assembly, which symbolizes faith that all the questions of human existence will be resolved within the structure of society, scatter in panic because of the rain, that is, the "force majeure," mocking the greatest modern effort to reshape human society and its members. Rain plays a similar role in the chapter called "Ancient Sorrow" (85; 62ff.).

Water, a dark natural element, has the power to wash away people and their houses, yet the same darkness lies within people, in the "bedrock" of their hearts, the "forgotten lairs," emerging in nightmares. At the novel's beginning the narrator has already mentioned Reuven Harish's "moist" slumber, the ferocious dreams that torment him, and he has pointed out that "even a pure man of sound principles cannot control his nightmares" (20; 14).

Regarding other characters, this darkness is not limited to the night alone. The members of the kibbutz and its schoolchildren are enthralled by "the dark forces" that motivate Oren's behavior and his revoltingly cruel deeds: "A kind of cold rage, the rage of dark forces, flashes within his eyes. What is that rage? we ask, for here we have no poor, neglected children, but the well-brought up offspring of pioneers. There are dark forces here, we say, and our hearts break with sorrow" (150). The cunning narrator of the novel also shrugs his shoulders signaling that he does not understand, but in other instances he proves to understand the reason for that behavior very well: he describes Oren as someone who comes from the sea, driftwood left on the beach. Immediately after the conversation between Oren and Zechariah-Siegfried, which compares Oren to a rotten apple, "the essence of putrefaction," the narrator describes a gnawed plank, rotting and tossed about by the ocean waves: "Sometimes the waves throw up a rotting plank on the beach. To and fro the water tosses the blackened object, alternately dashing it on the sand and dragging it back with a melancholy rhythmic ebb and flow. . . . Suddenly it abandons its baby, leaving it high and dry. From now on it belongs to the desolate sands, to the yellow vengeance of the scorching sun, a solitary black spot" (357–58; 279). The placement of that description, the narrator's insistence that "we are telling about Oren" (358), the emphasis upon rot, and the description of the plank as a "baby," suggest that Oren is that gnawed plank left on the sand by a treacherous sea. It is not surprising, then, that he answers the psychologist's question as to whether he suffers from nightmares by saying that sometimes he dreams about the sea (358).

Thus, the significance of water around and within the kibbutz is revealed through the mountains, the night, and rain. From a greater distance waters take the inviting and seductive form of Germany, the "elsewhere" of the title. In the novel, Germany is a decidedly psychic element, not a geographical, social, or political entity.[5] Germany is the good and beneficient womb, seductive and ferocious. Again and again it is characterized by its lakes and rivers, as are the people who are linked to it. Reuven Harish's Germany is "the land of murderers," the country that gave rise to the planners and executors of the Holocaust (82), and it is a land that also opens its mouth to swallow him, like the devouring mother (312; 241). Nevertheless, he also acknowledges that Germany contains the womb enticing man to rest within it, to fall asleep, to die (314; 248). Zechariah-Siegfried also links the woods and lakes of Germany with the presence of death: "There are forests and lakes there, and golden leaves and low gray clouds, and green dreaming hills. Calm death dwells there, and we are in his arms" (283; 221). Zechariah displays considerable expertise regarding that subject, "the juice of death" which nourishes German culture (292).

It is clear, then, that Oz didn't wish to examine sociological or other aspects of Germany in *Elsewhere, Perhaps*. "Germany," with its lakes and rivers, represents the rival, the fascinating and seductive unconscious, violent and instinctive. The people who chose Germany over Israel are repeatedly characterized as water lovers. Noga remembers that Eva, her mother, loved water (202), and evidence for that is also

---

5. In a conversation with Yehoshua Kenaz, Oz stated: "Germany in *Elsewhere, Perhaps* is not political Germany nor historical Germany, but a visionary Germany or a dream that exists in the minds of several of the protagonists. It is in fact 'elsewhere,' it expresses the deep forces that threaten some of the protagonists of that book. They burst out from within them, sometimes as yearnings, sometimes as a threat, and sometimes as an emotional outburst" (1966b).

found in the "two pencil sketches depicting a lake landscape and canals" (199) which Eva drew. She primarily drew lake landscapes while living on the kibbutz, and her house in Munich overlooks lakes (58, 364; 50, 281). The German climate, she points out in her letters, is cold and damp (181). Eva, who is infatuated with death ("death can be so beautiful. Death can be a festival" [88; 65]), leaves Reuven to his sighs and goes off with Isaac Hamburger and his "moist" laugh (156; 123). "Her drives ruined her," says Reuven, explaining to his daughter her mother's behavior (156; 124). The narrator reinforces the connection of those "urges" to water by comparing their emergence from their lairs with the rise of floodwaters (17, 21; 14). Let us also recall that in the alchemical tradition Eve symbolized the instinctual, primal aspect of woman.

Zechariah Berger, who presents himself as "a wintery man" (295; 231), loves water also. Moreover, he is the representative and emissary of the dark, watery world: in his first meeting with Bronka, his brother's wife, he arouses within her "a deep impression of a reptile or a frog" (261; 203).[6] In the pool his legs twitch like flippers, and he disappears "in the darkness of the depths" (272; 212). Thus, the narrator agrees with Zechariah, who describes himself as "a spy sent by a foreign power" (271, 349), as a "wicked fairy" vying for the soul of Noga Harish (351; 273). Like a water creature Zechariah is very familiar with the essence of water, and he points out some of its primary qualities: it is an eternal, mighty force (352; 274), as well as a female element ("The water's marvelous. Warm and caressing like a woman. Swimming in water like this is like petting. It arouses one's desire" [272; 312]).[7] Furthermore, water resembles the womb to which one comes when one dies. In speaking to the dying Reuven Harish, Zechariah describes death as a broad river sliding into the bosom of the sea (391; 305). Fittingly for one whose natural habitat is water and death, death does not arouse dread in him. On the contrary, he advises Reuven, "Don't think darkness. Think of a tunnel between light and light" (391; 305). He continues: "Who are you now, pure man? Now you

---

6. Campbell discusses the frog as a small dragon, a representative of the depths of the unconscious, but also as a herald leading to the treasure (1973, 51–52).

7. The narrator of the novel frequently changes his point of view and outlook. The complexity of his game is evident, among other things, when he describes the femininity of the pool, repeating Zechariah's words: "How good it would be only to jump into the swimming pool with no further ado. It has pure, clear, cold water that caresses you like a woman's hand" (236). Doubtless the narrator does not represent only the norms of the social arrangement, but also the opposites of those norms. I elaborate on this issue in *Toward Language and Beyond* (1988a).

are me when I was alive" (392; 305). His true being, like that of Oren Geva, resides within the sea itself. There he finds his light and his life.

While water is the life fluid of the "elsewhere" and its emissaries, it is not merely a negative element. Rain, which recalls the "elsewhere" (87; 64), simultaneously nourishes and purifies ("Siegfried left and the first rains came" [393; 306]). Eva's drawings, lakes and canals, are strangely fitting for Reuven Harish's poems for children (17–18; 11). The narrator, feigning innocence, pretends he does not understand the meaning of that "pure harmony," but Oz's familiar theme arises indirectly here: the struggle between water and dry land, darkness and light, conceals a common origin. Reuven, who fights against the dark river in his poems, cannot completely sever himself from his primary sources as such references repeatedly appear in the poetry he writes for children.

Noga Harish embodies this unity of opposites within water. First, her name shows her affinity with water, and the narrator takes pains to make it clear that "Noga is the name of a planet" (34; 27). Noga tells Rami that her name is Hebrew for Venus (344; 267), a name which identifies her with Dita-Aphrodite ("Purple Coast"). In addition to her name, Noga goes by the nicknames "turquoise" (a watery shade of bluish green), and "Stella Maris"—"Star of the Sea." Noga's mother gave her the latter nickname, which appears about half a dozen times in the book. Some say it shows Eva's attraction for watery landscapes (35; 27). Stella Maris emanates a constant inner flow ("Noga's feet are not still. They perform an inner dance on the running board, without changing positions" [30, 31; 23, 24]), her hair appears "thick and flowing," and her face is "lost within the cascade of heavy hair" (29; 22). Like Zechariah-Siegfried, she too loves the winter. "The summer is flat and empty, winter is dark and deep and alive" (346; 268). Her play among the sprinklers provides a paltry substitute for the "elsewhere" of which she dreams: "to go to the fish ponds before sunrise and wander there barefoot, to sing songs in the wind, to knit together forms, not to sleep on a winter night when the rain weeps and the wind laughs to itself. To sail to some other place on a ship, to strangers" (200). The much desired "elsewhere" also reveals itself to Noga in her own home. She makes Ezra sleep with her, using the power of "dark forces" aroused within her, and in making love with him she seems to return to the sea: "The ground beneath her stirred, sending quivering ripples through her. On spreading ripples her body floated. Torrents flooded over her, bursting out strong and cruel from forgotten lairs. Wave after wave after wave. . . . Boiling water battered her body" (159–60; 127). The continuation of that description develops those images of water, heat, and light. Here water is depicted as a primal psychic element, containing violence and venom as well as sweetness, heat, and dazzling light. That Janus-faced quality appears later in the novel in Noga's wish to be a goldfish (202; 158). The fish symbolizes the world of the depths and the unconscious, while gold is associated with light and the sun.

As in the case of her cousin Oren Geva, Noga Harish is not the product of a kibbutz education, but lives in an inner world almost completely cut off from normal social bonds (family, class, kibbutz members) and from the behavioral norms that characterize them. Her relations with Ezra Berger openly violate a social taboo, but even in making love with him she does not go beyond her own circle: "Ezra knows her body and does not know her body. Even as she gives herself she dissolves in violent rocking which is not intended for Ezra but for her dreams, the inner dance" (200). She relentlessly unmasks the deceit of her father's arguments when he attempts to separate her from Ezra, and her refusal to have an abortion further exemplifies her defiance of the commonly accepted norms of kibbutz society. The entire kibbutz joins in the effort to avert her decision, but Noga remains resolute. Unlike Oren, she is not a "rotten apple," nor does she desert to join the enemy camp. Like Venus, born of the sea, Noga has both blessed and cursed elements, contraries that provide the axis of the novel: Segal, the "good fairy," claims that she belongs to him, while Zechariah-Siegfried, the shadow and the "bad fairy," makes the same claim. Like a mathematical equation, both are equally mistaken, and both are equally right.

The symbol of the circle or ring, a primary symbol of the sea, hints at the unity of opposites within Noga's character. Like Dita in "Purple Coast," the novel links Noga-Aphrodite to the ring, the symbol of wholeness, of unity, the joining of beginning and end, life and death, the holy and the profane. We see the ring apparent in the "halo," in the way Noga sits, in the pomegranate, and in the snake. The cascades of her hair enclose her face like "a soft halo of shadow around the flame of a candle" (29; 22), and as she dances "her arms make a ring, closing around her head like a sort of halo" (149). As she dreams of "elsewhere," she sits "wrapped in herself," "her back is rounded" (37; 29), and upon various occasions she is described as "ingathered" and "drawn inward." After first making love with Ezra Berger she lies awake in her bed, "her body curls up compulsively, her knees drawn up to her chin, pressed against her breasts, her fingers caressing her skin. Drop by drop, like rain in a gutter, a song dripped inside: From the Dead Sea to Jericho / The pomegranate sweetly smells" (160; 128).

This passage associates her round, embryonic form with water and pomegranates (Noga had sung that verse after her first meeting with Ezra [31; 24]). Its shape and symbolic meaning associate the pomegranate with the circle: it reconciliates variegated elements within one, all-embracing structure (Cirlot 1983, 261).[8] The pomegranate, a symbol of constant renewal, recalls another symbol: the snake with its tail in its mouth, the dragon devouring itself and pregnant with itself in an infinite process of birth and death.[9] Rami shouts at Noga before he gives way to Ezra Berger: "Snake. Just like your mother. An evil snake" (121; 97), and Noga, with a fetus in her womb, is pregnant with herself, as it were: every night she has a mad dream, "to be a fetus inside your own body, to curl up in the enclosed warmth" (304; 239). Noga's cold, frozen hands are also connected to the cold-blooded serpent (202 and elsewhere). Like the snake with its tail in its mouth, Noga unites all opposites: the holy and the profane, blessing and curse, matter and spirit, male and female ("her figure is that of a boy" [29; 22]). She is grandma Stella (34, 201; 26) and her granddaughter at the same time; Reuven Harish's daughter while behaving like his sister, his wife, and his mother (157, 280; 125, 218); Ezra Berger's lover as well as his daughter (203, 225; 157).[10]

The meaning attributed to water throughout the novel sheds new light on the criticism voiced to the narrator about recent Hebrew fiction: "Reuven Harish continues, casting a cool eye upon us, saying that we take a strange pleasure in dabbling in ugliness, importing ugliness from brackish sources that do not flow from this land" (197). The narrator does not speak out in his own defense, but the novel provides a counterargument. First, the brackish sources lie beneath our feet, in the "primeval crack," in the land upon which the kibbutz dwells, far closer to the earth than Reuven Harish would wish to believe. Second, and alternatively, the true source is common to all mankind, and the limits of place and time form a thin and fragile crust over it. Third, the narrator could have used Harish's words against

---

8. In previous chapters the pomegranate was discussed as a symbol of the church.

9. Constant renewal is one of the most common attributes of the pomegranate; see Cirlot (1983, 261) and Ferguson (1961, 37).

10. Two other characters in the novel are closely linked to the circle and the ring: Ezra Berger, whose gold ring is repeatedly mentioned by the narrator (26, 90, 93; 19, 66, 69, and elsewhere), and the Secretary of the kibbutz, Segal, who listens to music with a rounded back (107; 82) and wears glasses with round frames. The narrator never tires of mentioning those special frames (280, 336, 339; 219, 259, 262, and elsewhere). It is not surprising that both Ezra and Segal exemplify the unity of opposites which is central to the novel.

him: the fields are irrigated with the brackish water flowing from the earth. The opposite of brackish water is not pure, clear springwater but drought. The novel also suggests that an affinity exists between brackish water and the "drop of stinking fluid," sperm ("Ethics of the Fathers," 3:1 and elsewhere in Rabbinic literature). Ezra Berger repeatedly uses that Mishnaic expression (67, 69; 58, 60) and the narrator too adopts it in emphasizing that "man is made of flesh and blood, and flesh and blood are not myrrh and frankincense but, as the ancient sages have it, 'a drop of stinking fluid' " (55; 47). These examples effectively refute Reuven Harish's argument: to his dismay the ugliness that disturbs his tranquillity derives from the source of his own being. If the narrator had been in a more contentious mood, he would, it seems, have sought to express his own view of the "pure harmony" knit between Reuven's verses and his wife's drawings.

## A Perfect Peace: This Is Home. All This Is Us

In *A Perfect Peace*, Oz continues to make use of water and sea symbols, but their significations vary in this novel. Whereas in *Elsewhere, Perhaps* water represented "elsewhere," both seductive and destructive, and the mountains were connected with it through their threat of destruction, *A Perfect Peace* presents the instinctual and destructive element of water in a more restrained fashion. Rimona exemplifies that restraint: on the one hand, like Dita and Noga, she represents the circle and the sea; on the other hand, she also represents the earth mother, who is stable, calm, and merciful.

Like the kibbutz depicted in *Where the Jackals Howl*, the kibbutz where Yolek, Srulik, and their comrades live adjoins the sea. The sea breeze and its odors contribute to the emotional atmosphere of the blue Saturday that "broke out" after the winter rains (127, 129; 115, 117). Upon leaving the kibbutz, Yoni sees that the land is beautiful and quiet "in the cool sea breeze" (228; 216), and later on the harsh winter winds become "a caressing sea breeze" (351; 343). The willful sea wind fondles "the hem of [Anat's] flowery skirt," to her joy as she calmly torments Azariah (140, 141; 128).

As noted, *A Perfect Peace* attenuates the sea's threatening qualities, which remain primarily in the fears of Monia Libersohn, the hardworking carpenter ("Why so many new hotels going up along the shoreline? Why this bulwark between the city and the sea? Lest worst should come to worst" [126; 114]), and also in the description of the mountains as "sea-like mountains like steep breakers that have arisen to the east and threaten to crash down westwards" (142; 130). Most of the other references depict the sea as an element beyond man's reach, like the earth, the mountains, and the stars, but not wholly violent and ferocious. The novel presents two distinct concepts of the sea: first, as a primal natural force, and second, as an element that human beings cannot conquer and that mocks all human endeavor to do so. In his journal Srulik writes about the illusion of socialism, which ignores the basic facts of existence: "I have lived my life here to the music of a marching band, as if there were no sea, no mountains, no stars in the sky. As if death had already been abolished, and as if old age had been eradicated" (236; 226). His journal describes the sea in other places, as well as the mountains and stars, as one of the eternal, mysterious components of the world. Azariah also speaks of the sea, the mountains, and the stars in one breath, as he proposes that the members of the kibbutz draw closer to the rhythm of the cosmos (154; 139). But Yonatan's reflections ("I'll plow the rocks and then the sea" [223; 211]), and especially Srulik's notes, depict the sea as a mighty, chaotic force that cannot be defeated. The kibbutz hastily proposes various solutions that Srulik compares to slogans scrawled "on the waves of the sea" (233; 223), emphasizing again the shortcomings of socialist ideology in its attempts to fundamentally change humanity and to cure its problems. Moreover, Srulik takes only the latter part of the Bolognesi's saying: "deep, convoluted, looking into the heart, frustrating like the waters cover the sea" (355), as a demonstration of the heart's eternal impulses and of time that grinds "to dust every mark of good and evil, of truth and deception, ugliness and beauty which we had thought to trace on things" (372). Frequently, he repeats the phrase, "like the waters cover the sea," which summarizes the bitter conclusions he has drawn about human nature (373, 374; 364).

Rimona's figure exemplifies the change in Oz's view regarding the sea's meaning. On the one hand, she is modeled after Dita and Noga: like them she represents the sea, the circle, and the womb, inviting every living thing to return to it. On the other hand, she lacks Dita's sexual aggressiveness and Noga's dark powers. "The mother of all life" (69), like Eve, she lacks the instincts and drives of Reuven Harish's former wife. Whereas *Elsewhere, Perhaps* plays out the tension between Eve (the instinctive side of woman) and Mary (the merciful side), in *A Perfect Peace* Mary emerges victorious. Only once in this novel does the water in Rimona threaten to rise up and burst out. Hearing Yoni's harsh words, Rimona

> glanced up from her embroidery and her eyes once again appeared to be tracing the music in the air. Indeed, at just that moment the fugue seemed about to overflow its banks, surging upward, beating against mighty walls. And right after that, a gentling took place. The melody relented, as though despairing of cresting the dam, and, surrendering at last, dove deep to burble beneath the foundations. The powerful current of the theme forked into several thin eddies, each flowing his way, each oblivious of the others, but swirling about one another with bashful desire, and slowly overcoming their forlornness to build up passionately to yet another floodtide. (73; 65)

This single threat of flooding quickly recedes. Here music flows like water, but not in a wild torrent sweeping away everything before it, but rather penetrating an area beyond words, beyond the boundaries of consciousness.[11] Water as the basis of the unconscious, prior to words, has here undergone a substantial change in form. It no longer represents instinctive and brutal impulses but, instead, the ability to communicate with the world soul without intermediaries.[12] The "animal" within Rimona signifies intuitive knowledge, unharmed by the development of consciousness, rather than blind urges: "Azariah was again bewildered by Rimona's eyes, which were resting on him poignantly, as one is sometimes watched by a house pet who remembered some primordial truth beyond all knowledge or words" (150; 135; cf. her "animal eyes," 32). The animal within Rimona does not express itself with fang and claw, but with a natural knowledge that comes from her childlike qualities (she is described as a little girl about a dozen times in the course of the novel), and from the *unio mystica* she enjoys.

Clearly, Rimona finds kinship with Noga Harish: like her, she is a "pomegranate" (*rimon* in Hebrew); her body resembles that of a boy

---

11. Rimona is characterized repeatedly by means of the music she listens to and her way of listening. Her development is shown, among other things, by the transition to the works of Bach: "Perhaps [she sees] the forms of the music that issued from the record spinning on the turntable—not the Magic of Chad, not the Mississippi blues given her by Hava, but a Bach violin concerto" (363; 353).

12. The connection between music and the world of the depths emerges from Srulik's notes: "From somewhere deep inside me came a feeling of indefinable peace. As if I were someone else. Or as if I had managed at long last to play a particularly difficult passage on my flute, one that for years I had been unable to master, and had acquired the confidence that I could effortlessly repeat it from now on without a single false note" (323; 313).

on the verge of adolescence, and she is the serpent pregnant with herself. True, the novel does not refer to Rimona as an "evil snake" as it does to Noga, but there can be no mistaking her identification with the snake eating its own tail: "Rimona sat curled up in an armchair, her feet tucked under her, her hands pulled up in the sleeves of her nightgown, as if pregnant with her own self" (187; 176). The hands gathered into the nightgown create a closed, rounded form. Moreover, previous passages explain that she holds her hands this way because of the constant, freezing chill of her fingers, a characteristic that also connects her with the sea and the serpent. The adjective "gathered" (Heb.: *asufa*) frequently applied to her (26, 77, 158, 363; 21, 69, 143, and elsewhere) also indicates Rimona's closed circularity, evident in the way she sits and places her hands, and also in the way she observes her surroundings without observing them directly.[13]

Nevertheless, along with the similarity between the women there is also a difference. Rimona represents not only the sea and the serpent, but also the earth mother. Yonatan thinks of her as a "steppe of taiga or tundra, beautiful snow in the blazing heat of summer" (33); before he goes out to renew his life, he remembers "the free-for-all in the big double bed a few hours ago. The sweat, the sordidness, the anger, the relentless sperm, . . . the silent submission of the woman, like earth giving way to the plow" (220; 208). Azariah, endowed with intuitive knowledge like Rimona, once again compares her to the earth during their Saturday excursion: "For Rimona does not cling to him at all, no more than the earth clings to a stone so it won't fly away" (138); "if she would only say what she knows, like the earth. . . ." (139). A few months later Rimona lies down next to the sleeping Azariah, "awake, listening as peacefully as the earth itself to Ephrat's breathing in the dark" (366; 357). As the sea and the earth mother, Rimona, unlike the devouring womb, does not entice one to death like the sea in *Elsewhere, Perhaps*. Often, she entreats those around her to rest: for example, Azariah, whose soul finds no peace (154, 182; 139), the young people of the kibbutz who are still in an uproar after their pursuit of the anonymous criminal (158; 143), Prime Minister Eshkol who complains of fatigue (289; 279), Hava (380; 373), and even a moth flying around the lamp in her room (175; 165).[14] For her, "rest" does not

---

13. Both the cold and the adjective "gathered" also characterize the figure of Noga in *Elsewhere, Perhaps*.

14. Rimona is preceded in that characteristic by the narrator's mother in "Mr. Levi" (1976b; 1978). She too repeatedly asks the people around her to calm down. The mother doubtless belongs to the gallery of figures discussed here (on her affinity with water,

mean death but peacefulness, to refrain from seeking what cannot be attained: "Wanting what it does not have or need. Its shadow keeps flitting over the marble counter. . . . Pretty little moth by the light, why don't you listen to me and take a rest" (175; 165). To rest means to find your rightful place in the cosmos, to become part of the *unio mystica*:

> Whoever is tired—will rest. And whoever has rested—will listen. And whoever has listened will know that it's a rainy night out. And that beneath the rain the wet earth lies quietly. And that beneath the wet earth the strong rocks are sleeping, the rocks on which light never shines. And that up above the clouds, up above the air, all is quiet too, the quiet between the stars. And that beyond the last star is the last quiet of all. What do they want from us? Not to disturb, not to make noise because nothing untoward will happen if we keep still. (181; 171–72)

These lines reveal a sharp contrast between Rimona and Noga. As one participating in the experience of "before words and knowledge," Rimona is at peace with herself and with the reality of her life. She does not yearn for other places and other people. She peacefully explains to Yonatan, who desperately wishes to change his life, that life is the same here as anywhere else: "Maybe you think new things should happen all the time, but that isn't so. . . . What should happen, Yoni? You're a grown man. I'm your wife. This is home. All this is us. And it's the middle of the winter" (74; 65).[15]

## *Black Box: Pandora's Box*

In earlier chapters we have seen that Oz's protagonists are torn between opposing psychic forces. This tension often dictates the way Oz's novels stem from each other. Thus, for example, *Elsewhere, Perhaps* is concluded with a harmonious scene, in which all the forces that had fought against each other are peacefully united. But this tranquil picture already includes elements of desolate routine. How

---

see 81; 96). The "soothing" side of woman is supported in this story by the figure of Bat-Ami, the narrator's girlfriend, who also pleads with him to relax (78, 82; 89, 95).

15. Rimona is, without a doubt, one of Oz's most complex characters. On Rimona as Persephone and as the moon, see Chapter 5.

long will Noga withstand this orderly existence, repressing her yearnings for the "elsewhere," for a type of life completely divorced from the kibbutz life? Indeed, a direct line leads from the peaceful last scene of *Elsewhere, Perhaps* to the author's next novel, *My Michael*. Noga's hidden dreams have not disappeared from the face of the earth but have been transmitted to Hannah Gonen, the protagonist of *My Michael*. The harmony achieved at the end of *Elsewhere, Perhaps* is fragile and temporary, and in *My Michael* it is utterly shattered.

The same development characterizes the transition from *A Perfect Peace* to Oz's next novel, *Black Box*. In the last chapter of *A Perfect Peace* all the rival characters and forces are reconciled and appeased. But just as Noga Harish had given birth to Hannah Gonen, Yonatan, Azariah, and Rimona have paved the way to Ilana and Alexander, the main characters of *Black Box*. The tranquil, peaceful routine brings about, as if in a mathematical equation, its own destruction. This pendulum movement, convincingly described by Schopenhauer (1948, 402, 404, and elsewhere), has turned out to be one of the main themes of *Black Box*: "Who does not dream occasionally of taking off, flying away, and getting singed on some faraway flame? There's no point in your making fun of me: I didn't invent the fixed choice between fire and ashes—I have my own closed circle" (1987, 155; 1988, 173). This tension explains the textual similarities between Ilana's first letter to her ex-husband, Alexander Gideon, and her last letter to her husband: from the secured life she has as Michel Sommo's wife, Ilana misses the junglelike existence she had experienced with Alexander, and she writes him a letter hoping to renew their relationship; however, once she has left her second husband and starts living with the dying Alexander and her son, Boaz, she misses her husband and invites him to join her.

Like Rimona, Ilana is depicted as the earth mother (93; 101). Yet Ilana's earthiness is manifested differently than Rimona's. Whereas Rimona tries to calm down everyone she meets, Ilana is the "whore" who, like earth, grants her gracious favors indiscriminately (8, 42; 2, 41, and elsewhere). Furthermore, unlike Rimona, Ilana is attracted to "the heart of darkness" (80; 84), and she yearns for its moisty, tropical air (79; 84). The author does not use sea imagery in this novel, yet "the heart of darkness" that allures Ilana is described in terms of moist, tropical rains and swamps.

In *Black Box* Oz examines the same phenomena he had tried to decipher in his earlier works. The novel revolves around the poisonous split in one's psyche, the result of which is the fact that the knight and the dragon, the beauty and the monster, are hidden in the same person. The uniqueness of the novel is the direction in which it develops this split. Oz's previous novels exposed the inner psychic struggle, the painful process in which one unearths one's "shadow" and learns to know it and to live with it. Human relationships were marginal to this inner struggle. Even such a novel as *My Michael*, which is ostensibly a "family novel," focuses on the protagonist's intricate inner world. The same is true of *A Perfect Peace*, whose core is the protagonist's spiritual "death" and his resurrection. In contrast, the inner split in *Black Box* is employed in order to study the war between the sexes, the possibility or impossibility of a lasting, meaningful relation between a man and a woman. The inner split, which tears apart one's world, also hurts one's relation with the opposite sex and does not leave any room for lasting affinity. To resort to a nickname frequently used in the novel, the "dragon" hidden in the soul is the image of one's spouse. By escaping from the dragon one escapes both from oneself and one's lover.

*Black Box* is an epistolary novel; the letters the characters write to each other are likened to the "black box" in an airplane that records all the details of a flight. Should an accident happen, the "black box" can decipher its circumstances. "The medium is the message": the epistolary novel embodies by its very nature the fact that an accident has happened, that letters are needed to bridge the distances between the addressees.

Seven years after he divorced her, Ilana writes a letter to her first husband, Alexander Gideon. The ramified correspondence that follows this letter gradually delineates the main characters' past and present. Why were Ilana and Alexander doomed to follow the records of the "black box"? Why was their marriage doomed to fail? In order to answer this question, first of all, the author differentiates between male and female features. Then, he applies these inner features on his main characters' relationship. The fact that the main characters' relationship has far-reaching meanings is implied, among other things, by allusions that connect them to mythical characters who in Jung's writings represent the anima and the animus. Ilana was born in Poland and her name there was Halina (34; 32), a name which is the Polish version of Helen. Indeed, like Helen of Troy, Ilana is repeatedly described as very beautiful. Alexander, on the other hand, is implicitly described as Hermes, the messenger of the Olympian gods. Hermes' mother was Maya, and Alexander's father, mourning his wife, calls her "Nusya maya" (Russian: my Nusya [92; 99]). Hermes' name is also introduced by Alexander's typewriter: Baby Hermes (194, 198, 200; 219, 223, 225). Furthermore, like Hermes who owned miraculous sandals, Alexander flies from one city to another, and Ilana's letter find him each time at a different address.[16]

Alexander is a typical hero: Ilana meets him when he is a successful army officer and she keeps describing him in terms of his military role. Importantly, Alexander's intellect is as sharp as his sword. Indeed, masculinity is embodied in the novel as a splitting, analyzing element, and as such, an element that leads to separation and alienation. The sword is a separating element, as is consciousness that conceives of the world by dividing it into its many components; the same is true of the intellect that analyzes the issues it has to cope with (see Alexander's descriptions when he argues with his friends and the summaries of the reviews of his book). At the same time, Alexander severs himself from the living world, from his own feelings, and from women. He admits to Ilana that he has never tried to cultivate his relations with women, and eventually he leaves Ilana and lives in complete solitude until Ilana's letter reaches him. Ilana, for her part, more than once, likens Alexander's sharp brain to a weapon: "I am not up to taking issue with you. Your razor-sharp brain always works on me like the barking of a machine gun: a deadly accurate burst of facts, inferences, and explanations from which there is no recovery" (108; 117). She uses the same military terms to describe Alexander's relationships with her and with their son, Boaz (110, 115; 119, 125, and elsewhere).

The feminine element, in contrast, is a uniting, assimilating one. Thus, as noted above, Ilana is the earth mother and the "whore." Unlike Alexander, she argues that there is happiness in the world, yet the way to achieve it is not through "advancement and conquest and domination," nor through "submission and surrender," but rather by "the thrill of fusion. The merging of the I with another. As the oyster enfolds a foreign body and is wounded and turns it into a pearl while the warm water still surrounds and encompasses everything" (109; 118). "You have never tasted this fusion, not once in your whole life," she writes to him (ibid.). Indeed, this fusion is the polar opposite of Alexander's barrier-creating character. Tragically, this contradiction turns both Ilana and Alexander into "predators." Ilana calls Alexander "a predator" for his wickedness and cruelty (144; 159 and elsewhere), whereas for him she is the predator, seducing him into joining her: "Have you ever heard of the carnivorous plants? They are female plants that can exude a scent of sexual juices over a great distance, and the

---

16. The appendix to my *Toward Language and Beyond* (1988a) includes a detailed discussion of this novel. Most of the themes and symbols mentioned here are further discussed in that appendix.

poor insect is drawn from miles away into the jaws that are going to close around him" (85; 91).

These mutual accusations are an integral aspect of the psychological notion developed in the novel. Alexander's and Ilana's letters reveal this picture: first, a primordial reality is concealed in every human being's heart. Its primal strength makes it a source of threat and fear on the one hand, and an endless attraction on the other. The stranger this reality is to consciousness, the more fearful and attractive it becomes. Second, the relation between the sexes is nothing but an embodiment of this inner schism. Men and women project on each other their dark shadows, and ascribe to each other utter baseness as well as holiness. The attraction for the other sex is characterized, then, as an attraction for one's innermost levels, and at one and the same time as an attraction for one's most distant and strange elements. Strangeness and closeness, attraction and rejection, are therefore inextricably connected: "The frozen ray at the touch of which I melt as though under spell. Right from the start. I melt and hate you. I melt and give myself to you" (40; 39). Unlike some romantic traditions that emphasized the need for openness and closeness between lovers, in *Black Box* strangeness is the source of attraction. The only time when Alexander shares his intimate emotions with Ilana, his virility lets him down in bed (148; 165). This is also the role of the "shadow of the third person" in the couple's bed: impersonating different characters Alexander remains an aggressive stranger, thus piercing both of them "with searing jungle thrill" (151; 168).

Indeed, since the connection between the two originates in their deepest psychic elements, it does not comprehend the various layers that culture has cultivated over these elements. The relationship between Alexander and Ilana is not based on affinity between equals, and there is no room in it for mutual understanding or intimacy achieved through openness and empathy. Ilana longs for her first nights with Alexander, in which, almost until dawn, they "used to drink each other like a pair of vampires. Our backs were covered with scratches and our shoulders with love bites" (146; 162). And she remembers "particularly the rainy winter weekends. We would stay in bed until ten o'clock, battered and exhausted from the cruelty of our night, almost tolerating each other, like a pair of boxers between rounds" (72; 76).

Alterman's poem at the beginning of the novel portrays a love relationship as a relation beyond time and place: the lovers were meant for each other and no one else could separate them. Alterman's lines are echoed in the letters exchanged by Ilana and Alexander, and both of them describe their bond as an unbreakable one. Ilana writes to her sister that, during the seven years since her divorce, she has tried in vain to forget Alexander, and she is convinced that he, too, cannot leave her memory behind: "Poor Alec, it was all for nothing that you tried to run away. . . . Hiding in your cloud and trying to open a new chapter" (61; 63). Alexander does not try to evade this truth:

> When I take into my bed some little admirer, pupil, secretary, interviewer, you appear and intrude yourself between us. If ever you forget to turn up, my sleeping partner has to help herself out. Or make do with an evening of philosophy. If I am a demon, Ilana, then I am a genie, and you are a bottle. I've never managed to escape. Nor have you, for that matter, Lady Sommo. If you are a demon, I am your bottle. (87; 94)

Here Alexander brings up a key point on his relations with Ilana. His words imply that the two of them are bound inseparably, yet it is a bond that is imposed on them. Both of them are imprisoned inside their lover, unable to break free. In one sense, this is a continuation of Alterman's theme: the two of them were meant for each other and cannot untie themselves from this connection. Yet Alexander's argument, that he and Ilana are simultaneously the demon and his bottle, has far-reaching implications. Alexander's image follows Jung, who interprets the demon in the bottle as the unconscious, primal psychic forces (1968, 193–203). Indeed, Ilana and Alexander represent both the wild element symbolized by the demon, and the bottle, the by-product of culture, that imprisons this element. Ilana accepts this legend as a pertinent analogy to her relation with Alexander, and later on she calls Alexander "my genie and my bottle" (153; 170).

The fact that each one of the main characters is both the demon and the bottle explains one of the most striking themes of the novel. Alexander is crippled emotionally, thus turning into a dragon; Ilana uses this nickname more than half a dozen times in her letters, and Alexander follows suit (59, 84, 95; 60, 90, 102). And the dragon is accompanied by all his symbols: Ilana repeatedly depicts Alexander as a "wolf," a "monster," and a "vampire." Typical of the psychological concepts explored in the novel, she is attracted to him not despite his draconic nature, but because of it: "I loved you not despite your cruelty; I loved the dragon itself" (149; 165). Ilana's own letters offer two answers for this attraction. First, she depicts herself as a slave girl attracted to her master: "But you were and remained my husband. My lord and master. . . . The master of my dreams at night. Ruler of my hair and my throat and the soles of my feet. . . . Like a slave girl I am thrall to you" (43; 43). In a later letter she further develops this idea:

> The icy malice that radiated from you like a bluish arctic glow . . . was what caught my heart. Your air of indifferent mastery. The cruelty that you exuded like a scent. . . . The murderous sharpness of your tongue at any hint of opposition. Your wolfish glee at the sight of the terror you spread. . . . I was drawn to you as though bewitched from muddy depths of primeval female subservience, ancient servitude from before words existed, the submission of a Neanderthal female whose survival instinct and the fear of hunger and cold make her throw herself at the feet of the roughest of the hunters, the hairy savage who will tie her hands behind her back and drag her, captive, to his cave. (143–44; 159).

Hannah Gonen, the female protagonist of *My Michael*, fails to experience true love because, in her concealed dreams, she wants to rule her lovers, to completely submit them to her will. Ilana exposes an opposing passion. She unearths in herself the impulse that led her foremother to surrender to the most cruel hunter. Why does she not try to cope with this primitive urge? Because she enjoys its results tremendously. This is the second part of her answer: true, Alexander is a dragon but he laid bare the dragon in her, and both enjoy the vital, primordial existence of the dragon's territory. Typically, Ilana chides Alexander that a scaly, bone-plated dragon like him cannot understand "grace and kinship and tenderness," yet she hurries to admit that her heart is with his junglelike existence:

> You have never had anything, and you never will have, besides your torture dungeons. Which my flesh longs for. Your tropical hell. The steamy jungles bubbling with warm decomposition, and glowing dimly in the half-light filtering through the foliage where the oily rain rises from the earth that simmers with fat wanton marrow, catches in the dense treetops, and spills back again, melting, from the treetops to the mud and to the rotting roots. After all, I was not the one who got up and ran away. It was you who smashed it all up. I was prepared to carry on, and I still am. Why did you bring me to the heart of darkness and leave me and run away? (79; 84)

Here Ilana paints a primordial existence, a moist womb devoid of any spirituality. Alluding to Joseph Conrad's famous novel, Ilana calls this experience "the heart of darkness." In a highly suggestive picture she conveys this innermost darkness, the abode of the "dragon," the "demon," and the "monster." She emphasizes that she is still ready to stay there, and mocks Alexander for beating a retreat.

Thus, Ilana is caught between two conflicting attitudes. On the one hand she numbers in her letters to Alexander all his flaws, yet she yearns for him and for his "tropical hell." She starts her correspondence with Alexander, pretending to be worried about their son, yet later on she admits that the real motive was her hope to renew her relation with the dragon. These conflicting attitudes are connected to one of the main themes of the novel: one's need to accept one's world and to give up unexisting worlds. Rahel, Ilana's sister, asks her: "What is it that drives you to throw away everything you have for the sake of something that doesn't and can't exist?" (106; 115). Later on Rahel admits that she is also torn by "the fixed choice between fire and ashes" (155; 173), yet she tries to channel her attraction for fire toward her family's well-being (ibid.). Ilana understands that she gambles with everything she has (117; 129), promises "to behave nicely and not to play with fire" (119; 131), but she cannot withstand this promise. She misses Alexander's hellish fire (the fire is alluded to by her last name, Brandstetter). In her last letter she uses the fire imagery once again: "Say in your prayers, Michel, that loneliness, desire and longing are more than we can bear. And without them we are extinguished" (229; 258). While fire represents the intensity of the sought-after experiences and their threat, water represents their nature: "Some jester in disguise has crept and seduced us into loathing what we have found. Destroying what was precious and will not return. Led us on with a seductive delusion until we strayed deep in the swamp and darkness descended upon us" (ibid.). The misleading swamp path was mentioned earlier in Ilana's letters. Pondering the possibility of staying with her second husband for good, she writes to Alexander: "But a persistent deluding light is still flickering over the swamp at night, and neither of us can take our eyes off it" (40; 39). In a later letter, describing the "hellfire" of their life, she once again mentions to Alexander the "deluding swamp light" (152; 168).

Unlike her predecessors, Ilana does not find a synthesis between the forces vying within her. Longing for the rainy tropical jungle, for the swamp, she cannot be satisfied with her secured, balanced life as Sommo's wife, eventually leaving behind everything she has "for the sake of something that doesn't and can't exist."

## Hard-Working, Responsible, Honest, Neat—and Utterly Boring

In the lineage of Oz's female characters, exemplified by Dita, Noga, Rimona, and Ilana, Hannah Gonen, *My Michael*'s female protagonist, is a noticeable exception. Decidedly "anima" figures,[17] these other female protagonists are witches and enchantresses, characterized by secret, intuitive wisdom, by their youth, by the combination of attraction and dread, and, of course, by the cold and damp. As representatives of the sea they draw a line between man and the instinctual, creative world of the depths. In contrast to Dita and most of her descendants, marked by the unity of opposites (the symbols of the sea, the ring, the serpent, the pomegranate, and others), Hannah's world is irreparably sundered. Moreover, a boundary exists between her and the sea—the horn of plenty enjoyed by Dita and her daughters—leaving her yearning for a lost paradise. In this sense, Hannah is a forerunner of Ilana (*Black Box*), though Ilana experiences a connection with the moisty jungle world as an adult, whereas for Hannah it is a distant childhood memory. Before discussing the place of the sea in Hannah's world, some of her characteristics should be discussed.[18]

In the novel's beginning, after her first meeting with Michael Gonen, Hannah tells about suffering from diphtheria as a child, how she had

---

17. Detailed discussions of the essence of the anima and its identifying outlines are found in Jung (1953a, 1959a, 1959b).

18. For a description of Hannah Gonen, see Shaked (1970). Certain of her important features are presented in Gertz's discussion (1980). Hillel Barzel convincingly argues that Hannah is molded after Jung's introvert type (1981).

Oz has called the writing of *My Michael* a personal necessity, liberation from an obsession that threatened to disturb his sanity:

> At the time I was writing *My Michael* I knew Hannah by heart, in my heart, I spoke in her voice. I knew more about her than I know about the people closest to me. I knew every detail. I remembered all her memories and I saw with her vision, and whatever pained her was not at all alien to me. . . . One of the reasons I wrote the book was to get free of her, so she would let me be. For a long time I didn't want to write *My Michael* at all. I told her, "Go to another author, I'm not the right one for this. Go to a woman writer. Leave me alone." But she entered my soul until she became an obsession, until the alternative really was to go crazy. So I wrote to get away from her, to separate from her. And she did draw back, she isn't a complete stranger to me, but she's getting more distant. (1974, 95)

True to his views of the character of the soul and the powers acting upon it, Oz describes Hannah Gonen as a spirit here, as a demon with her own life, whose claims had to be met in order to get free of her.

clung desperately to the disease, and about her recovery: "When I recovered, at the end of the winter, I experienced a feeling of exile. I had lost my powers of alchemy, the ability to make my dreams carry me over the dividing line between sleeping and waking. To this day I feel a sense of disappointment on waking" (17; 21). That Hannah was nine years old when she became ill (16; 20) is no coincidence, as pointed out by Mordechai Shalev (1968). The same year that Jewish Jerusalem was severed from Arab Jerusalem and the other Arab settlements around it, Hannah was cut off from Halil and Aziz, the Arab twins she had played with as a child. The novel presents that severance as a sundering from the sources of vitality and power (see the discussion of the Arab as representing the unconscious in the previous chapter). Hannah's anguish arises from the feeling of exile accompanying her recovery and awakening, or, in other words, the transition from unconscious psychic activity to consciousness. This makes her feel orphaned (115), and imprisoned: "There is a Russian steppe, there is Newfoundland, there are the isles of the archipelago, and I am exiled here" (80; 114). "I say those things so as not to sit quiet all evening and seem rude. The sudden pain: why have I been exiled here? Nautilus. Dragon. Isles of the archipelago" (121; 175).[19]

Hannah's lost paradise is a psychic state in which she experiences the utter opposite of consciousness, which sorts out, organizes, and truncates. She wishes, for example, to flee from the need to think (80, 169; 115, 246) and decide (17; 22). If consciousness is characterized by setting boundaries, in contrast, Hannah's world is that of flow and the blurring of borders, a world devoid of outlines: "I have fond memories of an attack of diphtheria I suffered as a child of nine. It was winter. For several weeks I lay on my bed opposite the south-facing window. Through the window I could see a gloomy expanse of fog and rain. . . . It was a winter world without details, a world of shapes in an expanse ranging in color from light to dark gray" (16; 20; see also 134; 194).

When Hannah imagines she has fallen in love with Michael, she returns to that world without lines: "I felt full to overflowing. I laid my head on Michael's shoulder and watched the screen sideways, until the pictures turned into a capering succession of different tones graded between black and white, but mainly various shades of light gray" (20;

---

19. Throughout the entire novel an explicit parallel is set up between Hannah and Jerusalem (see Shaked [1970] and Shalev [1968]). However, for Hannah the War of Independence did not end with the establishment of the Jewish part of Jerusalem but primarily with being cut off from Arab Jerusalem. Hannah was not liberated in the War of Independence, but, on the contrary, she was imprisoned in a world which was not hers.

25). That phenomenon, infatuation with a cloudy, vague world, free of forms, appears several times during the novel. Such a world allows no place for words that sort out and classify. In fact the Arab twins are characterized by their silence, the guttural sounds of their speech, and their sparing use of words (22, 73; 28). Michael Strogoff also battles with his enemies wordlessly (146; 212). Hannah herself has a tendency to lose her voice (35, 92, 124, 134; 47, 133, 178, 195). The main force active in Hannah's seductive world is the urge to control, as expressed in Hannah's dreams and in her treatment of the twins: "I ruled over the twins. That was a cold pleasure" (8; 9). "The twins acted the part of the submissive subjects. Sometimes I made them act rebellious subjects, and then I would humble them relentlessly. It was an exquisite thrill" (15; 18). Yoram Kamnitzer receives the same treatment: "He was mine. All mine. He was at my mercy" (159; 232). The urge to control appears again in the orders that Hannah, as a princess, issues to her subjects. Of course, such a world has no place for love, mutual affinity, equality, and reciprocal openness, but only for sex, another means of controlling others.

In Hannah's paradise we find a realm of experience characterized by flow, the blurring of boundaries, and freedom from the need to think and decide, a foggy world ruled by sexual urges and the lust for power as in ancient times. Hannah clings to this paradise, uniting with it through her dreams and illnesses. As a result, time becomes her bitter enemy, keeping her from that desired world and forcing her to grow up among her captors. In the name of that enchanted world, she denies Michael's values, the values of consciousness as it adapts itself to the world: "Hard-working, responsible, honest, neat—and utterly boring" (25; 31); "to be quiet and wise: how dull" (127; 183); "he fought back his surprise and silently nodded his head up and down as if expressing an understanding which made my blood boil" (73; 105).[20]

Hannah conceives of herself and of the world around her through her feeling of exile and the certainty of being distanced from the living, vital source. She sees a dual structure in everything around her, the nucleus of which is molten, worth more than its weight in gold but forbidden to the touch, yet its shell is cold and vapid. She feels sad that she cannot touch the delicate things "deep down inside my body" (72; 103), things hidden "in the caverns of my body" (136; 197), and thus Jerusalem is "shells within shells, and the kernel is forbidden" (77; 110).[21] That duality relates to the many geological descriptions

---

20. In Freudian terms, Hannah Gonen's problem is the transition from the pleasure principle to the reality principle.
21. The words Hannah uses in this situation (cave, ship, submarine) are blatantly

found in the novel, dealing, among other things, with the way geological forces "deriving from the action of the molten nucleus at the earth's center, from its gradual, uneven cooling" (94; 135). Hannah identifies those processes with her dreams: "the relaxed pose of his body in the armchair as he talks about volcanic eruptions, about the cooling of the crystalline crust. Those words have come out of the dreams I dream, and into the dream they shall return" (123; 178). Hannah finds herself drawn to characters and situations that have a similar ambiguity.

Yet another important element goes along with that dual structure of Hannah Gonen's world. Frequently, she imagines her beloved father as someone who always looks for "signs and hints of some truth which was denied him" (81; 117; see also 12, 39, 166; 14, 52, 241). Inheriting that characteristic from her father, she views reality as a cipher which must be decoded, finding hidden intentions in reality (the word "intention" is repeated about a dozen times in the novel). Unlike her father, however, Hannah considers that hidden wisdom to be contained in the hot, inaccessible core: "[Michael's] handwriting was neat and well-rounded, like a tidy schoolgirl's. But the words made me shudder: Extraction of mineral deposits. Volcanic forces pressing outward. . . . Once again I was startled by these words. I was being sent a message in code. My life depended on it. But I didn't have the key" (33; 44; see also 14, 62; 17, 88, and elsewhere). This transmission, coming from the deepest strata of the universe, "volcanic forces pressing outward," has evil intention (14; 17), as well as importance and vitality. The source of Hannah's code corresponds to both Jung's and Oz's view that the unconscious serves as a reservoir for wild impulses and also highest wisdom.

Although Hannah differs from Oz's other female protagonists, the rift within her aligns her with many of his other characters whose souls yearn for a treasure. Repeatedly, she notes her preparation for a journey, whether in a taxi, a plane (72, 151; 103, 220), or in a submarine (88, 121; 175). She does not realize that the archetypal journey in search of the treasure lies behind her desire to travel, but Oz hints as much by using the various symbols of the treasure. Hannah's professor discerns the symbolic nature of her marriage to a geologist: "Both geology, on the one hand, and the study of literature, on the other, delve down into the depths, as it were, in quest of buried treasures" (39; 53). Later on Hannah learns that "Michael and his colleagues did not deal with words alone but also searched for buried

---

sexual symbols, and her effort to renew contact with the forbidden kernel reaches its climax in an orgiastic ecstasy (136; 197).

treasures in the bosom of the earth" (96; 139). Hannah also dreams of the "great prize," the "decisive win" that again refers to a treasure (73, 150; 105, 219). A long passage describing her state of mind appears after the birth of her son, as she distances herself more and more from Michael: "I was contracted, withdrawn into myself as though I had lost a tiny jewel on the sea bed" (63; 89). Jewels serve as a common symbol of the treasure hidden somewhere in the depths of the sea, the recesses of the soul.[22]

The search also relates to the female protagonist's identification with the submarine *Nautilus* and the novel's abundant sea images. In fact, the interesting forces within Hannah Gonen's psyche are frequently conveyed through her affinity with the sea and water.

After her first meeting with Michael, Hannah talks about the war between light and darkness described in the literature of the Enlightenment, and about her love of darkness and sleep: "Awkward things sometimes happen in dreams, but some force always operates which makes decisions for you, and you are free to be like the boat in the song, with all the crew asleep, drifting wherever the dream carries you" (17; 22). Later in this passage she presents a more detailed description in which the drifting boat embodies eroticism and the heat of passion:

> The soft hammock, the sea gulls, and the expanse of water which is both a gentle heaving surface and a maelstrom of unplumbed depths. I know that the deep is thought of as a cold place. But it is not always so, and not entirely. I read a book once about warm streams and underwater volcanoes. At a point deep below the freezing ocean depths there is sometimes a warm cave hidden. . . . There are some rich nights when I discover a secret way through the watery depths and the darkness among green and clammy sea-creatures until I beat at the door of the warm cavern. This is my home. There a shadowy captain waits for me surrounded by books and pipes and charts. His beard is black, his eyes hold a hungry gleam. Like a savage he seizes me, and I soothe his raging hatred. (17–18; 22)

In her dreams Hannah discovers a warm cave under the frozen abyss, where wildness and Eros await her. Beneath the layer of consciousness

---

22. As noted, Jung interprets the search for the treasure as the search for individuation, combining all the forces active within one's psyche.

primordial and wild impulses surge. The strong link between darkness and warmth and the primal psychic strata emerges, among other things, from the timing of that description: the passage begins with the confrontation between darkness and light as presented in Enlightenment literature. Hannah, describing herself first as a fishing boat, becomes at the climax of this passage the water itself, which little fish traverse, creating within her "flickers of searing pleasure" (18; 22).

## Yvonne Azulai, The Opposite of Hannah Gonen

That stratified structure wherein life throbs beneath a layer of cold explains Hannah's identification with the submarine *Nautilus*, cruising in the "warm currents" under "the crust of ice in the Bering Straits" (72, 144; 104, 209). In her waking life Hannah unites with those warm depths only by means of sex. When she visits the seashore with Michael, desire overwhelms her, and she half seduces, half attacks him: "The sea joined in. And the sand. There were fine lashes of rough pleasure, piercing and searing" (187; 271). Of course that scene and the pleasure that accompanies it (cf. the burning pleasure she gets from the fish in her dream) can take place only at the seashore when the sea and the sand participate actively, as it were, in what happens. At one point, Hannah arouses Michael from his sleep, astonishing him with his own body and with hers: "Everything my own dreams had taught me. Flashes of quivering ecstasy. Floors of blazing spasms in the depths of an icy pool. . . . And yet I evaded him. I made contact only with his body: muscles, limbs, hair. In my heart I knew I deceived him again and again. With his own body. That was a blind plunge into the depths of the warm abyss" (178; 258–59). In what sense can a woman be unfaithful to a man while making love to him? Hannah communes with the primordial instincts of Michael's body, while ignoring the cultural layers covering the primal stratum. Hannah's lost paradise is characterized, as noted, by flow and the blurring of boundaries, and she seeks the same mingling in her relations with Michael: "Will we die, Michael, you and I, without touching each other so much as once? Touching. Merging. . . . Losing ourselves in each other. Melting. Fusing. Growing into one another" (178; 259). Hannah finds satisfaction in the erotic bond, but that bond only partially involves Michael. She can bring either Michael Gonen or his body into her game, but she cannot have him completely.

In addition to the warmth and pleasure beneath the ice's crust there resides immeasurable violence and destruction. When Hannah visualizes the mysterious island where Michael Strogoff has been sent, she sees someone lying in ambush, staring at her from the darkness, "beneath the surface of the earth," and she imagines her response to his violent power:

> Let him come live and snarling hurl me to the ground and thrust into my body he will growl and I shriek in reply in a rapture of horror and magic of horror and thrill I will scream burn and suck like a vampire madly whirling drunken ship in the night will I be when he comes at me, singing and seething and floating I will be flooded I will be a foam-flecked mare gliding through the night in the rain the torrents will rush down to flood Jerusalem the sky will come low clouds touching the earth and the wild wind will ravage the city. (148; 215)

The man lying in ambush is not a familiar character like Captain Nemo or Michael Strogoff, but an anonymous savage who ravishes Hannah. Her dread does not lessen her fascination for the envisioned man, but heightens it. She does not submit to her attacker, but unites with him willingly, renouncing the last remnants of human consciousness. The man's violence frees the violence within her, and she celebrates the liberation of her lust for sexual violence. The entire scene is one of total drunkenness, of the complete mastery of the demons who have been released. The delicate, passive fishing boat of her dreams (17; 22) becomes a ship thirsty for action, a vampire, a beast of prey. Unlike many of Oz's protagonists, Hannah does not wish to fight with the dragon but to be the dragon herself (cf. her repeated requests of the destroyer "Dragon").

The inundation of Jerusalem ("the torrents will rush down to flood Jerusalem") accompanies Hannah's inundation ("I will be flooded"). Other such descriptions appear in the novel. Hannah views her separation from the sea as exile and imprisonment (see above), knowing that success will come only when the sea returns to its original place: "I didn't forget that there was a British destroyer named Dragon, which knew me, which would be able to single me out from among all the others, which would come and save my life. But the sea would not return to the Free City until the new Ice Age" (92; 133). Confidently, she says to Michael, who has told her about the ancient sea that once covered the hills of Jerusalem, "at the end of time the sea will cover Jerusalem again" (43; 58). Since Jerusalem has no sea, Hannah dreams of the lake in Danzig-Jerusalem (91, 137; 131, 198), imagining the ways the sea can be brought nearer. The only news on the radio which interests her is the announcement that a deep water port will be built in Ashdod (88; 127), and she asks the British destroyer "Dragon" not to forget "the port of Haifa and Palestine and far off Hannah" (73; 104). She feels regret that Michael is a geologist and not an architect who could labor late at night for months in planning "the naval port in which the British destroyer Dragon might anchor" (79; 113).

Though unaware of the sea's meaning in her world, Hannah knows that it soothes her spirit. The peace she has experienced during her first meetings with Michael (9, 14; 9, 17) quickly disappears, leaving her with unrelenting restlessness. Only when she stays with Michael's father, swimming at the beach of Bat Yam every day, where the odor of the sea sticks to her skin, does that peace return to her. "The days were calm," she says several times (100, 102, 103; 144, 147, 149).[23] She repeats that sentence again when describing walks through Jerusalem on Saturdays when "it was as if the sea had come up and settled upside down over the city" (170; 247). It is no wonder, then, that she wants to visit the sea on Saturdays (173; 251; and her son Yair adds, "in a private submarine"), or else to live at the seashore (191; 277). But the real seashore ultimately remains a poor substitute for the other sea, the lost paradise.

Only once does Hannah actually try to return to that paradise. One very cold Jerusalem morning she has a pleasant memory of the time she had diphtheria as a child, and she felt "the interplay of shapes in the expanse ranging in color from light to dark gray" (134; 194). She tries to regain that experience that morning by pouring ice water on herself after Michael leaves for work. She becomes "a wild, disobedient child," "swept away by the violent floods of pleasure and pain" (136; 197). All the hidden caves of her body come alive and she rushes through the rooms of her flat like a madwoman, falling on her bed and imagining herself making love with "many friendly men."[24] At the climax of that scene she cries out: "Men are born for water, to flood cold and violent in the depths on the plains on snowy open steppes and among the stars. Men are born for snow. To be and not to rest to shout and not to whisper to touch and not to watch to flood and not to yearn. I am made of ice, my city is made of ice and my subjects too shall be of ice. Every one. The Princess has spoken" (136; 198). Here Hannah

---

23. That tranquillity is the opposite of the apparent tranquillity between Hannah and Michael at breakfast (113; 164).

24. Jung emphasizes that unlike an anima figure, conceived as a single woman by the hero, the animus tends to appear as a group of men (1959). See also *Touch the Water, Touch the Wind* (1973a, 66).

fulfills all her yearnings. She stands at the gates of the distant world of her childhood, a world motivated by power and sexual desire, a flowing expanse with blurred boundaries. That world is the complete opposite of her everyday life ("Yvonne Azulai, the opposite of Hannah Gonen" [136; 198]), and only there does she feel alive, taking part in events, and not a mere passive observer ("to be and not to rest to shout and not to whisper"). In her desperate effort to freeze that realm of experience, Hannah passes from water and snow to ice, to protect herself from any possible change and from dissolution: "We must be white and clear and cold else we shall crumble away" (137; 198). But that illusion does not last long. When the noise of military vehicles penetrate her room, she views their presence as a revolt against the princess by the destroyers "Dragon" and "Tigris," and by the Arab twins. Finally her husband rouses her from her dream. Typically, she sees him as one of the rebels who seek to harm her, one of her captors: "I still belong to the ice, yet already an alien power clutches" (130; 201). Hannah recovers from her illness, but she does not renounce her dreams: "When will the journey begin, Michael? I have grown tired of waiting and waiting" (151; 220).

Hannah Gonen makes her last attempt to transfer her hidden world to reality by coldly teasing the neighbor's boy, Yoram Kamnitzer. She becomes intoxicated with his desire for her and takes pleasure in controlling him (159, 161; 232, 234), but Yoram evades her control. With bitter certainty she knows: "But the defeat was mine. This was my last attempt. The menacing presence was stronger than I. From now on I would allow myself to float downstream, borne by the current, in passive repose" (162; 236). We can interpret this passage in light of the previously described two-layered structure: Hannah will no longer live in a warm cage under the crust of ice, a submarine cruising in the depths; now she will float on the cold water's surface, in daylight. Flow and life take place far below the surface of the water. To float means to die, to be put aside, to be silent (cf. "to be and not to rest"). She comes back to that description near the end of the novel when she thinks of her close friend's trip to Switzerland: "I don't mind, Hadassa. There's no sea in Switzerland. Dragon and the Tigris are laid up in dry dock in the harbor of the St. Pierre and Miquelon Islands. Their crews are roaming the valleys in search of new girls. I am not jealous. I am not involved. I am at rest" (189; 275). (In the Hebrew version Hannah repeats here the same adjective, *munahat* [lying, placed], that she had used in the previous description.)

Hannah's story could not have a happy ending or resolve itself in compromise. The forces struggling within her necessitate her defeat.

Finding a fertile unity of opposites does not exist for her. Everything to which she aspires while awake proves to be boring, repulsive, and unsatisfactory in her visions, and everything she dreams about proves to be threatening, violent, and destructive in daylight.[25] Her only option is that of submission, a renunciation requiring a fundamental, exhausted surrender. With this submission, Hannah gives up the possibility of a journey: "For some years Michael has been resting with his arms on the steering wheel, thinking and dozing. I bid him farewell. I am not involved. I have given in" (196; 285).

In this state of miserable renunciation, Hannah finds consolation only in the twins, Aziz and Halil, her childhood playmates. The novel links them to the sea (as deckhands, sailors, pirates: 8, 22; 9, 28, and elsewhere); they embody savagery, violence, and wordless animality. Hannah's relation to them indicates her desire for power as well as her desire to be conquered by their violence (35, 36; 47 and elsewhere). Those deckhands or pirates "cruise" on the surface of Jerusalem, "flowing" in its streets (82–83; 119). A similar image concludes the novel: in her imagination Hannah incites the twins to blow up the concrete reservoir, escaping before the explosion "like a light skiff edging through still, calm water" (198; 287).

Hannah is neither "anti-Zionist" nor an "Arab-lover" as several critics claimed when the novel was published. The Arab-Israeli political conflict does not concern her. Rather, she attempts to connect with her inner core: the hidden caves, the sea, the man in ambush, the unconscious. For her, the Arabs embody that fascinating and hostile force. This fascination is evident in the twins who occupy her dreams, and in her disappointment "that an Arab warship was burning alive in the sea of Haifa" (149; 218). She identifies the destroyed ship with the dual structure of the *Nautilus*: "Burning alive at sea—all this had happened before in the distant past. This wasn't the first time" (150; 218). At this point it might be interesting to quote Oz on the subject of Hannah and her twins:

> The Arab twins with whom she played in her childhood only exist in her imagination. They represent traumatic fear and ecstatic desire for another bitter confrontation, for another meeting of all the opposites. . . . For Hannah the War of Independence was a personal disaster. Her childhood was destroyed once and for all—everything that attracted her heart, everything that enchanted her, was lost. She is fearful

---

25. Nurit Gertz (1980) discussed that conflict from a different point of view.

of revenge. She yearns for revenge. From a certain angle the Arab threat is her only chance. Something has to happen. That isn't the end. (1972)

Oz's conception of the primal psychic forces appears throughout his works. Frequently he returns to the symbol of water and the sea, illuminating the eternal, unchanged urges and drives. As we have seen, a straight line leads from Dita through Noga to Rimona. Ilana, the female protagonist of *Black Box*, is the last offspring of this group. Hannah Gonen, though an exception in that line of descent, is also depicted through her painful attachment to the sea depths within her.

## A MEMORY
### Oz as a Soccer Player

Amos Oz first arrived at Kibbutz Hulda at age fourteen. At that time I was eight or nine years old. The various age groups at Hulda lived separate existences, and common activities in which children of all ages took part were fairly limited. There was no contact between us until a relatively late date. However, in one area alone all social barriers were broken: sports. In kickball, football, and basketball games all class and age boundaries disappeared and participation in them was dictated solely in accordance with the ancient laws of running speed, accuracy of hits, and so forth. Indeed, these laws were not merciful toward the young Oz. Years later, Michael Gonen would tell his wife Hannah: "At school, in Holon, I had a gym teacher called Yehiam Peled who always called me 'Goofy Ganz,' because my reflexes were rather slow. I was very good at English and math, but in P.T. I was Goofy Ganz" (*My Michael*, 141; 204–5).

Amos shied away from the game fields. At an early age he was known as an intellectual genius who would not waste his time on such things. Except, at least, on one occasion. At the side of our children's house extended a long patch of lawn that occasionally was transformed (not to its betterment) into a soccer field. One afternoon (Oz, it seems, was in one of the last grades of high school and I was in the fifth or sixth grade) Oz passed along the path that runs past the soccer field: for some reason someone called him to join the soccer game going on in the field and for some reason he agreed. I, as usual, was performing the function of goalie, and Amos joined the offense of the opposing team. I don't recall anything of this game with the exception of one picture: I am five or six meters from the goal when the ball flies past me, landing at Oz's feet as he stands in front of the goal line. I do not even attempt to run toward him to block the goal, because the situation, as I sorrowfully admit to myself, is hopeless. In my mind I have already added a goal to the credit of the opposing team when Oz, in a miraculous act, shoots the ball straight from the mouth of the goal, skyward. We are saved! My affection for this complex man, it seems, commenced at that moment.

# 5

## WAR AND PEACE
### The Element of Synthesis

Oz's protagonists have torn personalities. The tensions between the different psychic forces as well as between the flat, secured, and lifeless existence within societal borders and the intensive, vital, alluring experiences beyond these borders, find expression in the protagonists' struggles between light and darkness, God and Satan, spirit and body, man and woman, Jews and Arabs, culture and nature. Like a wound that cannot be healed, this tension underlies Oz's works, dictating their direction. His works attempt to find a cure to this problem by bringing the warring contraries together to live in peace. From its beginning, Oz's work has moved in two directions: on the one hand, it demonstrates an obsessive preoccupation with "elsewhere," an unceasing effort to delve ever deeper into the dark side of consciousness while heightening the contrasts between the opposing forces vying within his protagonists; on the other hand, it consistently attempts to bring these oppositions to peaceful coexistence and even to a fruitful, mutual relationship. In most of his books, the struggle ends with the discovery of the longed-for unity of opposites, but because of their contradictory qualities, the unity can only be temporary, another station on the way to a renewed struggle and a new book.

Oz's social and political articles also deal with the search for harmony. Consequently, we can say that there is no essential difference whether, as a member of Sheli (a leftist Zionist party) or the Alignment (the centrist Labor Zionist bloc), he works toward peace with the Arab countries, or calls for the establishment of a national unity government as he did after the elections of July 1984. In both cases Oz seeks, among other things, reconciliation with his own "other."

In describing the thematic structure of his works, Nurit Gertz writes:

> On the most abstract level of the plot it is expressed in the effort to obtain some sort of contact that can offer meaningful existence to the protagonists of the story, a contact possible only in destruction, violence, death, or war. That phenomenon undergoes several stages: the protagonist lives in the cultured world, which is barren, cut off from its environment, from man, nature, and the higher powers which could have directed and guided him. He tries, or, rather, he is drawn into making contact with those factors that are liable to shatter his isolation. But they themselves are disfiguring (savage nature, the cruel and malicious powers above, an inhuman loved one, etc.), and contact with them entails violence, war, or death. The protagonists destroy and are destroyed in that contact. (1980, 50–51)

This generalization is applicable to several of Oz's stories, but it certainly does not typify them all. Oz's protagonists do vacillate between conflicting urges, but their uncompromising struggle is, in most cases, merely external. Gertz applies an existential way of thinking to Oz, which allows no true dialogue between humankind and its world. However, the experiential quality of Oz's works is evidently dialogical as well as dialectical. The romantic "rift" is merely the point of departure, not the finish line. The structure of contraries characterizing his books does not take the form of a static spiral, as Gertz claims. In actuality, the structure develops, in most cases, toward the unity of opposites; this does not result in inevitable surrender, and certainly not destruction. Within that unity, good and evil, nature and culture, become both enemies and soulmates unable to exist without each other. Beyond the outer appearance of unconditional struggle Oz's fiction strives toward the discovery of harmony between the warring sides in which "evil," the "enemy," proves to be a reservoir of vitality and wisdom. We find this notion of unification in Oz's religious views (God and Satan embracing each other), as well as in his sea and water images (a fecund and murderous womb). The Arab characters also exemplify this dialectical outlook. The alien Arab enemy inspires a fear that is accompanied by a powerful attraction, by the desire for unity ("Nomad and Viper," *Elsewhere, Perhaps, My Michael, A Perfect Peace*, and others).

Beyond the "structure of opposites" by which Gertz seeks to encompass all of Oz's works, a thematic structure of no less importance emerges: the search for the treasure. The protagonists' divided world motivates their journey in search of the treasure. The treasure implicitly symbolizes a state of harmony where contraries peacefully coexist.[1] Symbols of the treasure are used by the author in *Where the Jackals Howl, Elsewhere, Perhaps, My Michael, A Perfect Peace, Black Box*, and *The Third Condition*. In these books the symbols signify the search for unified and whole existence. However, not all the characters achieve it. Hannah Gonen gives up hope and mourns for the pearl pin lost at the bottom of the sea, and the crusaders dreaming about Jerusalem perish before having all their desires fulfilled.

Oz's stories often violate the limitations of social taboo, lacking a moral fulcrum to restrain them. The author liberates the urges that society wishes to repress and bury. However, as his work demonstrates, the unity of opposites shows this interpretation to be one-sided. Doubtless, Satanic forces attract Oz's protagonists, but the stories do more than celebrate these dark urges; they suggest that a full life can be lived only through a person's reconciliation with his shadow. Thus Oz follows Jung's central ideas (cf. the process of discovering the "self," in Chapter 3). Neumann comments on this process, developing his teacher's views:

> What shakes the individual to his foundations is the inescapable necessity of recognizing that the other side, in spite of its undoubted character of hostility and alienness to the ego, is a part of his own personality. The great and terrible doctrine of "That art thou," which runs like a leitmotif throughout depth psychology, first appears, on a painful and most discordant note, in the discovery of the shadow. . . . To be obliged to admit that one is infantile and maladjusted, miserable and ugly, a human animal related to the monkeys, a sexual beast and a creature of the herd is in itself a shattering experience for any ego that has identified itself with the collective values. But the roots of the shadow problem go deeper still, and it

---

1. This is a typical Jungian concept. As noted, Jung interprets the search for the treasure as a projection of an inner journey toward individuation.

becomes a matter of deadly earnest when the probe reaches right down to the sources of evil itself, where the personality experiences its relationship with the enemy of mankind, the drive to aggression and destruction, in the structure of its own being. (1969, 79–80)

Further on Neumann notes the failure of the old morality that attempted to ignore the existence of the shadow, emphasizing the principles of the new morality:

> The only person who is morally acceptable in the eyes of the new ethic is the person who has accepted his shadow problem—the person, that is to say, who has become conscious of his own negative side. . . . The new ethic is based on an attempt to become conscious of both the positive and the negative forces in the human organism and to relate these forces consciously to the life of the individual and the community. The shadow who demands acceptance is the outcast of life. He is the individual form which the dark side of humanity takes on in me and for me, as a component of my own personality. (91–92)

Consciousness of the shadow will not destroy the individual but will provide a bridge between him and his world:

> The acceptance of the shadow involves a growth in depth into the ground of one's own being, and with the loss of the airy illusion of an ego-ideal, a new depth and rootedness and stability is born. . . . When the ego realizes its solidarity with the evil "ugliest man," the predatory man and the ape man in terror in the jungle, its stature is increased by the accession of a most vital factor, the lack of which has precipitated modern man into his present disastrous state of splitness and ego-isolation—and that is, a living relationship with nature and the earth. . . . We have in fact first to assimilate the primitive side of our own nature before we can arrive at a stable feeling of human solidarity and coresponsibility with the collective. (96–97)

Oz's work describes the tension between fascinating and powerful "primary experiences" which exact a heavy toll, that of madness and death, and battered and faded "secondary experiences" which guarantee the continuation of social existence. Thus he could not have written stories supported by conventional social morality. Hannah Gonen, along with other protagonists, wants to reject all social demands: "Hard-working, responsible, honest, neat—and utterly boring." Jung's and Neumann's ideas offer Oz a solution that neither requires him to distance himself from primary experiences nor to decide between primary and secondary ones. This solution, evident in Oz's earliest fiction, proposes a cease-fire through the unification of opposites, rather than a war of extermination.

Oz's characters who attain that unity can be divided into three main types:

1. Characters who combine primordiality and holiness, such as the female figures (Dita-Noga-Rimona-Ilana and others), and men such as Dov Sirkin ("Before His Time"), Matityahu Damkov, the jackal-god ("Where the Jackals Howl"), and Ezra Berger *(Elsewhere, Perhaps)*.

2. The members of the kibbutz's founding generation who did not fervently adopt the kibbutz ideology and did not allow it to emasculate them. They are aware of the inadequacy of values and ethics when contrasted with the mighty forces of nature surrounding the kibbutz and lying hidden within its members' psyche. What makes them special is that they find a golden mean, their ability to draw power from nature without becoming its victim. Their world, while not without tension, is reliable, and rooted, in contrast to the ideologues' false, deceptive world (Sashka in "Where the Jackals Howl," Shimshon Sheinbaum in "The Way of the Wind," Felix in "A Hollow Stone"). Herbert Segal *(Elsewhere, Perhaps)*, Ernest Cohen *(Touch the Water, Touch the Wind)*, and Srulik *(A Perfect Peace)* exemplify such characters, and, not incidentally, they are all secretaries of their kibbutzim. The people around them sense their inner strength and trust their judgment. Curiously, Herbert Segal and Srulik are "confirmed bachelors," as well as Kleinberger ("Strange Fire"), another figure embodying that unity of opposites. Apparently, the unity of opposites toward which Oz's works aspire has not yet assimilated woman, except in isolated cases.[2]

---

2. Interestingly, in *To Know a Woman* (1989; 1991) we find constant blurring of the borders between male and female. Jesus has a girl's face, whereas the protagonist's daughter has boyish features. Yoel's boss uses a feminine perfume, and the real-estate agent seeks Yoel's company "like a coy girl" (44; 54). One can find many other examples of this theme throughout the novel. Importantly, the crippled man the protagonist had seen in Helsinki "really did have the face of a girl. Or, rather, of something gentler still, gentler than a child, shining and wide-eyed as though he knew what the answer was, and quietly rejoiced over its unbelievable simplicity, though here it was, before your very eyes" (110; 145). On other occasions, this invalid is depicted as an androgyne, or as

3. Protagonists with sundered worlds, or characters who feel that their souls are dying, who try to restore their wholeness. Regarding the desire for the union of opposites, Oz's work shows remarkable unity. His first story, "A Crack Open to the Wind," concludes with the main protagonist's reconciliation with the jackal within him, the mending of the crack in his wall, and his firm decision to continue preserving the integrity of his house. A similar process, though varied and far more complex, unfolds in *Black Box* and *The Third Condition*, two of Oz's most recent novels.[3]

It is worth noting that even the characters who achieve the longed-for unity of opposites are rarely happy or content human beings (see, for example, the discussion of characters such as Dr. Kleinberger ["Strange Fire"] and Srulik [*A Perfect Peace*] below). Oz, as noted in Chapter 2, loves writers who "shattered those abstract patterns: floor and ceiling . . . negative and positive, good and evil," and he wants his writings to achieve the same effect (1978b). Yet the point of departure of his stories and novels is always based upon such oppositions. Binary concepts such as nature versus culture, light versus darkness, and the like, which the Zionist movement brought with it from Europe, were enhanced in Palestine due to historical and cultural circumstances: the need to "conquer" the land, either the marshland or the wasteland, was one of the main projects of early Zionism, and the tension between nature and culture is deeply rooted in modern Hebrew literature; in many cases the "cultured" European Jews envied the local Arabs and felt that in order to integrate in the area they had to imitate them, and yet, on the other hand, they looked down on them; clashes between Jewish and Arab aspirations created a constant tension between the two camps. Oz's private history strengthened this kind of binary world: his early childhood on the background of World War II; the constant presence of the threatening, hostile Arab neighbors; a right-wing family and an elementary school "with strong religious and national tendencies" (1979a, 206); a balanced, hard-working scholar as a father,

---

the Antropos, one of the main symbols of the philosophers' stone in alchemy. One of the implications in the novel is that the sought-after harmony is a situation in which the two sexes are merged into one. This theme implies, among other things, that, for Oz's male protagonists, harmony is achieved in a situation in which the world is no longer divided between males and females; males in such a situation do not have to confront the dread and seduction of women, nor do they have to cope with them as independent beings.

3. Gertz's claim, that "in any case, Oz's protagonists generally finish the story where they began it, whether it is an actual return, the semblance of one, or a metaphor" (1980, 51), is unsupported. Most of Oz's protagonists undergo an intense, accelerated experiential process, one that usually brings about a drastic change in their self-awareness, in their relation to society and to their world.

and a romantic mother who committed suicide when he was twelve years old. By opting for the kibbutz, as a fourteen-year-old boy, Oz took a daring step in order to turn his back on the world of his childhood, just to find out that he had brought his childhood patterns with him (1968b). The attempt to shatter the binary worldview was going to be one of the main thrusts in his writings. One cannot but appreciate the author's endeavor to extricate himself from the above binary concepts. Yet one cannot ignore the fact that Oz is inextricably imprisoned by them. The synthesis achieved by his protagonists takes place between diametrically opposed forces, and as such it constitutes a fragile, constantly threatened situation. In many cases it is more a sought-after goal than a real, lasting experience. Because of the opposing forces included in it, even when synthesis is achieved, rarely does it bring about feelings of harmony and tranquillity. Torn asunder by contradicting drives, Oz's protagonists unknowingly try to leave behind the Judeo-Christian world and to reach a world that is not based on divisions between God and Satan, good and evil, culture and nature, and the like. Imprisoned by his cultural and personal background, and trying to set himself free from this background, Oz is a living example of "civilization and its discontents" (to use Freud's famous title).

To sketch a general picture of these issues in Oz's work, in this chapter I will discuss "Strange Fire," the last story of *Where the Jackals Howl*, and the novels, *Elsewhere, Perhaps, A Perfect Peace*, and *Black Box*.

## *"Strange Fire": Degeneracy Is a Dialectical Phenomenon*

Although "Strange Fire" (first published in *Moznayim*, December 1963) was not the last story that Oz wrote for the collection *Where the Jackals Howl*, it is an exceptionally appropriate conclusion for the group. Oz arranged the stories as a single unit with interweaving parts (see appendix). Within this complex structure, "Strange Fire," along with the story preceding it, "A Hollow Stone," provides the final link. The book contains several stories where the struggle among the various powers of the psyche, between nature and culture, ends in the unconditional defeat of consciousness and culture. Geula wishes to be reconciled with the Bedouin, to enter his world, and she can do so only by delivering herself to the Bedouin's analogue, the viper, and its venom ("Nomad and Viper"). Gideon Sheinbaum discovers the wolf's teeth bristling in his brother Zaki's mouth and commits suicide for fear of losing his humanity ("The Way of the Wind"). The reformer of the world falls victim to the riotous nocturnal voices which descend upon him, and he too commits suicide ("Reforming the World"). Nurit Gertz makes these generalizations about the stories:

> In all the stories of *Where the Jackals Howl*, a struggle is waged between the cultured person (generally a kibbutz member), living sheltered by Zionist ideology, and threatening nature and its representatives—the jackals, the Arabs, the mountains. . . . In the course of the story the protagonist, who himself is composed of those very tensions, vacillates between violent contacts with the forces of nature and flight back to the barren life of society, until the climax or conclusion of the story, where that destructive contact ends either in disaster or surrender. (1980, 93)

Considering the entire thematic structure of the book, one finds that those generalizations hold true for certain stories but not for the book as a whole. On the contrary, the book ends with two stories the essence of which is the unity of the opposites existing between nature and culture. In the framework of that tense cease-fire, nature is threatening and destructive as well as purifying and fertile. These stories present the dark powers of nature: in the storm that nearly destroys the kibbutz ("A Hollow Stone"), in the zoo in Jerusalem, where senses are as sharp as in old times and the sexual instinct reigns supreme and unrestrained ("Strange Fire"). The stories show, however, that the primal world has a purifying function, symbolized by the strainer in the aquarium which gives the water its "marvelous clarity" ("A Hollow Stone"), and by the "purified" tops of the pine trees described in the closing passage of the book.

That "Strange Fire" functions as a kind of summary of the collection is evident in the analogies that can be found between this story and "Where the Jackals Howl," the first story of the book. The two stories describe the encounter between a young person and someone older who represents the night-time world. The older person proves to be the parent (in fact or metaphorically) of the younger one, though that does not prevent the pair from desiring an erotic closeness which shatters social taboos. In both, the plot takes place against a background of conflict between darkness and light.[4] We can also find a clear

---

4. Other details add to the link between the two stories. For example, in both of

line of development between them: while "Where the Jackals Howl" emphasizes the power of darkness, which threatens to destroy light, "Strange Fire" dwells on the purifying quality of darkness.

Dr. Kleinberger's response to his friend Yosef Yarden provides the central theme of the story. Yosef complains of the corruption that has spread throughout the state, but Kleinberger has his own opinion: "Degeneracy is a dialectical phenomenon, Yosef, for without the word degeneracy the word 'purity' makes no sense. The alternation between degeneracy and purity is like that between day and night. They seem to be contraries, but in fact one draws the other out, and neither can exist without the other, and that is what we must hope in this decadent age" (149). This passage, doubtless a key one in Oz's works, clarifies the story's concern with the interrelatedness of opposites. It suggests two possible ways in which their union may occur:

I. Cyclical, dialectical movement between two poles wherein day becomes night for eternity.
II. A dependent relationship wherein light draws on darkness and cannot exist without it.

Dr. Kleinberger, like Oz himself, is a great admirer of the dialectical views of thinkers like Heraclitus and Hegel, according to which every element achieves its particularity and meaning by evolving into its opposite.[5] We also find this principle to be a central one in Jung's theories:

> Old Heraclitus . . . discovered the most marvelous of all psychological laws: the regulative function of opposites. He called it *enantiodromia*, a running contrariwise, by which he meant that sooner or later everything runs into its opposite. . . . Thus the rational attitude of culture necessarily runs into its opposite, namely the irrational devastation of culture. We should never identify ourselves with reason, for man is not and never will be a creature of reason alone. . . . The irrational cannot and must not be extirpated. (1953a, 72)

Thus, with the support of Heraclitus, Schelling, Hegel, and Jung, Kleinberger tries to explain the complexity of reality to Yosef, and to

---

them the older person plans his moves "meticulously," careful not to bring things "to a boil too soon," and in both of them the color violet has an important role.

5. That principle is a key tenet in Schelling's system (see Chapter 3).

raise his spirits by pointing out that movement always oscillates between two poles. Thus "this decadent age" will not necessarily lead "to chaos," but in the future it might be replaced by significant and exalted activity.

The narrator, who identifies with the positions taken by Dr. Kleinberger, supports his view by means of frequent landscape descriptions: "As for the night birds, they roost in the heart of the suburb at night, but the first fingers of light drive them away to their holes hidden in the rocks in the woods outside the city. Here too a precise, cyclical principle is in control" (149). The myth of the sun's nightly voyage to the sea also refers to this cyclical principle. The narrator, describing the sunset in Jerusalem, presents the scene as a struggle between the sun and darkness. Since Jerusalem has no sea, the west becomes an "ocean" in which the defeated sun sinks: "A flock of twilight crows flies westward, pursuing the defeated sun as it drowns in the crimson ocean of the west" (154). This myth, a common one in various cultures, consists of these fundamental stages: the dragon devours the sun, followed by the imprisonment of the sun and its flight or return to life.[6] Thus the sun only drowns in the sea in order to be born again in the morning. The victory of darkness is merely temporary, and the dragon that swallows the sun becomes the womb from which it will emerge at dawn, warm and pure.

The comparison of the alternation of day and night with that of corruption and purity indicates a movement between poles entirely different from each other. However, as noted, from what Kleinberger says a new principle emerges: the poles are not homogeneous, but contain their opposites within them. Darkness not only parallels corruption, but also contains sparks of light. Threatening and destructive, darkness nourishes and supports light. "Strange Fire" expresses this central idea in the descriptions of Jerusalem (the streets, the trees, and the zoo), in the figure of Dr. Kleinberger, in the encounter between Yair Yarden and Lily Dannenberg, and also in the repeated myth of the search for treasure. Let us first consider the setting of the story—a Jerusalem that has "surrendered" to darkness (154).

"Strange Fire" presents Rehavia, the neighborhood where the protagonists live and where Yair's and Lily's journey begins, as a place whose arteries have been "clogged" by the many housing projects built around it (161). Who returns its dreams to it? Who sends new blood into its veins? The night, the ancient wind rising from the Valley of the

---

6. In Egyptian mythology there is a strong connection between that myth and several of the animals which appear in this story (the owl, the cat, etc.).

Cross: "The nights, they alone restore a few of the neighborhood's tattered dreams. The trees suckle renewed heaviness from the night. . . . An ancient wind rises from the Valley of the Cross, dragging the night birds along with it and the fragrance of pine, imbuing the neighborhood with restrained, monastic nervousness. The olive groves, climbing up towards the neighborhood, seep into its clogged arteries" (161). The olive trees planted in the Valley of the Cross give vitality to the neighborhood's ornamental trees (151). To explain the source of the olive trees' vitality, the narrator digresses, describing the secret of their strength: "In aggressive hunger they send out their root hairs into the depths of the earth. Their roots slip through the hidden cracks and crush the rocks blocking them. The treetops are caressed in the wind with a noble and moderate mien, but unseen their roots seek moisture with passionate powers" (158). Here we have a prime example of the unity of opposites around which the story revolves. The treetops move "with a noble and moderate mien" thanks to the moisture their roots passionately suckle from the depths of the earth. In other words, one does not gain nobility by ignoring the depths but rather by virtue of drawing upon them (cf. Lily's nobility [152] and that of the pines [161]).

In the human sphere, Dr. Kleinberger achieves that unity of opposites.[7] He repeatedly uses the term "dialectic" (149, 158, 166), and in his life he embodies the conceptions that he advocates. In speaking to his friend, he emphasizes the multiplicity of reality ("In fact every child has more than a single name" [150]; "every coin has at least two sides" [157]), and he advocates the "controlled release" of social protest (150).[8] Moreover, his creativity strives for "the marvelous unity of opposites": "Things approach their final goal, the marvelous unity of opposites. A strange fire sparkled in the man's eyes, shimmering on the lenses of his glasses. . . . The opposites are close to each other, flashing, glimmering ceaselessly, but the unification is unrealized" (173). The process of creation is not rational, planned, and tranquil (incidentally, in the second version of the story it turns out that the scholar is not, in this case, diligently adding another paragraph to his monograph, but rather trying his hand at writing poetry [133; 147]). The "wise light" in the doctor's eyes (166) becomes a "strange fire."

---

7. Both Lily and the cab driver, Abbu, also express this unity. See the discussion of their characters in Chapter 3.

8. The importance of that subject to the author can also be inferred from the fact that he even subjected marginal descriptive details to it. Dr. Kleinberger opens the window of his room to release the accumulated smoke, and the narrator quickly adds: "The smoke lost its advantage and spiralled out" (165).

The process of creation is a plunge into the world of the depths, the naming of "things," the preverbal contents of the strata within. The previous passage refers to those contents; words are confronted by "something that is not words": "Muffled and distant the cry of the jackals is heard. Words flee from him. Something that is not words seeks to be uttered but cannot be" (168).

In Dr. Kleinberger we find Oz's response to the tension between "primary experiences," powerful and pregnant with danger, and "secondary experiences," which do not allow a person to reach the stars but do guarantee him against falling. The dialectic, finding expression in Kleinberger, signifies the acknowledgment of the vitality of the depths, and the effort to live with these forces by giving "moderate release" to them. In this way a person can have a meaningful life without denying his individuality or depending on false solutions. One cannot be happy by choosing this path, however, because of the inevitable conflicts that arise from such a path. In Oz's world moments of happiness are few and as pungent as venom, but there are no happy characters. Kleinberger's fidelity to the unity of opposites finds expression in the restraint and "stoicism" that characterize him (149). Sorrow and sadness characterize the union of opposites throughout the story. The nights, which restore a few of Rehavia's dreams to the neighborhood, infusing its arteries with new vitality, imbue it with "monastic, restrained sadness," "tender sadness" (161). The pines, drawing up dew from the darkness, send out "secret breaths of sadness" (174).[9] The world-weary sadness spoken of by Lily Dannenberg (168) also reflects this idea.[10]

The plot of the story demonstrates the unity of opposites embodied by the Jerusalem landscape. Along with the sun going down into "the ocean of the west," Yair (both his name and that of his brother, Uri, derive from the Hebrew root meaning "light") meets with Lily (a name conjuring up the night [*layla* in Hebrew], and also Lilith). During the evening Lily lusts for Yair, her future son-in-law, proving to be a rival equal to her daughter. Against his will Yair is enchanted by her charms, and their meeting, beginning as a formal encounter between future relatives, becomes a tryst. An important key for understanding that encounter is the radio broadcast, "Treasure Hunt." Yair and his brother prepare themselves for that program, one of the most popular

---

9. Schelling discussed sadness as a necessary element entailed by the duality characterizing the world and God (see Chapter 3).
10. As expected, Lily is not a pole entirely opposed to Dr. Kleinberger. The strange fire in his eyes reminds one of the strange, dissolute light flickering in hers (171). The word "effort" also links the two of them (162, 173).

radio broadcasts in Israel in the 1960s, and they are "gripped by detective fever" when Lily appears and asks to speak to Yair. That conjunction hints at the location of the treasure. The search for the treasure appears throughout the story and it is responsible for its inner plot. It is not superfluous to recall that the myth of the treasure hunt is closely tied to the myth of the sun's nightly journey to the sea (Jung, 1953b, 335).

One of Bialik's well-known ballads gives us the first hint of the treasure's location:

> Not by day and not by night
> quietly I set out and walk,
> Not in the hill or in the vale,
> Where stands an ancient acacia tree. . . .
> (154)

Why did Oz pick that particular ballad, to which he refers about half a dozen times in the story? Bialik's lines fit into the unity of opposites that the narrator finds in the Jerusalem landscape. The words "Not by day and not by night" appear in the previous passage indicating the time when the diurnal birds meet the nocturnal ones; the mountain and the valley remind us of the Valley of the Cross, mentioned in the story, and the hills around it. The two negatives in the first verse of the poem also recall the two negatives in the words of the crazy woman whom Lily and Yair meet ("Not tomorrow and not yesterday" [162]). In the context of "Strange Fire," Bialik's poem describes a unitary situation in which the contraries of day and night, low and high cancel each other out. The acacia, a symbol of the eternal life of the soul (Ferguson 1961, 27; Cooper 1984, 10), also combines past (it is "ancient") and future ("It tells fortunes"). The eternal life of the acacia and the combination of opposites that it symbolizes explain why the narrator sets up a parallel between the acacias and the indestructible olive trees: "The olive trees can be replaced by acacias, and in that way things will be brought to some sort of rounding off" (158).

References to the treasure hunt abound in the story. Yair overhears the broadcast from a passerby's portable radio (160), and after meeting the madwoman he again hums Bialik's poem, which hints at the location of the treasure (163). Afterward the poem remains on his lips, and Bialik's words open section 7 of the story. Upon leaving for his forced stroll with Lily, Yair wonders, "Are there acacia trees in Jerusalem? —Perhaps the treasure isn't far from here" (157). Indirectly, the treasure hunt determines the route taken by Lily and Yair:

"No acacia tree that solves riddles and tells fortunes is to be found in the neighborhood of Nahlaot. There was no alternative but to leave the alleys for Jaffa Road and head for a dirty restaurant that caters to night cab drivers" (169). From the restaurant and its metaphorical animal (most of the description is devoted to Abbu, who is likened to a bear), the path taken by the pair leads to real animals: "Lily led the young man to the last stand of trees, the grove whose eastern rib is tangent to the zoo, and whose northern rib leans up against the border" (173). Here Lily's and Yair's night journey reaches a climax in one of the most suggestive descriptions in Oz's work. The pair have long since left words behind: "Let us leave them unwatched to exchange abrupt whispers, some of which are strange noises which are not joined into words" (172); "Their whispers are incomprehensible" (173). Now they reach a realm of experience where the senses, particularly those of smell and hearing, instincts, and primordial drives have powerful influence. Not incidentally the zoo is located next to the border between Israel and Jordan. Oz frequently uses the border as a symbol of the borders of consciousness (see, for example, Yonatan, who crosses the border to Jordan in *A Perfect Peace*). Indeed, Yair and Lily reach the border here, "the ancient matter" of the world and of the psyche.[11] They reach the inchoate source of culture, which still embraces the world of nature: "Moonstruck jackals wander about the valleys. From the depths of the fog they call their caged brothers. Their moaning sets the air ablaze and transfers the deeds to the realms of nightmare and even to the gloomy orchards of legend beyond the reaches of nightmare" (174).

In that evocative scene the dew becomes an important symbol. Like the acacias, the pines are also evergreens and symbols of eternity (Cirlot 1983, 256). Here eternity is bestowed by the night and its dew: the damp darkness, like an ancient womb, charges the pines with renewed vitality ("The trees draw renewed heaviness from the night" [161]; "The pine needles softly rattle and grope in the darkness for the dew" [174]). Yet the images also suggest purification: "Out of the depths of your terror lift up your eyes and see the tops of pine trees. A halo of violet light, pale light, crowns the treetops. Refined and shining peacefulness floats over the pure treetops and soothes them

---

11. The metaphoric significance of the border, dividing the conscious activities of the psyche and the unconscious strata, is indicated, among other things, by the similarity between the strange lights flickering across the border (174) and the strange, dissolute light flickering in Lily Dannenberg's eyes (171). As could be expected from the worldview implied in this story, on the other side of the border there is not absolute darkness, but rather "strange lights."

with caresses" (ibid.). The dewy darkness gives the pines shining, bright, glowing peace and soothes them. The pine achieves nobility like the olive trees, through encountering the moisture of the darkness and depths. The adjective "refined" ("refined . . . peacefulness") also indicates the nocturnal purification of the pines, as does violet, the color of self-purification and repentance (Ferguson 1961, 152). The peacefulness denied Lily Dannenberg in the early evening (151) will be granted to her here, in the "pine grove" extending between the border and the zoo.

The double significance of the dew repeatedly emerges in the writings of the alchemists, who saw the "primordial material" in the dew, like mercury (Jung 1953b, 317; 1954, 121), and at the same time viewed it as the pure water of baptism (Jung 1963, 132). Mention of alchemy in this context is no coincidence. The entire scene is one of magic, of changing matter, of an overwhelming desire to touch the foundations of existence, to be touched by it and be saved. Moreover, most of the details mentioned in that description served as typical alchemical symbols. The mist ("A bluish mist rises from the valleys") represents the transformation of something corporeal and material to something which is incorporeal. Moreover, Jacobi points out that a blue mist acts as a kind of intermediary link between the two areas of the soul, belonging to the lower, watery area and also to the higher, blue area, uniting them in significant fashion (1974, 165). Mist and fog unify heaven and earth; through these elements the world of "primordial matter," that of "the bad animals," will purify itself and evaporate (162). The animals in the cages and the jackals represent the lower waterlike world of the bad animals (as noted, the narrator has already mentioned that the jackals are "in [the story's] basement and turn its wheels"). The jackals wander in the valleys from which the bluish mist rises, calling to their brothers who are trapped "in the depths of the fog."[12] The word "depths" here has the connotation of water and the sea, emphasizing the jackals' primality: the jackals do not seem to be somewhere in the distant valleys, but rather somewhere in the dark, damp depths. The purified tops of the pines, wrapped in violet light and refined peacefulness, symbolize the "higher" area in this scene. Stony fields extend between the depths and the treetops "as dry as death." The rocks, like human beings, occupy an intermediary position, between the lava of creation and the treetops. They have pure whiteness ("The moon brightens everything and it cleaves to the

---

12. In the aforementioned discussion by Jacobi, vapor and fog overlap with each other, as indicated by the name of the section: "The Blue Fog or Vapor" (160).

whiteness of the rocks as though bewitched") and, at the same time, poison ("tumors of glistening venom stand out on the moonlit boulders, like a malignant cancer"). That acute tension gives birth to hopes for redemption which will have, like the existence of the pines, a mixture of damp depths and light. That desperate hope concludes the story: "Only the rocks, the rocks are as dry as death. Give them a sign" (174). The timing of the description, the personification of the fields, and the cancer that shows on their face ("cancer" is also mentioned in Lily's and Yair's conversation and in Yodef Yarden's reflections) suggest that they are metaphorical extensions of the characters.

The "whiteness" of the rocks is, I believe, connected to the Lily and Yair plot. Their story suggests the second stage in the alchemical process, in which the meeting of darkness and light results in whitening ("albedo"), the white stone. According to alchemy, changing darkness into light can be accomplished through the war against the dragon and by means of the "holy union" of the brother and the sister or the mother and her son. The story alludes to both methods. The sun's nightly journey to the sea is a fine example of the struggle against the dragon: Lily, who was once married to Yair's father, is thus a possible mother of his, and she even calls him "my child" (167–68). Abbu too, with a taxi driver's sense of humor, says, "By God, he could be your son" (170). The tryst between the future mother-in-law and the man who is to marry her daughter, while violating a social taboo, turns out to be a necessary stage in the discovery of the treasure, "the marvelous unity of opposites," the pinnacle of the process of individuation. Will the treasure be found? The story does not offer an unequivocal answer. The radio game ends without the treasure being discovered. The concluding passage of the story, in contrast, unifies the purified pines and the parched stones of the field that await redemption. It seems to me that the name of Yair's fiancée, Dina, is not coincidental. The name sounds like Diana, the goddess of the moon, suggesting that Yair could achieve the highest stage of the alchemical process, obtained through the union of the sun and the moon, and of male and female.

"Strange Fire" does not finish with the discovery of the treasure, but it suggests where the treasure can be found, and which path leads to it. The treasure lies hidden in the dark bottom of the sea, across the border, in the "primordial matter" of the world and the psyche. To ignore it leads to a life of morbidity ("the house is empty, Yair, there is only cancer at home" [171]). The encounter with it, by contrast, offers a chance for renewal and purification. In "Strange Fire" Oz presents this topic in an extremely concentrated and condensed way, and he expands these same concerns in his following works.

## *Elsewhere, Perhaps:* The Phallus as an Assassin's Dagger

*Elsewhere, Perhaps,* like the stories in *Where the Jackals Howl,* depicts a torn world in which good order and savagery, valley and mountain, Jews and Arabs, life and death are constantly vying with each other. The "good order" that the kibbutz tries to impart to its members is broken through time and again in the human, social, and political spheres (13, 37, 44, 194; 29, 36, 154). Reuven Harish, "a pure man of sound principles" (20; 14), finds himself helpless in the face of the urges that dominate his nightmares and the fears and attractions that Germany arouses in him. "Dark forces" act on his daughter Noga and on Oren Berger. The kibbutz, trying to impose "the straight lines, the clean shapes, the neatly ruled concrete paths and rectangular lawns" (11; 5) on the environment, is helpless at night, surrounded by darkness that might steal in "and wreak havoc on the good order with its slashing teeth" (194; 154). The longings of the kibbutz to save the world, mentioned about half a dozen times by the narrator, receive blow after blow in the flight of Eva, Reuven Harish's wife, in the complicated relationships arising from Reuven's ties with Bronka, and in the friendship between Noga, Reuven's daughter, and Ezra, Bronka's husband. The kibbutz members, exposed to a psychic and social rift, find themselves in yet another arena, that of the Arab-Israeli conflict. Throughout the entire novel that front threatens to explode, and in fact, the climactic scene of the novel occurs during an artillery duel between Israel and its Arab neighbor.

As in the stories of *Where the Jackals Howl,* in *Elsewhere, Perhaps* the outer struggle covers an entirely different structure of relationships. The mutual relations between the warring sides take a very interesting turn in this novel: while *Where the Jackals Howl* concludes with emphasis on the dialectical movement between the dark and light poles, in *Elsewhere, Perhaps,* along with that dialectic, there is complete identity between the sides: the acts of hostility are like the acts of love, the death wish is merely an intensified desire for life. In other words, the longing to obtain wholeness and unity is identical with the longing for self-annihilation. That identity is found in the psychological and philosophical infrastructure of the novel, and the main characters in the novel must struggle with it. This topic, at which *Where the Jackals Howl* only hints, becomes central in *Elsewhere, Perhaps,* and it will continue appearing in Oz's works. Thus, for example, in *A*

*Perfect Peace,* Yonatan oscillates between "the charms of death" and his attachment to life.

As noted, the bitter struggle described in the novel extends over every level of existence: the psyche, society, the landscape, and politics. In each of those areas we find struggle and dread, along with mutual attraction. The reciprocity seems likely to lead to a nourishing and fertile synthesis, but also to mutual destruction. The novel focuses on this second alternative. We can find many examples to illustrate this destructive attraction in the relations between the kibbutz and its Arab neighbors. The hostility between the sides is repeatedly expressed in geographical terms: the kibbutz is situated in the valley while the Arab peasants and soldiers inhabit the hill rising above it. Reuven Harish associates the bare hills and wildness with the bullets of the Arabs who attack the peaceful valley (41, 83; 33). His poems also identify the hill crests with the Arab enemy: "A barren mountain plots / To bury our village alive" (129; 104). The narrator uses similar terms to describe the nightfall: "The mountains are trying to bury us alive in an avalanche of heavy shadows. The last rays catch some metal objects for an instant, a flashing sign of the menacing presence of the enemy positions on the mountainside" (47; 39). In fact the mountain does rise above the kibbutz as a constant threat, evident in the bullets fired at the kibbutz from time to time, in the ambush where Tomer Geva is wounded, and finally in the attempt to thwart Israel's intention to cultivate the lands right up to the border. The narrator supports Reuven Harish's position throughout the novel, presenting the Arab-Israel conflict as a war that opposes culture, good, and light with nature, evil, and darkness. However, the narrator has many masks. Indirectly the reader can infer that this biased viewpoint conceals a far more complex structure of relations. The hills arouse dread, but they are also a focus of stifled yearnings.

It would seem that the kibbutz members should hate the Arab hill that constantly threatens them. What, then, is the meaning of that yearning for the hostile hilltop? The hills represent one aspect of the "elsewhere" that attracts the characters. Like Germany, the hills are also linked to water and darkness ("A pool of absolute darkness" [195; 155]; see also 47, 56; 32, 48, and elsewhere). It is, then, no surprise that Noga declares, "I belong to the mountains" (202; 158), and that several descriptions support that declaration (31, 292, 346; 24, 268). The narrator does not define the character of "our errors lusting for feverish matters" (231), but he juxtaposes that sentence with a description of the hills. Moreover, the term "lusting" shows that the previous description of the dogs, "the cry of the dogs lusting for the mountains"

(195), represents the feelings of the kibbutz members no less than it refers to the dogs.

That attraction for the mountains is one of the best-disguised subjects of the novel. The narrator does not speak directly of this attraction, leaving the task to descriptions of the landscape. The opening chapter provides abundant examples of the hostility between "the valley, with its neat, geometrical patchwork of fields" (10; 4) and the wild, gloomy savagery of the hills. At the same time, in that chapter, the narrator emphasizes that the border does not coincide with the natural boundary: "The soil of Israel overflows the limits of the valley and spreads up the lower slopes of the hillside, along the approaches to the desolate nakedness" (9–10; 3). These lines suggest that the struggle is not one-dimensional. Moreover, the phrase "desolate nakedness" introduces an erotic element, emphasizing the phallic character of the crest of the hills.[13] In addition, the kibbutz vineyard branches outward toward the hilly land in "a gentle curve like the bend of a soft, relaxed knee"(13). In the same reference the cunning narrator repeatedly emphasizes the "marked contrast between the cultivated plain and the threat of the hill," but indirectly he compares the hill and the valley to a man and a woman about to make love. The female, erotic character of the vineyard is confirmed further on in the novel, when the fourteen-year-old Ido, seized with desire, looks at Hassia, sitting at his side: "He breaks his mental vow and squints again at the uncovered knees. They are white, he sees, and gently curved like the rows of vines when they reach the lower slopes" (98; 74).

It appears that the hostile hilltop is not only the moist and dark womb, but also the erect, fecundating phallus. Once again the Arabs are identified with primality, vitality, and power. Here that view leads to a highly interesting change in the way Oz portrays Israel. In many ways *Elsewhere, Perhaps* develops the confrontation, familiar from Oz's earlier works, between consciousness-culture-man and unconsciousness-nature-woman. Israel represents, according to that view, the masculine, cultured side (the kibbutz expresses light, sanity, order, the good). However, this notion embodies a contradiction. Although the kibbutz is indeed an island of culture, of order and of the good, it is situated in the valley, "the primeval crack" (40; 32). In a nutshell, this contradiction reveals the principal features of Oz's world. The kibbutz lacks uniformity: its "masculine" elements are built upon decidedly "feminine" elements that are manifest in various phenomena

---

13. On mountains as a phallic element, see Freud (1965, 391).

which interfere with good order (see the previous chapter regarding phenomena connected with the sea that occasionally terrorize the tranquillity of the kibbutz), and similarly in the desire for the nudity of the hostile hill. The hill itself simultaneously represents both "masculine" and "feminine" elements. Nevertheless, its masculinity, unlike that of the kibbutz, does not arise from an effort to impose the rule of consciousness and culture upon nature, but on the contrary, from its natural, phallic element. The struggle between Israel and its Arab neighbor, which had at first seemed like the familiar struggle between culture and nature, becomes the struggle between a man-woman and another man-woman. The opposition between the "masculine" and "feminine" sides brings about the mutual attraction, which leads, slowly but surely, to the destructive embrace characterizing their relations.

The erotic tension latent in the opening chapter emerges with a huge fanfare in the climactic scene of the novel in which the narrator views an artillery duel as sexual intercourse. For a better understanding of this comparison, we must go back to Tomer Geva's reflections on the mighty power of erotic pleasure: "Our lives cascade from gulley to gulley till they drain away into the sand for a fleeting sensation in the lower abdomen" (380; 298). In the description of the battle, the narrator repeats Tomer's words: "A dialogue of cannons here. The only result is the deception of feverish senses. It is its own end. It's a marvelously moderate dispute, subject to an exacting rhythm, producing a kind of sublime satisfaction with its noises. Also: a short distance from here, to the west, the east, the north, and the south, an obedient, blue, calm day. . . . Here is merely a fleeting sensation. The empty and terrible breath of the distances. As ever. As always" (387). In what way are the results of the battle merely a deception? The "fleeting sensation," the erotic release experienced in battle, explains the first part of the passage: the battle brings strong, primal pleasure with it, and it, then, is its own purpose.[14] This idea rejects the Marxist theory of the powers that motivate humanity. Instinctive desires motivate the battle, allowing primal needs to be expressed. Other explanations are merely "the deception of feverish senses." The entire passage reveals a gloomy worldview: each side needs the other to find harmony, to breathe in rhythm with the "breath of the distances" and

---

14. That conception was already implied in the stories of *Where the Jackals Howl*, through metaphors drawn from the area of music used to describe the Israeli reprisal raids (82–83). Freud has dealt extensively with the instinct of aggression and destruction (e.g., 1961b and 1969).

unite with them; only acts of hostility can fulfill that mutual need, and yet they cannot eliminate the emptiness of the expanses. Nevertheless, the destructive encounter also has other aspects. The Arab side appears here as a source of fertility and might. Encountering it will bring, along with destruction, the reinforcement and inner fulfillment of the kibbutz society, the fortification of its resolve to achieve its goals. Paradoxically, destruction is a source of renewal; death gives birth to new life.[15] To clarify this point, we must consider a character who specializes in that area, Zechariah-Siegfried Berger.

Zechariah Berger, referred to as a "negative figure," and the "angel of evil," is ostensibly the emissary of Satan. Yet the narrator's gloomy worldview, although hidden behind seven veils, indirectly supports Zechariah's philosophical and psychological ideas. Those ideas are first seen as produced by the imagination of someone who has sold his soul to the devil; however, they are in fact an open and exhaustive formulation of the narrator's implicit views. To Noga, his niece, Zechariah explains the meaning of German-Jewish cooperation:

> The murder victim and his killer are not like fire and wood, not like throat and sacrificial blade. There is a hidden thread riveting each to the one he hates, and the enemies are shackled to each other for all eternity, like the bond between a man and woman whose mating was successful and crossed one upon the other. The child is their absolute crossing. . . . If the mating of murdered and killer is not withdrawn, they are crossed in death. An eternal crossing, a confirmed murderer and a victim pining for his killer with desire as strong as death. (285)

The Hebrew expressions used here have Biblical overtones: the adjective translated as "confirmed" is *nirtsa*, referring to the slave who refused to leave his master and consequently had his ear pierced (Exod. 21:6); and the phrase "as strong as death" comes from the Song of Songs (8:6). These references point to the inverted relations at the root of things: the killer is bound to his task like the slave whose ear was pierced, and "as strong as death," rather than referring to love, refers to desire of the murder victim for his killer. The phrase "riveting each," which can have both a psychological meaning (enchanted, unable to take their eyes off each other) and a physical one (joined together,

---

15. See Ezra's remarks about the kibbutz reaction to Ramigolski's death: "We have come to celebrate his death like a carnival, as if it was good that someone should have died early on, good from an educational point of view, as it were" (140; 114).

gripped by each other), emphasizes the power of the bond uniting the two camps. Before us we have the vital core of *Elsewhere, Perhaps*. Zechariah depicts the relations between the murderer and his victim not as a one-sided relation, but as a mutual one. Moreover, he compares their relationship to the act of lovemaking: the murderer's dagger and the phallus are the same thing.[16] Each side wants to be rehabilitated through the other side, but the attempt to obtain the yearned-for harmony makes the phallus an assassin's dagger. At the pole of the absolute, wholeness and the void are the same. The narrator indirectly corroborates this point describing the Israeli and Arab searchlights as they duel with each other at night: "The two beams of lights remained locked in a furious embrace, piercing each other's eyes, bitter and stubborn, like knives poised for murder or like drunken lovers" (247; 189). Doubtless we have here a realistic demonstration of the argument advanced by Zechariah. Here too we have deathly hatred, in which the two sides grasp each other (cf. the thread that shackles them in Zechariah's remarks). Here too the two sides either embrace each other in love or with an assassin's knife. That identity is also central to Zechariah's second "lecture": "Some say of death that it is the feminine element, a symbol. And the opposite, life, is the masculine element. . . . According to that doctrine, by the way, it too was produced by a German sage's spirit, the man's act is the extermination of the woman, the extermination of death, but it is also breaking back into the womb and the warm, embryonic slumber of the black interior of the female symbol, death" (292).

True to himself, Zechariah here returns to the basic principles of his outlook with breathless excitement. The dialectic flow between the two poles that concluded *Where the Jackals Howl* becomes, in his words, movement in two directions that destroys itself. However, even in that movement, as we have seen above, there is an aspect of synthesis, but that aspect is not the main one. Its essence is the identity between the two poles: yearnings for a life endowed with significance and intensity are longings for death.[17] The entire novel

---

16. That identity hints at its two wings, at the violence inherent in sex and at the erotic vitality of death. As noted, that comparison is not foreign to the narrator himself. Thus, for example, in describing Ezra Berger returning weary from his work, he writes: "Sleep comes on the man suddenly. Like an ax blow. Like a woman" (72; 62).

17. That subject explains, among other things, Oz's deep affinity with Berdyczewski. This is how Oz describes Berdyczewski's protagonists: "[They] are not relegated to a position in which they must choose between good and evil, between righteousness and happiness, between destruction and ruin, but rather, they must choose between life and death, and in order to prevent any over-simplistic assumption, I shall add that that choice is particularly difficult in Berdyczewski's stories, since life is similar to death and

illustrates this view, in the various axes of the plot, in the yearnings for "elsewhere" (especially the German womb, moist with water), as well as in the protracted conflict between Israel and its Arab neighbors. The Jungian conception, which holds that the dread and fascination aroused by the "enemy" derives from the fact that the "rival" is the dark, repressed side of one's psyche, is varied here with the addition of Freud's death instinct.[18]

The death instinct appears again in various forms in the course of the novel. Eva desires death ("Death can be so beautiful" [88; 65–66]), and the picture of death she depicts (ibid.) is congruent with the seductions of the German landscape and its slumber about which Reuven Harish tells his daughter (314; 248). Those seductions, with the sounds of the bells and the black birds, keep arising in Reuven's mind like an incomprehensible memory (89, 297; 66, 232). In his poems Reuven exalts the kibbutz's steadfast power, as it fights with an enemy who plots to bury it alive, but at the same time, Reuven struggles with his inner desire for death.

Two kibbutz members, Ezra Berger and Herbert Segal, fly the banner of "life." Herbert Segal, who also comes from Germany, is well aware of the yearnings for "elsewhere." He finishes his eulogy over Frumma's grave by saying, "Now, in this place, when death surrounds us and fate seems to be celebrating its cruel, evil, stupid victory, we are sworn not to surrender to the black powers. To the black powers within the soul. Death is not the law of existence. Existence is the law of existence" (342). At the start of his eulogy, Segal has mentioned the blows that fate has dealt to Frumma, the death of her husband, the loss of her son, and the power of her existence. There is no apparent connection between those words, according to which fate is an external power, and the final sentences; but his declaration, "Death is not the law of existence. Existence is the law of existence," shows that he knows very well that the black powers, the powers of death, lie within the very soul itself. That declaration does not state a fact but expresses a wish to fly a banner. Segal has indirect knowledge of the

---

death resembles an eruption of the senses" (1979a, 31). Further on, Oz claims that in Berdyczewski's world there are two possible structures of experience, "primary experiences, which exact a heavy price (madness, death) but which contain the spirit of life," and "secondary experiences, which are faded and miserable and worn out" (36).

18. Against the background of *Where the Jackals Howl*, with its decidedly Jungian infrastructure, the influence of Freud is conspicuous in *Elsewhere, Perhaps*. As we shall see below, the three Berger brothers illustrate the structure of the psyche as described by Freud. The war between light and darkness is also resolved here in a Freudian manner.

enormous power of the longing for death, while at the same time he defies it. His eulogy is not addressed to the late Frumma, but to himself and his fellow members.

Ezra Berger also values life. To Reuven Harish, sitting at his side, Ezra says: "Now, at our age, we must realize one fact: the important thing is not to die gloriously, it's to die as late as possible. Another ten years, another twenty years" (140; 114; cf. 174; 141). In comparing himself to his two brothers, Ezra is thankful for his very existence in the world: "I just live and exist, thank the Lord, the Creator of the universe."[19]

Through the descriptions of the kibbutz and the plot development, the narrator supports Ezra's and Segal's positive views. The death wish exists and cannot be completely repressed, but one can struggle against it. Attraction for death will make new life blossom. While the pretext for the struggle with the enemy is a fascination with death, this impulse will also lead to the expansion of the land toiled by the kibbutz and to the strengthening of the kibbutz society. In the end, the kibbutz continues its routine, which, more than anything, demonstrates that "existence is the law of existence." Noga remains on the kibbutz, married to Rami Rimon, and gives birth to Inbal. Einav becomes pregnant again and Ezra dwells in the bosom of his family as in days gone by. The mountains are as threatening and fascinating as ever, but the narrator turns his eyes away from them with a determined decision: "The mountains are as they have always been. I turn my eyes from them" (395; 308), taking leave of his readers with a description of a calm evening in the Berger home.

The struggle with the Arab enemy represents the other struggles undertaken in this novel: those between order and wildness, culture and nature, Israel and Germany, and others. Twice the narrator uses general language, quoting Reuven Harish: "The war of light and darkness, barren and sown, mountain and valley, says Reuven Harish, is an eternal war" (196). But the narrator reveals his own opinion of that war in describing the masses of people who eat and disturb the good order of the dining hall:

> How pleasant is the sight of the hall at this hour. . . . We almost regret the approach of the masses of voracious people about to burst in here in their gray or blue overalls, to raise a

---

19. This subject, the longing for death and the desire for life, is developed in *A Perfect Peace*.

predatory uproar, to do away with good order, to leave, after a few moments, stacks of greasy utensils, dirty tables, turbid puddles with leftovers floating in them. Anyone looking for an example or symbol of Reuven Harish's views about the war between order and turmoil which is a law of life need only join us now and observe, as we do, what happens here. (234)

That example, identifying the dining hall set up for dinner with good order and the meal itself with predatory turmoil, shows that the narrator, to whom good order is, as it were, precious, knows very well that wildness and turmoil are vital fertile elements without which life is impossible. Freud also presents eating as an example of the way in which the life and death instincts mingle: life is maintained thanks to eating, but the process of eating itself is one of destruction, of biting, chewing, and swallowing.[20]

The narrator thus vacillates between two different ways of unifying opposites. On the one hand he presents Zechariah's view, which holds that the two poles (life and death, love and hatred) cling to each other indissolubly, but that their opposing characters necessarily lead them to destruction, doing away with any possibility of productive bonding. The unity of opposites represented by Reuven Harish, in contrast, does not argue with the absolute identity of the two camps, but proffers a dialectic movement in which destruction and struggle are the source of renewal. The latent plot of the novel revolves around the conflict between those two views. The element of synthesis implicit in it is expressed, among other things, in the victory ultimately achieved by Reuven Harish's views. The narrator does not reject Zechariah's psychological conclusions. As a denizen of the world of the deep, Zechariah certainly knows what forces are at work "on the floor of the soul" (285). The novel asks this question: what is a person to do with that knowledge? On the one hand one can embrace those dark powers, like Zechariah, or on the other hand, one can attempt to restrain them, harnessing them to the wagon of culture as it slowly moves forward. That second possibility does not suggest that we ignore or repress those forces, but that we should draw power from their primal strength while blocking their destructiveness: let those forces help pull the wagon, yet not send it flying over the precipice.

---

20. See Freud (1969, 6). This issue is also hinted at by the role gossip plays in the kibbutz society: "Gossip is normally thought of as an undesirable activity, but with us even gossip is made to play a part in the reform of the world" (16; 9).

## *The Blue Flame*

*Elsewhere, Perhaps* presents the dialectic unity of opposites in the plot development (Noga remains on the kibbutz, Ezra returns to his wife), and in some of the main characters' qualities: Noga Harish, Rami Rimon, and, of course, Ezra Berger and Herbert Segal. In the previous chapter we saw that Noga brings together all the oppositions: holy and profane, blessing and curse, matter and spirit, male and female. Noga also contributes to the topic of the unity of opposites within the plot. For a while she wanders between the kibbutz and the "elsewhere" to which she is drawn, between the good angel, Segal, and the bad one, Zechariah. After her father's death she demands that Zechariah be sent away from the kibbutz and determines to stay herself. The kibbutz society, fearing the "wild spirit" that Noga brings to it (307) and wishing to rid itself of her, ultimately finds a place for her. She becomes a full-fledged member of the kibbutz when she marries Rami and gives birth to Inbal. I do not consider this solution forced as other critics claimed when the novel was first published. In Noga all oppositions struggle with each other and achieve a synthesis, and her remaining on the kibbutz is merely another aspect of that synthesis. It is true, however, that the struggle was not ultimately decided and is not likely to be decided. In the concluding scene of the novel, Noga, occupied in the kitchenette, carries out a wife's tasks with practiced expertise: "Bronka and Noga confabulate in the cooking alcove. There is warmth between them. Stella Maris. A paraffin heater burns with a blue flame. On the rag, as always, are two babies" (395–96; 309). Blue is the color of Mary and Venus, who are, as noted, a background for the character of Noga.[21] The blue flame of the stove unites warmth with the sea, which was mentioned previously, symbolizing the entire scene: the fire is kept to human dimensions, the depths of the unconscious have been restrained to the proportions of society. Noga finds here, if only for a short while, the blue flower of her dreams.

We find synthesis in the scene also expressed by the bell and its clapper: "Outside the wind may howl and the rain beat down. The house is an inverted bell. The people inside are like the clapper" (395; 309). The bell, which appeared earlier as the seductive voice of death (88, 89, 297, 314; 66, 232, 248), here stands for the warm home, protecting those within it from the storm. The opposite meanings of the bell, good and bad, eternity and death, sky and earth, male and

---

21. See Cooper (1984, 40) and de Vries (1981, 45).

female, once more point out that the tranquillity described here arises from the struggle between contraries.[22] Throughout the plot, Noga is identified with the clapper of a bell (203, 248, 304; 159, 189, 239); she even names her daughter "Inbal," which means the clapper of a bell.[23] Now she finds her proper place in the protective bell of the family and the kibbutz.

At the same time, the tranquil concluding scene reflects routine and barrenness: "Ezra is seated, wearing his glasses, which make him look old and resigned. . . . Einav drops off to sleep with a newspaper over her face" (395; 309). What will be the fate of those longings for another place now that Noga has become a married woman, with a child, soon to assume the yoke of the quotidian routine on the kibbutz? That question might best be addressed to Hannah Gonen, the main protagonist of Oz's next novel; her story begins, as noted in the previous chapter, where Noga's leaves off.

We find synthesis also embodied in some of the characters surrounding Noga. Her brother Gai (meaning "valley" in Hebrew) complements her tempestuous character, which belongs to the hills. Again we have another example of the central opposition between hill and vale: the kibbutz, settled and masculine, is located in a valley; so too is the composed and responsible brother whose name means "valley," whereas his sister claims that she belongs to the dark hill. In contrast to dark Noga (whose name means "brightness"), Gai "is fair-haired with a matching complexion" (36). True, his eyes "cradle a warm darkness" (ibid.), but the inner struggle he wages does not penetrate or delve as deep as the one threatening his sister. He leads a gang of kids in war games, which displeases the kibbutz members, but the narrator admits that Gai and his companions are "only making a lot of noise" (109; 85). Furthermore, when Noga's pregnancy becomes known, a total change takes place in his behavior (297; 232). He acts like an adult with his father and sister (361), and becomes Segal's trusty ally.

In contrast, Oren Berger is the image of Zechariah, the agent of evil and of the depths of the sea. Like Noga he is not the product of kibbutz education or of influences he absorbed unknowingly at home: his father is generally a diligent, upright man, and his mother is one of the kibbutz educators. "Dark forces" direct his actions, and he promises

---

22. For the symbolic meaning of the bell, see Cooper (1984, 20) and de Vries (1981, 44).

23. The fact that Noga identifies with this phallic symbol is typical of her character. This identification is integrated with her attraction to the mountains and with the male-female nature of both Israel and her Arab enemy.

Zechariah, his spiritual mentor, that he will not fall from the tree, but rather infect all the apples with his putrefaction (357; 279). Nonetheless, Oren too appears in the final, harmonious scene of the novel: "Gai and Oren are here too, standing at Ezra's desk, heads together, bright hair touching dark hair, their shared stamp collection spread out in front of them." Oren remains as "dark" as he was, but in this family scene his darkness is balanced by Gai's lightness. Further, both boys are busy with their stamp collection here, a common symbol of good order in Oz's work. The narrator does not clarify what happened to Oren between the previous descriptions, where he was shown as Zechariah's ally (356; 278), as a piece of driftwood left behind by the sea waves (358; 279), and the present one. Oren's story does not find completion within the novel. It seems to me that the thematic element, the desire to conclude the novel with a synthesis embracing all the opposites, overcomes the element of plot and psychology here.

Rami Rimon, Noga's husband, also appears in the concluding scene of the novel. In the beginning of the novel, Rami was an awkward kibbutznik, dreaming of conquering Noga and of military exploits. The encounter with death gives him a new way of seeing and completely changes his scale of values. During one of his leaves from the army, he accosts Noga, despite the fight that had taken place between them, and he tells her enthusiastically about miscellaneous events in the army. At that stage, he still identifies wholeheartedly with the way people think in the army and on the kibbutz, and he is impervious to his interlocutor's reactions. But that evening a change takes place: to prove to himself he is no coward, and to strike out at Noga with his death, he plays Russian roulette. He presses his luck to the verge of suicide, and stops. The encounter with death suddenly opens his eyes: "A new thought occurred to Rami. It soothed him like a gentle caress. Not all men are born to be heroes. Maybe I wasn't born to be a hero. But in every man there's something special, something that isn't in other men. In my nature, for instance, there's a certain sensitivity. A capacity to suffer and feel pain. Perhaps I was born to be an artist, or even a doctor" (216: 172). Henceforth, his ways change.[24] Segal formulates that change, even before plotting to marry Rami to Noga: "The lad went off to the army full of blazing ambition. Now I can see a different quality in him, a kind of contraction of desire, some withdrawal. Now one notices . . . a kind of sensitivity and attentiveness. Signs of a weighty man" (340: 263–64).[25] During the mourning period

---

24. A total change in the wake of a possible encounter with death also takes place in Yonatan's soul in *A Perfect Peace*.

25. The adjective "heavy" or "weighty" (Heb.: *khaved*) is one of the most loaded ones

after the death of his mother, Rami shares the change that has taken place within him with Noga, supporting her decision not to have an abortion. In the issue of whether or not to work the disputed land, Rami also supports Noga's position (339; 262). On his following leaves he no longer tries to divert her with stories about the army. His decision to deviate from the social norms to which he had been subject until then and to make his own choices gives him the necessary power to propose marriage to the girl he loves, though she is pregnant by another man.

Synthesis is suggested by Rami Rimon's family name (Hebrew *rimon* = pomegranate) and by his frequently being compared to a horse.[26] The narrator mentions his horselike expression about half a dozen times, and Noga, when she is angry, also uses that expression. At the same time, Noga knows that a horse contains a contradiction: "a horse can be miserable and obedient like a donkey or a mule, but there's a contradiction in it. It can also be wild and roar through the valleys" (203; see also 157–58; 125). Like other characters in this novel, Rami achieves a synthesis comprising both the wild stallion and the mule. The horse is a prime example of the unity of opposites expressed in the novel. On the one hand, it belongs to the world of nature, but on the other hand it lives harmoniously with humans, an animal hitched to society's wagon.

Two other figures in the novel embody the principle of the unity of opposites: Ezra Berger and Herbert Segal. Both are linked to the symbol of the ring-circle, and both win the praises of the narrator for their moderation and the sense of correct proportion. Ezra Berger is instructive, perhaps more than any other figure, about the element of synthesis implicit in the novel. That element within him is indicated, among other things, by his place between his two brothers. He occupies the middle position between Nehemiah, the scholar in Jerusalem, all of whose ways "are enveloped in desiccation" (128), and Zechariah, the emissary of the world of darkness. Like Nehemiah, Ezra has spirituality (26; 19), and he reads all his brother's writings. On the other hand, there are similarities between him and Zechariah, as both his wife and son notice (263, 357; 205, 278). It is hard to miss

---

in the novel. When used by the narrator, it is connected with earthiness, rootedness, and nobility (70). Ezra is characterized by his weightiness (70, 71, 158, 159; 62, 127), as is Grisha (165, 362; 279). The treetops enrich the kibbutz with "a dimension of weightiness" (9; 3), and the twilight shadows "endow the ornamental trees with a heavy look" (46; 38). Zechariah adds to it an element of strength (332, 357).

26. On the meaning of the pomegranate, see the discussion of Noga's character in the previous chapter.

the parallel between that structure of relations and the structure of the personality as described by Freud: the id, the ego, and the superego. Doubtless Ezra is like the ego, compromising, in the name of the reality principle, between the pleasure principle of the id and the demands of morality and conscience. The reality principle is embodied in his character and expressed both by his being a practical man, as the narrator emphasizes (26, 138; 19, 112, and elsewhere), and also by the positive value he places on life. The narrator summarizes that by saying, "Ezra Berger, then, is unique among his brothers. Ezra Berger married and had children, and helped to establish Kibbutz Metsudat-Ram. His life is not doomed to sterility" (128; 103).

The unity of opposites expressed in the figure of Ezra is also symbolized in his bearlike nature. Noga sews a little bag for him to carry his sandwiches, embroidering on it, for some reason, the picture of a bear (118, 144; 93, 117). In thinking about him she frequently calls him a bear, a frightful bear, yet a tame, good, and wise bear (202, 203). Here Noga hints at the contradictory characteristics that have been attributed to the bear. In Christianity it represents the evil spirit, cruelty, and malice, but also the church itself in its power to reform the image of idol worshipers (Ferguson 1961, 12). In the hero myth it is linked to the sun, but in many other myths it belongs to the gallery of moon figures. The bear is a symbol of cruelty but also of heroism, nobility, and wisdom (de Vries 1981, 38; Cooper 1984, 18). In alchemy the bear represents the *nigredo* of the primal matter, related to the primary and instinctive stages of development. Similarly, Jung sees the threatening aspect of the unconscious in it, but in the light of its contradictory characteristics, Jung also sees it as a symbol of "self" (1959b, 226).

Ezra thus represents the compromising element, uniting opposites: both the ego, in Freud's view, and the self, in Jung's. Appropriately, he wins the narrator's praises, not for being entirely blameless, but for knowing limits and proper measure: "Even in his merriment there is nothing rowdy or ill-mannered. Ezra may be only a simple driver, but he knows one thing his brother will never learn: how to keep things within bounds" (322; 254; see also 70; 61). This knowledge elicits the highest praise accorded anyone by the narrator who refers to this quality as "an element of nobility" (27, 70; 19, 61). Nobility, then, does not belong to the realm of the superego, nor is it achieved by pure monasticism, by distancing oneself from the vanities of the world. Nobility is the virtue of the man who affirms life, who takes part in active life, who, like Ulysses and the Sirens, makes his way between two opposing forces without succumbing to the seductions of either, but also without silencing them completely. Like other figures in the novel who embody the union of opposites, Ezra is also linked to the circle. The narrator draws our attention to the gold ring Ezra wears, saying that it is of exceptional appearance (26, 90; 19, 166). The ring is mentioned further on, when Ezra and Noga are in the stable looking for rope (93).

Herbert Segal is, from many points of view, another Ezra, although there are some differences between them. Like Ezra, Segal is both a practical and spiritual man (44; 36), and like him he wins the narrator's praise for his moderation, and for the correct equilibrium in his behavior (44, 151, 230; 36). He is blessed with "sensible, sensitive tact" (45; 36), which he tries to impart to the children of the kibbutz (289; 226). At the same time, unlike Ezra, whose views "were formed in his early youth [and] are clear, well-defined and easygoing" (26; 19), Segal is a "solid and severe" man (79), "a straight and severe type of person" (307). Reuven Harish describes him as someone who lives "dead straight. Calmly," but "with clenched lips" (314; 248). The narrator corroborates these words in some of his descriptions (151, 344). What are those lips trying to hide? More than Ezra, Segal is aware of the forces hidden in the bottom of the human soul and of the need to restrain them. He knows that "the black powers" exist within the soul (342), and that "folly lies in wait for all of us. Insanity is aiming at us" (341). Like other characters in Oz's works who live in sharp awareness of the world of the depths, Segal too is very interested in music. He is the director of the local music group (and his predecessor in that position was none other than Eva Harish!), and he plays violin a little. The meaning the narrator attributes to music emerges from the implicit connection between descriptions of it and descriptions of the universe. Segal reflects that "there are different layers in music. Layer within layer" (107; 82). Interestingly, in the description of the artillery duel near the end of the novel the narrator repeats these words: "A hot autumn day. Sun, sky, earth, thick darkness. Layer within layer" (387). It appears that music is like the cosmos itself, and its deep levels penetrate to "the thick darkness." It is thus no wonder that listening to music carries Segal "elsewhere" (107; 82), or that when he feels the weight of his loneliness, he is drawn to music "as an alcoholic longs for wine" (344; 267). Music is an interesting example of the unity of opposites between nature and culture. It would appear to be a purely cultural product, addressing the refined, aesthetic side of the listener. On the other hand, its roots lie in the primal instincts, and the fact that sounds, unlike words, have no fixed, defined meaning, allows them to express those instincts, to reach territory beyond words and beyond consciousness.

Unlike Ezra, Segal remains unmarried. If he took a wife, "we would say of him that he had found the correct balance in life," notes the narrator. Is knowledge of the forces at work within him what prevents him from marrying? So his clenched lips fear to be opened by a kiss? Or perhaps it is fear of exposure to the threatening forces of woman, to the seductive pleasure of "elsewhere"? That point remains locked up tightly like a safe, the owner of which fears to show its contents in daylight. Nevertheless, like Ezra, Segal is also symbolized by the circle. Listening to music he brings his head down between his shoulders and "rounds" his back before his spirit is borne "elsewhere" (107; 82). The first time he is introduced the narrator mentions his round spectacles, referring to their round frames about half a dozen times. "The round hoop of steel" encircles the lenses (339; 262) and represents, it seems to me, Segal's inner wholeness, achieved through the struggle between opposing forces. That inner wholeness gives him a central position on the kibbutz, expressed, among other things, by his appointment as secretary of the kibbutz. In fact the place occupied by Ezra among his brothers is occupied by Segal within the entire kibbutz. He reconciles adversaries, soothes those bitter in spirit (see his conversation with Frumma, who complains about the corruption spreading on the kibbutz [230]), and he preserves the integrity of the kibbutz framework in getting Noga and Rami to marry. Segal's power does not derive from ignoring the "dark forces." He struggles against them and, at the same time, draws power from them. That combination makes him an adversary equal in weight to Zechariah in the struggle for Noga. Zechariah is confident of victory, for he sees in Segal merely "a man with progressive principles" (351; 273). He is well aware of the fundamental weakness of such people. But Segal's progressive principles, inured by inner struggles, finally win out.

The implied author does not support many of Segal's opinions concerning culture and art (86; 63), literature (111, 197, 231; 86), or education (162; 129). In most of those arguments, Reuven Harish's views receive the implied author's support. Nevertheless, Segal, unlike Reuven Harish, does not live a life of slogans and self-deception. While Harish's epithet, "a remarkable man" (14; 7), soon proves to be ironic, the representation of Segal as "a remarkable man" (289; 226) remains convincing and valid. Together with Ezra Berger he represents the thematic axis of the novel: the rejection of the temptations of pure light, on the one hand, and of utter darkness on the other; walking in the middle of the road, acknowledging the opposing forces vying with each other and attempting to bring them to coexist; valuing the kibbutz, including its barren routine, more highly than "elsewhere"; holding for life, with its pains and joys, rather than death.

## *A Perfect Peace: The Treasure Hunt*

In the novel *A Perfect Peace* the union of opposites finds its most complex and well-elaborated expression. That union is expressed in this novel not by one plot axis alone, but by two axes which support this union and firmly hold the novel together. I refer to the double course taken by Yonatan Lifshitz and Azariah Gitlin. Yonatan wishes to leave the circle of the kibbutz, and Azariah tries with all his power to gain entry into that circle. The unity of opposites is found in both directions of that movement. Moreover, that double motion ultimately ends within the kibbutz framework, where both Yonatan and Azariah serve as Rimona's husbands, as though becoming a single figure. A key figure such as Srulik also contributes to the portrayal of synthesis in the novel. He is clearly an extension of Segal from *Elsewhere, Perhaps*.

Two major literary devices express that central idea: first, most of the characters come to resemble each other by means of a technique of indirect parallels. That process, increasing in strength toward the conclusion of the novel, creates a kind of mystical union among the characters. Second, the many human triangles among the characters also illustrate a decided process of the unification of opposites. The number three proves to be the number of "the true heart" and of perfect peace.

*A Perfect Peace* begins with Yonatan's firm decision "to set out and begin a new life." His life on the kibbutz, which has been marked by the constant need to give up what was his own and adapt to the strictures of society and its expectations, made him into a "barren desert." He feels that life is slipping away from him, and that he must grasp it firmly. His various efforts to define his destination, a trip to America, studies, a career, merely give familiar outlines to a longing for the free and intense existence which is "life" (65, 225; 214 and elsewhere). In the end Yonatan sets out on a treasure hunt, in search of "life" and its meaning. That is how Rimona (243) and Azariah (296), who both have an unerring intuition, define it, as does Yonatan himself (225, 281; 214, 269). Paradoxically, life is revealed to him in Petra, presented as the diametric opposite of life, the underworld. Thus

Yonatan abandons culture and finds its absolute opposite. In his night trip to Petra he reaches the bottom of his soul, its primordial matter. He flees, pursued by horror, back to Israel, back to culture. Here he returns to Alexander Tlallim and serves as his assistant before returning to the kibbutz. Thus we have a prime example of the process of individuation.[27]

Yonatan's development can be seen in several reflections on the true nature of "the home" and of "life." Rimona, who senses the disquiet increasingly taking over her husband, tries to persuade him: "I'm not telling you to look at other people, but if you do look at them anyway, you'll see that new things don't happen to them every day either. What should happen, Yoni? You're a grown man. I'm your wife. This is home. All this is us. And it's the middle of the winter" (74; 65). Yonatan, eaten up by incomprehensible longings, does not accept the fact that "this is home. All this is us." He wants to be another man, in another place. Thus, when he leaves Beersheba in a military car and heads south, it is as if he were indirectly replying to Rimona's statements: "Flat earth bounded by soft hills, flat earth stippled by droplets of light, all the way to the edge of the world, with only a single road to spear it like a black arrow, answered only by the roar of a motor. This is life. And the world. And me. And love. Just wait peacefully and you will receive it" (275; 264). And the next morning, after a night of pleasure with Michal, he once more reflects: "What have I done with my life all these years? From the citrus groves to the dining hall, to a dead double bed to this committee, to that meeting. Here, praise be, I've come home at last. Here, I'm no longer theirs" (285; 274). But even that "home" is rejected a short while afterward in the face of "true" existence in the desert. As he sets out at night, Yonatan tries once more to define his life and his home: "Azariah himself wasn't real. And neither were all those years. Or home. And neither are Michal and that old madman. What's real is my life that's beginning now. In truth there are only stars and darkness. The desert really exists" (344; 337).

But "real life" is the path to death, the underworld, as Yonatan discovers to his horror. With the last remnant of his vitality he flees back to his prison, to Israel. Now that he has known the other side of life, the deadly side of the existence for which he yearned, he is reconciled with his world. During the time he spends in the desert as Sasha Tlallim's assistant, he is farther than ever from the lands of which he dreamt and the way of life that had enchanted him, but yearnings no longer separate him from the reality of his life: "I'm

---

27. This process, as well as the meaning of Petra, is discussed at length in Chapter 3.

beginning to understand. And my heart is getting true because everything changes for the better. I am here" (350; 342). "Life" is no longer a distant treasure beyond reach, and "home" is no longer a malignant wish. Life and the home are here and now. At that point Yonatan can return to the peace of his home and his kibbutz. He does not return in order to subject himself to all of society's regulations. The synthesis he reaches does not entail total obedience to social morality, but is achieved through finding equilibrium between that morality and the forces which threaten to shatter it.

The synthesis which Yonatan achieves and the individuation he obtains are indicated by his comparison with a tortoise. Azariah secretly calls the tortoise he gave to Yonatan and Rimona "little Yonatan" (157; 142), and Yonatan himself seems to identify with the captive tortoise and announces that the next day he will free it (161; 146). The one who actually goes free is Yonatan himself, of course, who seeks life in the desert. Even before that he had been described by his wife while sleeping on his belly, "his arms and legs spread out to the four corners of the bed" (174), a description reminding one of a tortoise. Because of its shape (a half sphere lying on a flat plane, a rounded body with a sharp head), the tortoise has been viewed as a symbol for heaven and earth, masculine and feminine (de Vries 1981, 471; Cooper 1984, 171). That duality permits it, according to Jung, to serve as a symbol of God in the form of an animal, and of individuation (1959b, 226). We should not be surprised to discover that the tortoise is also one of the symbols of Mercury, whose connections with Yonatan were mentioned at length in Chapter 3. Oz develops the tortoise's androgynous character in his description of Yonatan, who imagines that he feels "the moving baby in his own belly" (345; 338). Of course the tortoise is also connected to the question of the location of home. After his nocturnal adventure in the desert Yonatan understands that his house is not somewhere off in the distance but that, like the tortoise, he carries his house with him all the time. Yonatan must try to leave home only to return willingly.

## *Death Is Disgusting*

In his search for life, as noted, Yonatan reaches its opposite. A substantial aspect of the process of synthesis is oscillation between yearnings for death and the travails of life. Like many of the protagonists of *Elsewhere, Perhaps*, Yonatan is quite familiar with the seductions of death. Thus he searches for life in Petra, a "ghost city." Petra is depicted by Sasha Tlallim as "the bottom pit of hell" (337; 329), and Yonatan himself calls it "hell" (347; 340 and elsewhere). For Yonatan death is the attraction of the underworld, the complete opposite of consciousness and culture.[28] But it is also a "perfect peace" for him, balm to a weary heart:

> As flies paraded across his face, he envisioned his death that night from a burst of bullets in the chest or a curved dagger between the shoulder blades. There was no fear in the thought of such death. . . . his blood soaking into the dust like a venom purged from his body. In such a death, he might at last find perfect peace. . . . Yonatan yearned for a death as gentle and painless as this, one that would turn him into just another rock in the stony desert, one that would leave him without a single thought or longing, cold and existing, cold and existing. And forever still. (333; 325)

Yonatan repeats the phrase "cold and existing," as though it were a longed-for vision, twice more on the night of his journey (340, 344). The desire for death finds an ardent adversary in this novel in the figure of Sasha Tlallim, the surveyor. He is presented as an opponent of the Foul Fiend that entices Yonatan to his death: " 'Pull over right

---

28. Rimona reflects on the attractions of death that seduce her two men and the male sex in general: "Just a rumor or a whiff of war is enough to make them both more dangerous, more handsome, more passionate, more alive to me. . . . They have this thing inside that's always hungry and thirsty. Always gnawing at them. And making them suffer. It's not just wanting to have sex. It's something else too. Something harder and more lonely. . . . The smell of death makes up for what they're missing" (175–76; 164–66). The narrator affirms these intuitions in describing the disappointment of the young men of the kibbutz, after their storming of the mosque is fruitless: "A moment later the charms of death faded away and a kind of barren pall crawled in and filled the heart" (157).

As we have seen, that subject accompanies Oz's works all along the way. It is no coincidence that Oz identified a similar attraction in Moshe Dayan:
> This is the place to point out a kind of pleasure in death, betrayed by the man's tongue to the heedful ear (including all the following: excavations beneath every mound, the attraction for caves, the flirtation with death expressed in his daring gallop to any place where shells are falling). And all this, with a deep affinity with Alterman, with the poems of the dead rising up in the windows of the living. Till it became an obsession: the charms of death inspire Dayan. . . . Beyond these faint words one glimpses a poetical, romantic lust for death which I would gladly accept in a poet or author, but which inspires dread in me when it is expressed by a man who makes decisions concerning the lives and deaths of many people. (1979a, 28–29).

here,' said Yonatan. 'This is where I get off.' 'Ay, mama,' groaned the old man, 'I have been foiled by the Foul Fiend again' " (342; 335). He himself is a "devil of a fellow," as he says (336; 328), "the Devil's own" (341). But he is a kind of beneficent demon, a demon clinging to life.[29]

That function emerges from the timing of his appearance (exactly at the stage in which longings for death take over Yonatan [333; 325]), and of course, from what he preaches to Yonatan. Oz puts in Sasha's mouth a response to romantic longings for death as such. To the frightened Yonatan he describes death not as a peaceful and reconciled event but as a process involving infinite suffering. In short, "Death is disgusting! Revolting! Abomination! It stinks! Not to mention that it will not run away" (337; 329); "Death is filthy. Feh! Dirty! And it hurts too!" (339; 331). He clings to life, though he knows that suffering and pain are indissolubly bound up with it: "Live, you bastard! Live and go on living! . . . You spoiled brat! You little snot! Have a good cry and live! Crawl on your belly and live! Go crazy with pain, but live! Suffer, you bastard, I say! Suffer!" (336; 328). When he sees how firmly Yonatan is resolved to go to Petra, Sasha seeks a last line of retreat: "Well, go to hell then. Only take my advice. Don't spend the night. Come back to Shash. Steal across the border if you must and have a peek to Transjordan. No harm is likely to come of it. Just don't go beyond their road. And then as soon as you reach it, turn around and come straight back. . . . Come back to my royal palace tonight and stay for as long as you like" (341; 334). Unwittingly Yonatan obeys the good spirit fighting for his life: in the middle of the night he returns to Sasha's caravan without having reached his destination, and he becomes Sasha's assistant. The desire for life overcomes the death wish, and now he is full of strength because he has wrestled with death and overcome it.

The life instinct has another advocate in the novel. Following the antideath prophecy spoken to him by Sasha, Yonatan remembers Benya Trotsky, his mother's lover, who shot at Hava, Yolek, and even himself, but missed. Now Yonatan understands the meaning of his second father's strange, poor shooting: "He must have missed on purpose because death stinks. Crawl and live! Suffer and live!" (340; 333). Oz is careful to strengthen the possible thematic link between Sasha and Trotsky through the old parabellum pistol. Importantly, the same parabellum revolver that Trotsky fired at his lover and himself (8) appears again at the end of the novel, hanging from the

---

29. For a psychological interpretation of the various kinds of demons, see Jung (1959a). On the "good" demons, see also Langton (1949) and Fletcher (1982).

ceiling of Sasha's caravan (336; 328). Yonatan himself adopts the principles he attributes to Trotsky, and the author emphasizes the similarity between them: Yonatan, firing in every direction in the dark desert, lets out "a dog's yap" (349), like Trotsky running "with the piercing howl of a shot dog" before shooting at Yolek (8; 5).

## *Yonatan and Azariah: Brothers and a Husband*

A complementary aspect of Yonatan's story is the process of achieving the synthesis experienced by Azariah Gitlin. At first the two move in opposite directions: one moves outward from inside the circle, the other moves from the darkness beyond the circle inward toward the center. In contrast to Yonatan, who seeks life far from the kibbutz, on his first evening there Azariah imagines "how, behind each fogged window, families laughing, straw mats piled high with babies' toys, the smell of bathed children, heaters burning with blue flames, women in woolen bathrobes. There, within, life was flowing truly and unhurriedly such as you have never known it, such as you have longed with all your soul to touch, to be part of, so that you need no longer to be the outsider in the dark" (43–44; 35). That realm of experience, which Yonatan flees as though from a prison, is a much desired treasure for Azariah, the blue flower (the blue flame in the stoves is later explicitly compared to a blue flower, 187; 176 and elsewhere). That opposition between them emerges again from Azariah's answer to Yonatan, who proposes they race each other: " 'I have run quite enough in my life,' said Azariah, taken aback but with some semblance of self-respect. 'I came here to stop running' " (143; 131). The parallel opposition between Yonatan and Azariah is also demonstrated in the plot: Yolek adopts Azariah as a son, and when Yonatan disappears Azariah takes his place as Rimona's husband and the one responsible for the garage.

Azariah, who came to the kibbutz like a jackal emerging from the dark, moist womb (38–39; 31), gradually takes root in the kibbutz. Despite his strangeness the members of the kibbutz like him, and finally, on Srulik's initiative, they accept him as a member. The little wrinkles that race restlessly around his eyes (107; 96) are calmed, and he adopts the behavior and tone of voice of the young kibbutzniks (359; 350). While he was a proponent of Spinoza's views upon his arrival at the kibbutz—unsuccessful as he was in fulfilling the obligations implicit in them (246; 235)—under the influence of life on the kibbutz the disparity between his opinions and his behavior is reduced (368–69;

359–61). Several months after his arrival at the kibbutz he is capable of helping others, of advising and consoling them (370; 381), and even carrying out key functions on the kibbutz with good humor (360, 371; 350, 362). When he came to the kibbutz Azariah could not reconcile the sense of destiny throbbing within him and the appetites welling up inside him. On his first evening in Rimona's and Yonatan's house he looks at Rimona's "Christian" beauty and swears he will never reveal "how vile and despicable" he is (106; 95). On the Saturday excursion with the members of the kibbutz he reflects on the "filthy appetites" of his body and his "bad desires" (137, 138). He even calls himself a "dirty, polluted man" (143). After that excursion he stays overnight in Rimona's and Yonatan's house, calling himself "filth" to Rimona. The spiritual and erotic bond with Rimona and Yonatan puts his instincts in the right place. The appetites and desires that were satisfied cease to be a threatening, base, and debasing element. Azariah's reconciliation with the nature within him is expressed by an image from nature: "Upon leaving the dining hall after supper he would put an arm around Rimona's waist, his green eyes glinting with the unspoken arrogance of a male who has taken another male's female and might do it again any time he wants" (368; 360).

The opposing motions of Yonatan and Azariah thus culminate in a synthesis in which the two meet at the very same point, a point simultaneously within the framework and outside it. They live in reconciliation within a social framework with a strict code of behavior, but they live their lives in loyalty to their "true heart," a loyalty which is an utter violation of social morality.

The two axes of the plot seek, as noted, the unity of opposites. Oz was not satisfied with that and ultimately strengthened this element by combining these two figures into a single one. The first chapters of the novel emphasize the basic difference between Yonatan and Azariah. In contrast to Yonatan, born on the kibbutz, trying to uproot himself from the soil of his homeland, Azariah, the persecuted refugee, wants to take root in that soil; Azariah has a "spark" (113; 101 and elsewhere) and Yonatan lacks it, in his father's opinion (169; 157); Azariah believes that it is possible to break barriers with words (85; 75), and a "flood of words" bursts from his lips, whereas Yonatan does not like or trust words (90; 81). In addition to these differences in personality and aspirations, there is the fact that both struggle for the same father and the same woman, so that one might think that eternal hostility would reign between them. As expected in Amos Oz's world, that is not what happens. Yonatan takes a liking for the young stranger despite his strangeness. When he makes his acquaintance, he tells his wife, "He's a loudmouth, a cheat, a brown-nose, and a bullshitter . . . and yet you can't help kind of liking him" (112; 100). Later he defends him against Udi's cutting remarks (151) and even invites him to sleep in his home, which Azariah accepts because of the rain (161; 144). Rimona, feeling the closeness developing between the two (182; 173), sleeps with one and then with the other, creating a "holy trinity." Yonatan is about to leave the kibbutz, so he is glad to bring a kind of heir and substitute into his house (208, 263; 197, 247), but before setting out he shares his bed and wife with the young stranger. On his return to the kibbutz he also accepts Azariah as a full partner in his life and marriage.

Why is Yonatan drawn to the stranger whom he ought to hate with every fiber of his soul? It seems to me that we have here a variation of Yonatan's being drawn to another, dark life, the unknown side of existence. Yonatan's reconciliation with Azariah, who is depicted as a cat (56, 87; 47, 78), "a lost, wet puppy" (90, 220; 81, 208), is like the reconciliation of the kibbutz member with the wet jackal cub in Oz's first story, "A Crack Open to the Wind." In other words, that attraction is merely another aspect of the process of individuation undergone by Yonatan (Chapter 3 deals with that process at length). Yonatan's path to inner wholeness must pass through the stranger, the rival. As Azariah says upon arriving at the kibbutz: "That's why I've come. I want to join you and change my life for the better. And in relating to others, I believe, one relates better to one's own inner self" (40–41; 33).

Just as Yonatan's attraction for Azariah is similar to his yearning for "life," so too Azariah's affinity with Yonatan is merely another aspect of his affinity with the orderly and protected world of the kibbutz. Azariah adopts Yonatan as a brother, as part of his desire to live on the kibbutz "among good comrades. Among Jews. Among brothers" (397), as part of his desire to live among "brethren" (144, 157). From his very first days on the kibbutz Azariah sees Yonatan as his big brother. "Most pleasant have you been to me, my brother Yonatan," says Azariah (129; 118), repeating the words spoken by King David, and he also tells Eshkol and Hava that Yonatan is his brother (296, 370; 285).

The psychological and plot connection between the pair is emphasized by many parallels. Although the differences between them are brought out first, as the novel proceeds the similarities increase, until in the end the two virtually become a single character. Let us look at some of the details that link the two: at first it seems that only Azariah is "tormented" (53; 44), but in the end it turns out that Yonatan too is "tormented" (341). Like Azariah, who is called "boy" throughout the novel (55, 150, 174, 186–87; 46, 136, 176, and elsewhere), Yonatan too becomes a "boy" in the words of Michal (284; 273) and the surveyor (336, 350; 328, 342, and elsewhere). Both of them inwardly call themselves "filth" (182, 222; 172), and both of them, at the same time, are "good" people: Yonatan was always a good boy (72; 64), a good husband (73, 277; 65, 265), and now Azariah becomes good, as Rimona tries to persuade him (135, 182, 364; 172, 354, and elsewhere). We should also note that both of them work in the garage and Azariah's fingernails are blackened like those of "his brother" (369). Yonatan feels utter alienation in his relations with Rimona, but in making love with Michal he finds release and is completely "opened" like Azariah. This is how Rimona describes Azariah's response at the moment of orgasm: "When he comes there is a short, sharp yelp like a dog that has been wounded. Then his mouth and nose drool and then there are tears" (175; 165). That is just what happens to Yonatan: "Suddenly, like a dog that has been shot, he also cried out and burst into a flood of tears and sperm as if every wound in his life had opened at once and the very blood of his life was pouring out" (284; 272).

Yonatan's friends notice the process by which he comes to resemble Azariah and even give him Azariah's nickname, "Chimpanoza" (192; 179). Yonatan contributes indirectly to that identification by introducing himself as Azariah to the surveyor (339; 332). Thus, in the end, Yonatan virtually becomes Azariah and vice versa. After Yonatan's return to the kibbutz they are described in fully parallel fashion: "Every morning they rose early and went to the tractor shed, returning only at nightfall because there was plenty of work. Then they would shower, drink cold tea or coffee" (377; 369); "At the end of that summer Azariah and Yoni decided to make their own wine for the winter to come" (378; 370); "Sometimes Yoni and Azariah both sit on the sofa, next to each other, looking in silence and surprise" (379); "Yonatan and Azariah built a dog house for Tia in the garden" (380; 372); "In late May, both Yoni and Azariah were mobilized. . . . On their discharge, Hava baked them a cake" (380–81; 373). Rimona also does not appear to distinguish between the two: "Sometimes she would spread a clean diaper on one of their shoulders and give them the baby to walk around" (380; 372). It is thus no accident that the question of the paternity of Rimona's daughter Na'ama remains unresolved. Azariah and Yonatan have virtually become one flesh in fathering a daughter with Rimona. The mystic unity is also hinted at in the wine they prepare for the winter. The wine illustrates their intermingling both in the traditional aspect of wine as blood (all the more so with two figures who have been compared to Jesus) and in its capacity to blur the borders of consciousness. Wine is also related to the Eleusinian mysteries, which took place during the winter, and which evoked the story of Persephone, the goddess of agriculture and the queen of the world of the dead. But in order to grasp the full meaning of wine, we must now take up the third side of this triangle: Rimona.

## Rimona: The Goddess of the Underworld and of Vegetation

Without doubt Rimona is one of Amos Oz's most puzzling characters, and critics have completely mistaken her role in the novel. That sorceress (as Yonatan calls her), who knows what is going to happen, and who maintains links with the forces of nature and with the souls of the dead, is quite different from the way critics have depicted her (e.g., as a retarded woman). In Chapter 4 I pointed out that Rimona carries on the lineage of Oz's female figures representing the sea. The sea as the source of life and its end fits in well with the element of synthesis embodied by *A Perfect Peace*. However, the sea is just one aspect of that complex figure. Another aspect, congruent with the sea, emerges from the parallel linking Rimona with Petra, the world of the dead. That equation is one of the best disguised focuses of the novel. Yonatan emphasizes the coldness and frigidity wafting up from Rimona, she being "a barren desert," and he describes their bedroom as the land of the dead: "At three in the morning on a wide, arid sheet beneath a wide, arid ceiling with everything gleaming like the bones of a cadaver in the light of the full dead moon in the window, wide awake yet abducted by some white nightmares in a snowy polar wasteland, wide awake but alone with a corpse" (69; 60).

That fact prepares for the associative link between Rimona and Petra. Reading in the pamphlet about Petra, that it is "a red-rose city, half as old as time," Yonatan thinks of his wife: "He repeated the words over and over to himself, moving his lips silently, only to have his wife Rimona appear, lying cold and naked on the snowy sheet of their bed in the pale light of a summer moon that was turning corpse-white in the window" (331–32; 323). Further, Yonatan's enormous desire to reach Petra, the dark side of culture and life, is parallel to his desire to penetrate, if only once, to the source of Rimona's existence: "Once and for all to grab the bread knife and plunge it into her soft skin, into her veins and her arteries, and down deeper yet, to open her up, to rampage through the dark lymph of her and the fat and the cartilage, to the innermost nooks and crannies, to the marrow of her bones, to carve her till she screamed" (70; 61–62). Thus, Yonatan's journey to Petra is like a journey to Rimona, a journey guided by mighty desire to touch the bottom of existence. Yonatan sets out for Petra to find the treasure (on his journey as a treasure hunt, see Chapter 3). The connection between Rimona and the underworld could well remind the reader that the pomegranate (*rimon* in Hebrew) is one of the most common symbols of Persephone, the goddess of the world of the dead. The source of that association stems from the pinnacle of the mythological story: after a long search Demeter finds her daughter, who had been kidnapped by Hades and brought to his kingdom, and she seeks to bring her back to the world of the sun. Here it turns out that Persephone had eaten a fruit from the world of the dead, a pomegranate, and that fact binds her forever to the kingdom of Hades. The struggle between her mother and Hades ends in compromise: Persephone is to spend the winter months in Hades and return to her mother in the spring.[30] That possible link between the character of Rimona and that of Persephone explains Rimona's "death," her comparison to Petra, and the fact that she soothes everyone about her as though seeking to make them sleep in her bosom; it also explains her bond with her dead daughter (as the queen of the underworld, she rules over the souls of the dead).

That Yonatan finds life in Petra, the world of the dead, fits in well with the dual function of Persephone in Greek mythology. The goddess of the underworld is also the goddess of agriculture: the seeds that sprout in spring were "buried" in the earth beforehand. The dark and gloomy world, the realm of Hades, is not only a cold tomb, but it is also a womb producing new life. That dual role is merely another aspect of Rimona as a "sea" figure, and it is also responsible for the structure of the novel: the first part of the book is called "winter," in parallel with the period spent by Persephone in the gloomy kingdom of Hades, and the second part is called "spring." In fact Rimona, who miscarried her first fetus and later had a stillborn child, gives birth to a healthy baby in the second part of the novel, and even Yonatan returns from the dead with a treasure in his heart.

The function of Rimona-Persephone in the kingdom of the underworld and as the goddess of agriculture is also illuminated by her

---

30. The pomegranate is also a symbol of the unity of opposites embodied in the figure of Rimona: the pomegranate is the symbol of reconciliation of many and various powers within a single unity (Cirlot 1983, 261; Cooper 1984, 134).

being compared to the moon. In the thoughts of her husband, Rimona is connected to the moon (69, 332; 60, 323), and toward the end of the novel the narrator would seem to affirm that connection, although now it no longer represents death: "The freed nipple was elongated and dark like a finger and did not stop dripping. But on her rounded face a thin glow shone, like the nimbus around a full moon" (379; 372). The moon is the dwelling of the dead in various mythologies, and, like Persephone, it is responsible for the cycle of sprouting and withering, ebb and flow in the world.[31] Rimona, whose nipple reminds one of Persephone's horn of plenty, is the sea and the moon, the goddess of the underworld and of growth. Her figure thus represents the unity of opposites described in the novel: life and death are not eternal enemies. Winter is not absolute death, but prolonged pregnancy, the fruit of which is spring. It is a recurrent cycle in the world. There is no spring without winter or winter without summer and autumn.

## *Toward Mystic Union*

The "perfect peace" to which the title of the novel refers is the repose found by Yonatan and Azariah, each one separately and both together, and the perfect peace enjoyed by Rimona, uniting life and death in her being. The element of synthesis in the novel is emphasized by two other central means: the parallels among the various figures and the triads that populate the novel.

The technique of parallels is not applied only to the figures of Yonatan and Azariah. Most of the figures appearing in the novel are gripped by each other, if only partially. I do not refer to complete parallels here, such as that between Yonatan and Azariah, but to partial similarities pointing at traits common to various characters. Another central task of those parallels is to indicate the growing *unio mystica* between the main protagonists of the novel. Let us take a deep breath and try to point out the main features of that complex network of relations.[32]

---

31. It is no coincidence that the moon appears on the cover of the book. The moon as the dwelling place of the dead appears explicitly in the novel: " 'The winter will end,' said Rimona, 'then spring and summer will come. We'll go somewhere on vacation. Maybe to upper Galilee, or to the seashore. We'll sit on a balcony in the evening watching the stars come out or the full moon rise. Do you remember once telling me that the moon has a dark side where everyone goes when they die?' " (75; 66).

32. Some of the details in that network of connections have been mentioned by Gershon Shaked (1985).

The figure of Yonatan is connected, among others, to Yolek, his father, to Srulik, and to Rimona, and also to Trotsky and to the Bolognesi. Yolek, disappointed in Yonatan, points out the absolute contrast between them, but the author hints that the contrast is not complete. Let us mention several details linking father and son: both feel that something vital has been extinguished in them and gone cold (14, 119; 10, 108, and elsewhere); Yonatan harbors the wish "to get up and go before the time is up" (125; 113), and intuitively he knows that his father is driven by the same wish (148). The inspiring bond with the world experienced by Yonatan on his first morning in the desert reminds one of the religious experiences familiar to his father from his walks at night on the kibbutz (see Chapter 3 for a detailed discussion). The father and his son both suffer during the winter "from a slight allergy," and if that is insufficient, Yonatan's movements become similar to those of his father: "Tensing his neck, he thrust his head forward on the bias, a movement that resembled his father's attempts to hear" (75; 87; cf. 338; 331). Another figure from the generation of the founders to whom Yonatan is close is Srulik. Like Srulik he sees "pain and suffering everywhere he looks," and like him he sees that as a cruel practical joke (270; 258; cf. Srulik, 358; 349). Yonatan emphasizes that similarity by adopting Srulik's position according to which "our task is to reduce pain" (277; 266). Srulik, for his part, wonders "with what weapon can we repel these interior barren deserts within us?" (372; 363), like Yonatan who seeks redemption from the "desert waste" to which he is prey.

There is also a certain similarity between Yonatan and Rimona, his wife. Like her he "soothes" Azariah and asks him to rest (100; 90). Like her he understands that "you have to be good" (183, 228; 173, 216). And, like her, he wishes to belong to silence (181, 344; 172). Thus while living in the desert with the surveyor, one day he discovers to his surprise that his smile is "an exact replica of Rimona's, a woman who had been his wife," and unwittingly, he repeats her words, "Everything changes for the better" (350; 342). On the other hand Yonatan also has some of the traits of the Bolognesi, the repentant murderer, and of Benya Trotsky. His body size is, surprisingly, the size of the Bolognesi (22, 27; 16, 21), and he imitates his manner of speech on various occasions. He also compares himself explicitly to the Bolognesi and Trotsky from the angle of his murderousness (29; 23). Like Trotsky, Yonatan uses the name of Azuva, daughter of Shilhi (8, 145, 221; 5, 132, 209), and in his frequent memories of him he compares himself to him (63, 145, 286, 340; 56, 132, 275, 333). In the end Yonatan understands that Trotsky, like himself, found "the true heart" and thus he never hit anyone with his pistol. Oz did not feel his work was complete before creating a parallel even between Yonatan and his bitch: "As I was walking, something sprang out of darkness behind me, giving me quite a start. Is that you, Yonatan? But the something, which proceeded to trot in front of me, was only Tia, his German shepherd bitch" (327; 317); and Yonatan enjoys sitting without a thought in his head, "like Tia" (267; 254).

Azariah too is woven into a complex tissue of parallels. Various details hint at the possible affinity between him and Yolek, Srulik, Sasha Tlallim, Rimona, and also Trotsky and the Bolognesi. Like Srulik he is a "music lover," and like him abhors the hatred, cunning, and illnesses of Yolek and Eshkol (292, 314; 281, 304). Azariah is right, then, when he talks about Yolek confusing him with Srulik (45, 110; 37, 99), in emphasizing that he does not believe in "pure coincidence. Everything happens for a reason" (110; 99). Like Yolek, Azariah interprets Zionism as a process whose goal is "the reconciliation" of the Jewish people with its land (117, 212), and like Sasha Tlallim he interprets Yonatan's flight from the kibbutz as a "punishment" (337, 370; 329, 362). Azariah's fingers are long and delicate like those of Rimona (97; 88), and both of them are graced with never-failing intuition. The Bolognesi and Trotsky join the picture: on his first evening at the kibbutz, Azariah is sent to sleep in a room next to the Bolognesi's, and the next night Rimona gives him the coffee previously intended for his neighbor. Moreover, like Azariah, whose fate illustrates that of the persecuted Jewish people (278; 266 and elsewhere), the Bolognesi constantly mumbles verses concerning the suffering and redemption of the people. Like Trotsky, Azariah falls in love with another man's wife, and like him he is called vermin (193, 202; 181, 191). Of course Azariah, like Yonatan, also partakes of the vitality and serenity of the bitch, Tia (175–76; 164–65).

Rimona projects her personality upon those around her. I have mentioned the bonds increasingly joining her with her two husbands. In addition, one must mention the affinity created between her and Srulik, an affinity expressed in the deep understanding between them (232; 222), and also in their relation to silence: "And that up above the clouds, up above the air, all is quiet too, the quiet between the stars. And that beyond the last star is the last quiet of all" (181; 171–72). "The silence is hovering over the darkness—in the valleys, in the mountains, on the sea—mutely but insistently demanding a response from us all, man, dog, bird" (234; 224). In his journal Srulik even repeats what Rimona had said about the ancient urge to pursue the wild ox and kill it (371). It is impossible to mistake the similarity between her and Tia, Yonatan's bitch: both of them look "softly" at Yonatan (19, 31), and Tia receives all the adjectives used to characterize Rimona:

> Rimona put down her embroidery and rose to open the window to air out the smoke-filled room. Tia rose too, arched her back, and moved closer to the table, panting in short, rapid breaths ... her eyes glued on her master and her ears cocked forward, as if straining not to miss a word or a move. She was like a good and well-organized student trying with all her power to concentrate and make a good impression. (108; 97; cf. the descriptions of Rimona, 31, 33, 150; 25, 26, 135, and elsewhere)

Nor shall we neglect the place of the Bolognesi in this structure of parallels: "Rimona took a long look at him. With a diffident, delayed-action smile as though she has been asked a delicate or even dangerous question" (12; 8); "He spoke little with his feminine voice, as though careful always to respond with enormous caution to questions liable to confuse him or embarrass the questioner himself" (24; 18).

Let us now turn our attention from the triangle of Rimona and her two husbands to Yolek and Srulik. Yolek, Eshkol's enemy and friend, comes increasingly to resemble him. He uses the saying from the Ethics of the Fathers, "Judge not your friend until you have been in his place," which he had been in the habit of reciting to Eshkol (162; 148), and in his letter to the Prime Minister he points out that both of them are afflicted by an evil spirit at the time (163), and both of them are reprobates (164) who received no pleasure from their children (166; 153). Azariah, looking at them during Eshkol's visit to the kibbutz, also senses the similarity between them (289, 293; 279, 281). As expected of a religious malefactor, a "murderer" like Yolek, there are also similarities with the Bolognesi, with Trotsky, and even with Sasha Tlallim. In her anger Hava compares her husband to the Bolognesi (198; 186), and that very night Yolek extends the comparison, as it were; "Yes, even before the evildoer, some gate ought to open. Like that Bolognesi man who was a cruel killer and now he's repented and sits and knits sweaters" (205). In the end Hava's "wishes" nearly come true and the Bolognesi comes and teaches Yolek how to knit (although Yolek soon tires of that work). In his letter to Trotsky Yolek curses him vociferously and sees him as a symbol of the "poisonous cancer in the body of the Jewish people for generations" (202; 191). Behind Yolek's back the narrator points out the similarity between him and the man he hates. Like Azariah and Yonatan, Na'ama's two fathers,

Trotsky and Yolek are Yonatan's fathers: Hava does not tell Yolek whether he or Trotsky is Yonatan's true father, and to himself Yonatan calls Trotsky "his second father" (145; 132). Let us also recall that, like Trotsky, who fell in love with Hava "against all his principles" (84), Yolek wishes to treat his grandchildren in a way that goes "against all principles" (204; 193). Another aspect of Yolek is illustrated by the comparison with Sasha Tlallim: both of them are "Tolstoyan" figures (203, 280; 191, 268), and both of them make fun of Yonatan, calling him a "philosopher" (167, 341; 155, 334).

Srulik, who abhors Yolek's cruelty and cunning, ultimately replaces him as the Secretary of the kibbutz, discovering within himself the love of power and honor that had characterized Yolek (372–75; 364). On the other hand he longs for a "caress" (232; 222), just like Yolek walking about at night in the kibbutz courtyard (204; 193). I have already discussed the complex of relationships between Srulik and Azariah, Yonatan, and Rimona. Some similarity also exists between him and the Bolognesi. Late at night, when the entire kibbutz is asleep, only those two are awake, and Srulik points out: "No doubt he's sitting like me, muttering his charms and incantations" (326; 316). In the course of that night he again compares himself to the Bolognesi: "Some day, when all this is only a memory, I'll ask Hava to have Bolognesi over to my place for tea. No good can come of such solitude. No good has come from my thousands of lonely nights of flute playing and journal keeping" (328; 318).

This short survey shows that in the tissue of themes and motives in the novel the secondary characters play a role far more important than their function in the plot. All the main characters share some of the identifying traits of the Bolognesi. To the figures related to Trotsky (Yonatan, Azariah, and Yolek) must be added She'altiel ha-Palti and Hava, who also try to use a pistol to solve their problems (121, 240; 110, 229). I have mentioned the similarity between Trotsky and Sasha Tlallim above: the old parabellum pistol like the one Trotsky shot at Hava and Yolek is discovered in Sasha Tlallim's caravan, and Yonatan links the two in their advocacy of life. Sasha Tlallim has some of Yolek's features and has, as noted, something of Azariah and Trotsky, and even of Eshkol and the Bolognesi: like the Prime Minister who keeps calling Rimona "krasavitsa" (lovely girl, 295; 284), Tlallim calls Yonatan "krasavits" (335; 327); the stench of garlic and alcohol arising from him (338; 330) is also an echo of the arak wafting from the Bolognesi's mouth (23; 18).

Without doubt, then, a central technique in this novel is that of erecting parallels, gradually binding together all the characters. It seems to me that two different but connected purposes must be attributed to that complex network of parallels: first, it shows that people are not made of a whole cloth. Everyone has something of the Bolognesi ("Each one of us is a bit of a murderer," as Srulik writes in his diary [381; 374]), of Trotsky, of Azariah, and of Srulik. All the main characters, upon various occasions, are compared to a "child" and to a "murderer," two of the most common terms of comparison in the novel. Thus, everyone aspires to break out of the framework to which he is subject, and at the same time, to strengthen and adopt it, everyone embraces both the stars and the dust, sanctity and sin, life and death. Second, that structure of parallels in which every character is somewhat similar to others creates a kind of circle (in the context of the kibbutz and of the mysteries: a circle of dancers), in which everyone exists for himself but is bound to two other figures and takes part in the experience of the whole circle. From the citations and page numbers given above one finds that the structure of parallels is built up gradually, reaching its climax in the concluding chapters of the novel. The main protagonists gradually achieve "perfect peace," the apogee of which is a kind of *unio mystica*. That phenomenon clearly characterizes Yonatan and Azariah, and it also exists, but with less force, for the other characters. The characters all mingle with one another, and thus they mix within themselves the sparks of sanctity and sin.

## A Perfect Peace: The Holy Trinity

Another central means that sheds light on the process of synthesis in *A Perfect Peace* is the human trinities within it. Some of the trinities in the novel were disbanded while still in embryo (Hava-Yolek-Trotsky), and others achieved full life (Rimona-Yonatan-Azariah). Some of the trinities moved from potential to actual existence (the central trinities mentioned above are emphasized by those created by the secondary characters, Eitan R. and his two girlfriends, and others), and some remain merely potential (Srulik, in love with P., never opens his heart to her). In addition to the aforementioned trios, all of which are variations of bonds between men and women, we must add the trinity created by Yolek and his two "sons," Yonatan and Azariah. These triads fit in well with the traditional meanings of the number three, a number standing for both multiplicity and unity at the same time. The wholeness of that number, unlike that of number one, is not obtained by virtue of uniqueness and unity of a phenomenon but rather by virtue of a process of synthesis that exists among rival forces. The synthesis implied by that number is not a static situation but a dynamic equilibrium attained by the several actions exerted upon the powers struggling with one another (de Vries 1981, 363–64; Cooper 1984, 114). It is the number of the self, in which the conscious and the unconscious parts of the soul live together, struggling and reintegrating (Jung 1958, 391).

In his article on Berdyczewski Oz differentiated, as noted, between "primary" experiences, the cost of which is madness or death, and "secondary" experiences, barren and lacking life. All of Oz's protagonists, as we have seen more than once, vacillate between a secure, pallid, and arid existence within the borders of human society, and strong, tempestuous experiences that entail, without exception, breaking the social framework and threatening its very existence. The trinity is the solution Oz found to that vacillation. In the novel under discussion it represents life both within and outside the framework. It is the pattern of a couple taking in a third figure, a stranger. The third person necessarily brings struggle and tension—both in his disruption of the equilibrium of the pair, and also in the strange, dark characteristics he bears with him—but he also preserves the vitality and fertility of the framework. The one who bursts through the framework assures its wholeness. In that sense the number three represents "the true heart": life within a social framework without giving up the movements of the heart, the desires that are inconsistent with the demands of social morality.

The number three is, as noted, the number of the "self." It is thus no wonder that the only trinities that were actualized in the novel have Yonatan and Azariah as two of their members (Yolek-Yonatan-Azariah; Rimona-Yonatan-Azariah), the two characters who attained, each in his own way, individuation. The number three recalls the Holy Trinity. That possible connection is no coincidence. In Chapter 3 we saw that certain details link Yonatan and Azariah with Jesus, and that Rimona is depicted as "angelic," and her beauty as "Christian." The Holy Trinity is composed of three personae, the Father, the Son, and the Holy Spirit, which create a single entity of one God. Several aspects of that theological conception are important for understanding the triads in *A Perfect Peace*: the fact that each of the personae exists as an entity in its own right while, at the same time, the three make up a total unity; the connection implied between God and man (Jesus was born to Mary by the Holy Spirit, and he has both divine and human nature; Jesus is constantly present among his believers, and he guides them through the Holy Spirit); the tension between sin and redemption (man as a creature imbued with sin, on the one hand, and the possibility of redemption by God, on the other).[33] In contrast to "Before His Time," *A Perfect Peace* does not reject the possibility of redemption (see Chapter 2). However, that redemption does not mean freedom from sin and base drives, but rather the achievement of an equilibrium and harmony among all the components of one's psyche.[34]

The trinity is thus the number of the "true heart," of individuation, and thus it also represents the image of God that the main characters of this novel discover within themselves. The trinity, symbolizing both life within a framework and the bursting out of that framework, at the same time symbolizes life and the underworld, as well as heaven and earth.

## *Black Box: Between Helen and Hermes*

On the surface, no sign of the synthesis achieved in *A Perfect Peace* is found in *Black Box*. The war between the sexes is waged unchecked in *Black Box*, and, like Hannah Gonen *(My Michael)*, Ilana is torn between forces that exclude each other. And yet, the same process of mystic union, depicted in the final chapters of *A Perfect Peace*, is hinted at in *Black Box* as well: despite the bitter contradictions between the main characters, they long to merge with each other.

The differences in mentalities as well as jealousy and mutual suspicions do not seemingly leave any room for reconciliation between Ilana's two husbands. Michel sees Alexander as "a confirmed evildoer and rogue imbued with the spirit of Belial" (185; 208), and he asks him bitterly: "Are you a Jew or are you an Amalekite? Are you a human

---

33. On the tenets of Christian dogma and their consolidation, see Lonergan (1976) and Rusch (1980).
34. That dialectic meaning of the trinity is emphasized by Jung:
> The trinity is an archetype whose dominating power not only fosters spiritual development but may, on occasion, actually enforce it. But as soon as the spiritualization of the mind threatens to become so one-sided as to be deleterious to health, the compensatory significance of the Trinity necessarily recedes into the background. Good does not become better by being exaggerated, but worse, and a small evil becomes a big one through being disregarded and repressed. The shadow is very much a part of human nature, and it is only at night that no shadows exist. (1958, 193)

True to his system, Jung emphasizes that Jesus is the symbol of the self, and he sees the Holy Trinity as a demonstration of the process of individuation (ibid.).

being created in G-d's image, or are you, Heaven forbid, some kind of a demon?" (ibid.). He wants him to suffer (190; 215) and for a moment he even thinks of killing him (187; 210). Alexander, for his part, sees Michel as an incorrigible zealot, inferior to his own intellectual caliber: "You irritate like a mosquito. You have nothing new to offer me. I have long since finished with your sort and turned to more complex types. Take the money and run well out of my range" (204; 230). Nevertheless, along with the mistrust and mutual accusations, an entirely different kind of relation is established between the two. First of all, they are analogical to each other by the very fact that both of them married Ilana. Indeed, when he lives with Ilana and with Boaz, Alexander mentions to Ilana that, after all, she is Michel's legitimate wife and begs her not to neglect that role (223; 251). Second, both of them serve as Boaz's fathers and Boaz is likened to both of them. The analogy between them has interesting language aspects. Both of them ask each other to treat Ilana "graciously," and both use the same Hebrew allusions. "A lover who knows neither laughter nor levity is getting closer and closer to you," Alexander warns Ilana (85; 92), and Michel uses the same allusion to God in his letter to Alexander: "It would be better for you not to forget that there is One Who dispenses retribution to the arrogant, One before Whom there is neither laughter nor levity" (186; 209).

Moreover, Alexander bequeaths his assets to Michel, as if Michel were his offspring (213; 240), and he describes the money he is sending to Michel as a blood transfusion (84; 90). The affinity between money and blood is highly important in the novel. The author does not let the reader forget that the word *damim* in Hebrew means both blood and money (28; 24). Thus Alexander's and Michel's blood is merged into one, and this blood unites with Ilana's and Boaz's blood, who also enjoy Alexander's money (blood). The same process typifies, as we shall see later, the plot of the novel.

It turns out that, while they exchange blame and terms of abuse, there exists mutual appreciation between Michel and Alexander. Importantly, they wish to exchange places and even to blend with each other. Michel tells how much he used to admire military men such as Alexander in his youth (187; 211), and Ilana palpably senses his desire to merge with both Alexander and herself (229; 259). Alexander himself admits that Michel is a "better man" than he is; he learns to appreciate his "excellent qualities," and develops "a certain esteem" for him (194; 219). Reading Michel's complaints, Alexander answers that, if he had more time left, he would have tried to take Michel's job at the cinema, and adds: "Would you like to change places with me,

Mr. Sommo?" (197; 222). Through the harsh complaints that are included in Michel's last letter to him, Alexander senses the deep closeness between the two of them, and his answering letter expresses this affinity, in its content as well as in its details. This is Alexander's most detailed and most intimate letter, in which he tells about his family and childhood for the first time, and it is concluded in a tone of great closeness.

The main characters' yearning for a state of conciliation is expressed by the invitations they send to each other. Michel invites Alexander and Boaz to his place, and hopes to convince his rabbi that Ilana should be allowed to join them as well. For their part, Boaz, Ilana, and Alexander, each of them in turn, urge Michel to join Boaz's commune where they are all staying. In her last letter to Michel, Ilana longingly describes her previous life with him, and hints that she might return to him in the future (221; 249). She finishes her letter emphasizing that she is waiting for him. Upon his coming, the wife and her two husbands will be able to join together: "When you desire me I'll attach myself to you and his fingers will slide over our backs. Or you can attach yourself to him and I'll caress the two of you. As you have always yearned to do: to be joined to him and to me. To be joined in him to me, in me to him. For the three of us to be one" (229; 259). This sought-after union will make the three of them a part of the cosmos itself: "For then from without, from the darkness, through the cracks in the shutter shall come wind and rain, sea, clouds, stars, to close in silently on the three of us" (ibid.). Michel's answer is quick to arrive: "Thus is written in the psalm, 'Bless the Lord, O my Soul' [Psalm 103]: 'The Lord is merciful and gracious, slow to anger and plenteous in mercy. He will not always chide: neither will he keep his anger forever" (230; 259). Citing Psalm 103, one of the most forceful expressions of God's grace and mercy in Psalms, Michel hints that he might also forgive Ilana for having left him.

Elements of reconciliation and synthesis are also found in the relationship between Ilana and Alexander, and to a greater extent in the character of their son, Boaz. As noted in the previous chapter, Ilana and Alexander characterize each other as a demon, a monster, and a predatory animal. Yet the psychological concept expressed in the novel follows the idea that the origin of the war between the sexes lies in the fact that the beloved represents the deepest psychic layers, those which are the polar opposite of one's conscious life. Thus, the stronger the attraction, the stronger the rejection. Alexander's letters imply that closeness and reconciliation are possible only when his hatred and evil powers are weakened (213; 240 and elsewhere). Yet that weakening means old age, ailment, and death. In *Black Box*, a synthesis between the sexes is possible only in the shadow of a pending death.

Still, the novel hints at another possibility. Alexander was raised in a mansion in Zikhron Yaakov. Since he is living abroad and his father is staying in a mental hospital, the mansion has been completely neglected. In order to find a place and a purpose in life for his son, Boaz, Alexander asks him to take care of the neglected asset. Suffering from cancer, Alexander returns to Israel to live with his son in the house of his childhood. When he arrives at the house he finds out that Ilana, who had left her husband, also lives there. Alexander's new encounter with Ilana, in Alexander's "palace" of childhood, takes place with the legend of Beauty and the Beast in the background. Alexander himself alludes to this legend ("Stories of Beauty and the Beast," 62; 65); indeed, Ilana is repeatedly described as a beautiful woman, whereas Alexander is depicted as a monster and a beast. According to the legend, to save her father's life, Beauty volunteers to live with the Beast in the palace, where she comes to know the generous and noble character of the ugly creature. When vacationing out of the palace, she hears that the Beast is fatally ill. She hurries back to the palace to find the Beast dying, but her grief and love suddenly breaks the Beast's terrible spell. The handsome prince is liberated from his beastly form; healthy and very much in love, he is ready to marry Beauty. Can Ilana's love perform the same miracle? The novel does not give an unequivocal answer. True, Alexander has been changed since his arrival. He does not ignore his feelings anymore, and, contrary to his previous behavior, he tries to communicate with the people around him: "Attentiveness and hesitancy characterize my present relationship with those around me (even though I am not certain that they are aware of it). If only there were more time left, I might suggest that you and I should try to meet someday and see each other from roughly the same height" (195; 219–20). On the other hand, this new attitude is an expression of Alexander's weakness, the weakening of the snake and the wolf in him, and Alexander knows well that he does not have time to set things right. It seems that the synthesis in the relation between Ilana and Alexander is achieved too late. A more complete example of synthesis is embodied by their son, Boaz.

In the first letter to her first husband, Ilana underlines Boaz's similarity to Alexander (7, 8, 9; 1, 2, 3). Like Alexander, Boaz is a "monster" (9; 4), and like him he is an aggressive loner. Throughout the novel, this analogy is enhanced by their pantherlike walk (144, 194;

160, 224), their aggression toward authoritative figures (47, 211; 46, 238), and their slow, seemingly apathetic tone of voice. Ilana thinks of "the tragic similarity" between the two of them (61; 63), and writes to Alexander: "this child is you" (75; 80).

Yet the similarity between father and son is partial only. Unlike his father, Boaz does not ignore his emotions and does not become a dragon and a demon. Like some of Oz's previous protagonists, Boaz reaches inner harmony not by accepting societal regulations, but rather after breaking through the familial and societal frameworks and checking the nature of existence beyond their borders. Apparently, first he goes from bad to worse: he is thrown out of his school for misbehavior, detained for possessing stolen goods, and after beating his boss he finds refuge in the Sinai desert and works on a ship. Like Yonatan Lifshitz in *A Perfect Peace*, Boaz is reconciled with himself and with his world only after shattering the borders and rules of family and society. Upon returning from the sea and the desert he is not like his father only, but like his mother as well. Watching him after returning to Israel, Alexander attests: "Despite his physical size I do not find him at all reminiscent of my father, who was thick and bearlike. But, rather, somehow, of Ilana. Perhaps in the softness of his voice. Or his long, supple strides. Or his drowsy smiles, which strike me as childish and shrewd at the same time" (199; 224–25).

As in his previous works, Oz employs major alchemical symbols in *Black Box*. Whereas Alexander is characterized by mercury (in alchemy, the *prima materia* of the world), Boaz is depicted in terms of gold, the symbol of a complete balance between all the metals, the symbol of enlightenment and redemption. Back from the desert, Ilana sees him as "Bedouin Viking, sun-scorched, smelling of sea and dust, his shoulder-length hair white-hot, like burnished gold" (74; 79). Alexander also describes his son's golden hair, comparing him to another figure who symbolizes the unity of opposites: "His dull golden hair descends in waves to his shoulders. His soft blond beard, his half-closed eyes, his lips, which do not close but hang slightly open, all give him the look of Jesus in a Scandinavian icon" (199; 224). Later on he tells Michel that "some enamored girl has painted over an entire wall the image of Boaz, naked and radiant, striding with closed eyes over a calm patch of water" (202; 228).

Boaz's adventures, his aggressiveness and his frequent complications with the law, imply that holiness is not conceived of in *Black Box* as fulfilling one side of life (purity, sublimation, ignoring the bodily and the earthy). On the contrary, holiness is achieved by turning the opposing elements of life into a fruitful, reconciled unity of opposites.

Jesus symbolized this synthesis in Oz's earlier novel, *A Perfect Peace* (cf. Yonatan and Azariah). As noted in previous chapters, Jung repeatedly argues that Jesus is a symbol of the Self, the psychic harmony comprehending all contradictions. The peacock in Boaz's yard (170, 226; 191, 254, and elsewhere) is another symbol of the synthesis that Boaz has reached, both as a symbol of Jesus and as a symbol of the totality in which all colors are blended (de Vries 1981, 360). The tortoise Boaz received in his childhood (62; 65), and the tortoise he finds in his yard and gives to his sister (210, 213; 236, 240), is another illustration of the union of opposites embodied in Boaz. As mentioned above in the discussion of Yonatan Lifshitz's character, because of its shape the tortoise is a traditional symbol of sky and earth, female and male.

Unlike his father, Boaz is not an intellectual, not a man of words and theories. Time and again he reprimands his mother for her tendency to pour out her heart in words, and suggests that she choose some job. Boaz is "Mowgli the wolf boy; Tarzan king of the jungle" (124; 137). He settles down in the "jungle" his father gave him, not in order to live there like a wild man, but rather, to restore the place and to turn it into a blossoming (vegetable) garden. His faulty spelling well exemplifies the fact that he is not a man of words and that he lives inside and outside societal borders at one and the same time. In this sense, Boaz is the complete opposite of his father. Whereas Alexander is afraid of his feelings and cultivates his intellectual faculty only, Boaz does not sever himself from his roots and lives peacefully with the wild forces in him. Thus, Alexander turns into a monster, a snake, and a demon, whereas Boaz gains an element of holiness. Interestingly, Alexander, after he has reconciled with himself and with those around him, is likened to a "Scandinavian village pastor, on his face a strange mixture of mortification, meditation and irony" (226; 256).

The fact that Boaz is completely anchored in his time and place and, unlike his mother, is not captivated by dreams and fantasies, is conveyed by the character he gives to the house he restores. He does not try to reconstruct the melancholic splendor of the house, with the exotic flowers his grandfather ordered from the Far East. The beds of rare roses are replaced by beds of vegetables, the glorious tiles, by plain cement, and the goldfish, by carp (196; 220). The authentic, aboriginal nature of Boaz's commune is implied by its comparison to an Arab village (199, 226; 225, 255, and elsewhere).

Returning home from the desert, Boaz has a clear-cut worldview. This is how Ilana formulates her son's Ten Commandments: "I. Pity them all. II. Take more notice of the stars. III. Against being bitter.

IV. Against making fun. V. Against hating. VI. Bastards are still human beings, not shit. VII. Against beating up. VIII. Against killing. IX. Not to eat each other. X. Cool it" (143; 158). In the agricultural high school where he studies, Boaz is a complete copy of his father: "a bitter, wild boy whose hatred and loneliness have invested him with astonishing physical strength" (9; 4). Yet when he returns from his adventures in the Sinai desert, he is against hatred and against being bitter. Unlike his father, he does not create any barrier among people. Even bastards have room in his "state." With his physical strength he could have become a typical "hero," yet he channels his strength to restoring the neglected house he has received; now he is against aggression (128; 141) and the army will have to give up his good services (129; 142). Reporting about Boaz's Ten Commandments, Ilana correctly tells her first husband that "these halting words are the exact opposite of you" (143; 159).

At one and the same time Boaz is also "the exact opposite" of Ilana. Ilana cannot put up with reality; vacillating "between fire and ash" she longs for "something that doesn't and can't exist." Boaz accepts reality without complaints and does not yearn for other places and times. In this sense Boaz is the polar opposite of Ilana and her two husbands. In his letter to Michel, Alexander argues:

> What is the obsession with redemption? Only a mask for a complete absence of the basic talent for life. This is a talent that every cat is endowed with. Whereas we, like the whales that dash themselves against the shore in an impulse to mass suicide, suffer from an advanced degeneration of the talent for life. Hence the popular urge to destroy and annihilate what we have so as to hack a path to regions of redemption that have never existed and are not even possible. (205; 231)

Alexander himself is severed from the vital flow of life, and eventually asks "not to exist at all. To cancel my presence retroactively. To make it so that I am not born" (202; 227). Ilana turns her back on the family she had created with Michel, and, like Alexander, all she wants in the end is to disappear: "What is there left for me except to accompany my obsession to his grave? And then to disappear. Not to exist" (225; 254). Michel also finally discovers that he is left empty-handed, and, at least for a moment, he hopes for death (187; 210). Boaz is smart enough to realize that the difference between him and his three parents lies in their attitudes toward life: "Take you and your husbands for instance. Not one of the three of you knows what it means to really live. You just fuss all the time instead of doing something. Including that saint and his mates from the territories. You're living off the Bible, living off politics, living off speeches and arguments, instead of living off life" (128–29; 141).

In this issue also one can discern the element of synthesis in Boaz's character. Although he is now "only in favor of working and taking it easy" (ibid.), he does not approve of focusing on the individual and his needs only. Much to her surprise, Ilana learns from him that he is a Zionist: "A Zionist. Wanting everyone to be okay. And for everyone to do just a little for the country, even something really tiny, just half an hour a day so they can feel good and know that they're still needed" (ibid.). One's contribution to society is not expected to be a sacrifice or to take over all his activities. This contribution cultivates the bond between someone and his society, gives that person a sense of meaning, and prevents alienation.

Boaz is conceived of by those around him as a noble savage and as Jesus. Yet the author is far from idealizing his character. He rules the young men and women of his commune like a feudal lord, and in this sense he is a direct continuation of his father and grandfather. Like them he actually does not know the meaning of love. He endows his sexual graciousness to the women on his commune equally, but he does not have a meaningful relationship with any of them. He proudly tells his mother about his "fucks," but when she asks him if he has ever loved, it turns out that he loved only her and Alexander (128; 141). Furthermore, his concepts and behavior are, to a large extent, a continuation of his mother's romantic longings. Not incidentally she admires him and comes to live with him. His Tolstoyan worldview might fit the small commune he manages, but it is far from answering the needs of the whole society.

## *Michel: A Human Diamond*

Most Israeli critics have described Ilana's second husband, Michel Sommo, as a right-wing fanatic, citing descriptions made of him by Alexander's lawyer, Manfred Zakheim, and by Alexander himself. Yet, one should bear in mind that one of the most interesting facets of the novel is the degree of reliability that can be granted to each of the characters. Thus, for example, Ilana starts the correspondence with Alexander, pretending to be concerned about their son, yet later on she admits that she had employed Boaz's story as a pretext only. Each one of the letter-writers has his or her own motives and biases, and the reader cannot take their observations at face value. Needless to say, Zakheim wants to prevent any connection between his rich client, Alexander, and Michel; knowing Alexander's political views he intentionally depicts Michel as far more fanatic than he really is. Alexander, for his part, has never met Michel; he knows him mainly through Zakheim's biased letters. As is the case in Oz's previous works, the attitude of the implied author of the novel is conveyed through implicit analogies and confrontations between the main characters. On the surface, there is nothing in common between Michel, the soft-spoken, polite, and ruthless fanatic (23; 20), and Boaz, who carries the banner of "live and let live." Implicitly, it turns out that, for better or worse, there is an element of similarity between the two.

No doubt, Michel's character is much more complex and balanced than the figure portrayed in the letters of Zakheim and Alexander. First of all, being "a human diamond," as Ilana puts it (15; 10), Michel may embody the treasure Ilana desperately seeks. Several descriptions of him reveal a strong element of synthesis. Watching him cuddling their daughter and folding her inside his sweater, Ilana imagines that he had been pregnant with her (222; 250). Indeed, at home he fulfills the traditional role of a wife and a mother, and he is the one who protects the wholeness of the family framework (see, for example, 19–20, 39, 141–42; 15–16, 38, 156–67). The Arab existence is conceived of in the novel as a rooted, authentic, sought-after existence (74; 78; see also the frequent comparisons of Boaz's commune to an Arab village). Born in Algeria, Michel is both an Arab and a Jew. He keeps complaining that in Paris people considered him an Arab, and Ilana enjoys studying "his strange family songs, tunes in which guttural joy almost verged upon wailing" (111; 121).

This element of synthesis explains the analogy between Michel and Boaz. Apparently, Boaz, the Sabra, the high, strong, and handsome savage, who mocks religion and its regulations, is poles apart from Michel, the short newcomer, who espouses Judaism and its commandments. Yet several elements create an implied analogy between the two. Thus, for example, just like Boaz, Michel is compared to Jesus (28; 24), and like him he suffers from a kidney disease (12, 34; 6, 32). Not incidentally, the two of them appreciate each other, and after a short period of tension they learn to know and like each other.

Unlike Ilana, who cannot put up with her reality and is caught in the frustrating pendulum between fire and ash (see above), Michel happily accepts his responsibilities as a husband and a father, and, at least as a family member, he embraces the here and now without any reservations. Typically, Oz does not create a one-dimensional character. In the political arena, Michel is a different person altogether. In the early 1970s he is among the founders of a right-wing group whose aim is to buy territories on the West Bank and to vacate Eretz Israel from its Arab inhabitants by offering them money for leaving. Thus, Ilana's personal tension between reality and some dreamed-about world that cannot be reached takes a political nature in Michel's character. Referring to Michel's offer to pay the Arabs for leaving their homes, Zakheim mocks him: "To finance this migration we would have to sell the whole of the state, and would still be in debt. Is it really worth selling the State of Israel to buy the Territories?" (97; 104–5). This ironic answer is materialized later on, when Michel and his group get a piece of land west of Bethlehem in exchange for a piece of land inside the Green Line. As noted, Michel's political activity is analogous to Ilana's inability to accept reality. And yet, unlike Ilana, who vacillates between two options that destroy each other, Michel wants to keep both Israel and the West Bank. One can argue, like Zakheim, that Michel's activity might jeopardize the existence of Israel even within its 1948 borders, but surely Michel does not think so, and surely he is not interested in such a result.

Michel, then, is not exactly the fanatic believer described by Zakheim and Alexander. Nor does he represent Oz's unfavorable attitude toward the Sephardim, as some Israeli critics have claimed. On the contrary, according to the inner code of *Black Box* and of Oz's work in its entirety, he has some clearly favorable features. Unlike Ilana and Alexander, he calmly fulfills his own duties, as husband and father, and the unity of opposites embodied in his character protects him from the emotional imbalance of these two. Depressed as he is after losing his wife and daughter, he resists his family's advice to go to the police in order to get his daughter back, and prefers to address Alexander directly. After reading Alexander's letter, Michel asks him to forgive him "for the harsh and unnecessary insults" he had cast at him (214; 242), urges him to receive the appropriate treatment at Hasassah Hospital, and invites Alexander and Boaz to stay with him in his house. His last letter to Ilana implies that he is ready to forgive her as well.[35]

---

35. In an article published at the time *Black Box* was published (1987c), Oz argued that the most interesting phenomenon in the last two decades in Israel has been the appearance of a new Sephardic middle class. He claimed that this new class, which already holds the key to any important political decision, has synthesized eastern and western values, as well as secular and religious options. This class is politically hawkish,

From the start, Amos Oz's work is typified by a sharp confrontation between heaven and earth, God and Satan. Upon close examination of this conflict we have found that the grappling forces hide within themselves elements of their bitter rivals. In fact, the struggle takes place between heaven-earth and earth-heaven, or between God-Satan and Satan-God. In this struggle neither side strives to totally subdue its enemy. Oz's protagonist seeks to join his opponent and to be redeemed through him. The way to tranquillity, the way to light, passes through utter darkness. This line of synthesis stretches throughout the course of Oz's literary career. From his first story, "A Crack Open to the Wind," in which the protagonist is able to mend his house only after he comes to terms with the jackal within himself, to his latest novel, all his main characters take pains to reach a peaceful, fruitful agreement between their opposing elements. In many of his books the struggle ends with the discovery of the longed-for unity of opposites. Yet because of the contradicting features of the forces that the protagonists try to unite, that unity can only be temporary, a springboard for a renewed struggle and a new book. Fending off his jackals and trying to live peacefully with them, Oz has contributed to modern Hebrew fiction one of its most complex and spellbinding chapters.

---

yet it rejects messianic fanaticism. Without a doubt, Michel Sommo is a representative of that class.

# APPENDIX
## On the Structure of *Where the Jackals Howl*

Oz's first collection of stories, *Where the Jackals Howl* (1965), was greeted enthusiastically by the critics when it first appeared, and its young author was acknowledged as one of the most prominent representatives of the "new wave" in Hebrew fiction. The nine stories included in the book were interpreted in the early critical reviews, and most of them have also been studied in later, individual articles. Nevertheless, critics missed one of the most important and most interesting keys to understanding the stories.

When one notes the many links among the stories in *Where the Jackals Howl*, it becomes clear that Oz wrote them as a single unit whose parts are all interconnected. Oz did not intend for each of the stories to stand by itself, which is the usual practice, but rather sought to write a book in which all the stories would become part of a single, unified structure. That unified structure was achieved through the subjects of the stories as well as by many reciprocal connections that shed light on their respective meaning.

In the course of that process the first stories became the foundation upon which the later ones were built. The symbols forged in the early stories appear in the following ones, to be interpreted in light of their earlier contexts. In many cases the reciprocal connections among the

---

This appendix first appeared in Hebrew in *Ma'ariv*, May 5, 1984.

stories provide the key for understanding them. Thus, for example, in "The Trappist Monastery," the shots fired in the Israeli retaliatory raid against the Jordanian village are compared to orchestral music: " 'The orchestra is tuning up. Those are the sounds before the start,' Nahum said with forced cleverness as the isolated volleys fell silent" (82). Describing the battle, the narrator adds:

> Gradually the sounds of battle evened out and submitted to a rhythm which was wild but subject to strict harmony. . . . The shriek of mad strings played its part and then fell silent behind the pounding of the unsettled drums. A joyful whirlwind of percussion instruments went wild, and the whine of mournful violins burbled below all the other sounds, submissively obeying the dictates of the hidden conductor. Finally the orchestra fell into disarray and split apart in precise tempo. (83)

In the context of this story, that metaphorical description reflects the way the author conceives of warfare, with its manifest and latent motivations (see Chapter 5). Yet we find the very same metaphor in "Before His Time," which is placed before "The Trappist Monastery" in the volume, giving the description just cited new and unexpected meaning. "A distant jackal emitted a broken grinding noise, like the concertmaster playing first to tune his comrades' strings" (65). That metaphor attracts one's attention to other similarities between the cited description of the battle and the jackals in "Before His Time" (62, 64).[1] The metaphor, beginning in one story and developing in the following one, juxtaposes the howling of the jackals and the noises of the battle between the Israeli soldiers and the Jordanians. The meaning of that confrontation, indirectly supporting the author's views regarding the causes of war, is clarified, as noted, only when one has perceived the structural principle binding the stories into a single unit. That example and dozens of similar ones show that Oz did not work on each individual story by itself, but that he had a single pattern in mind, in which the stories fit according to a predetermined thematic process, and in which they are interwoven, shed light on one other, and support one other.

In order to bring out that structural principle I shall first describe the connection between the first two stories of the book, "Where the Jackals Howl" and "Nomad and Viper."

---

1. The paragraph quoted here also calls to mind the descriptions of the jackals in the first story, "Where the Jackals Howl."

## Between Galila and Geula

"Where the Jackals Howl" (first printed in *Keshet*, January 1963) was preceded by "Before His Time" and "The Trappist Monastery." Nevertheless, Oz had good reasons for beginning the collection with it. This story presents the main components of the author's worldview in a well worked-out fashion, and it can be read as a sort of dictionary of his symbols. In its center is the encounter between Matityahu Damkov, a refugee who came to the kibbutz toward the end of World War II and remained there in isolation, and Galila, the sixteen-year-old daughter of Sashka and Tanya, who were among the founders of the kibbutz. The story depicts the vitality of nature as opposed to any fixed, limiting, petrified framework. It is the vitality of a cruel and evil beast: at night the kibbutz lands relapse into their primal, natural state, and they are described as nocturnal beasts of prey (16). This aspect was reinforced in the revised version of the story. The inanimate objects that come back to life at night are also enriched by a "cold and rustling tremor, a poisonous tremor" (14). The world of nature is symbolized by the jackals, by their riotous evil; "the lands of the jackals" (the literal translation of the Hebrew title) are natural realms in which eternal, undisturbed darkness reigns. This characteristic of the natural world gives rise to uninterrupted battle between that world and culture. Every fragment of culture is like a piece of land wrested from nature by force, and nature seeks to regain it and take vengeance upon the invaders. This process is portrayed by metaphors of a struggle between kingdoms, between bitter enemies. That struggle reaches its climax in Damkov's vision, in which masses of black, apelike people descend from the mountain and completely eradicate the culture that has been created between the mountains and the sea.

Damkov, the protagonist of the story, is indirectly shown to be the representative of the "lands of the jackals." As noted in previous chapters, he is analogous to an ape, a jackal, and a horse in heat. In the center of the plot is his meeting with Galila, a daughter of the kibbutz. Damkov has initiated this meeting with the intention to tell the girl that he is her true father (see Chapters 3 and 4).

"Nomad and Viper" also takes place against the background of the kibbutz, but its plot is entirely different. Here we have the fatal encounter between Geula, born on the kibbutz, and a bedouin nomad who brings his herd of goats into the kibbutz orchards. At one point, the nomad lets Geula know that he desires her, but when she responds to him he gets up and flees. Upon her return to the kibbutz Geula hallucinates the rape that the nomad supposedly committed against her. At the same time an enormous yearning to become part of the alien, dark, and liberated world of the nomad is awakened within her. As she is lying on a flower bed, she is bitten by a snake that is implicitly described as an analogue of the bedouin, completing what the nomad had begun but not finished.

Thus, the plot would seem to be entirely different from that of "Where the Jackals Howl." Nevertheless, dozens of details link the two stories. First, in both of them we find the encounter between a daughter of the kibbutz and a man who represents the world of nature, a man whose ugliness has something fascinating about it, and in both stories the kibbutz girl is overwhelmed by his charm. The women, who even have similar names (Galila and Geula), respond with desire to the concealed courtship of the man, violating a rigid social taboo that they were trained to observe, indicating the power of the frustration entailed by social life with its frameworks and prohibitions.

The struggle between nature and culture is presented in both stories, among other things, through a full range of contrasts between light and darkness. In both stories the vitality of the night world is linked to moisture and dampness, while the barrenness of life within a social framework is conveyed by the "fatigue" of the light (an "old" light, in the first story, an "old" sun in the second one).

That similarity in theme and situation is supported by other connections in language and situation. The bedouins, who flee northward from the threat of drought and hunger, are described in terms used to describe the masses of black people in Damkov's vision (flow, steady stream, revenge). In both stories the woman reacts first with panic and "coldness," and in both of them, as noted, she ends up being carried away by the attraction for the man (there is also a correspondence in the most marginal details: in both stories the man offers the woman a cigarette). The women's reaction is connected with the discovery of a deep world that had previously been unknown to them, and when it rises to the surface, both of them respond with a "strange" voice: " 'Yes,' said Galila, with a strange voice" (19); " 'You don't have a girlfriend yet,' Geula interrupted his prayer, —'You're still young,' her voice was loud and strange" (35). The landscape in both stories is the same, and the descriptions of the cypress trees, for example, is common to them both: "A wall of old, dusty cypresses surrounds the orchard" (15); "Far off, in the orchards, stand dark cypresses, heavy with dust" (41). I might add that in the revised version Oz heightened the link between the stories. Thus, for example, Geula listens to the "sounds of the night" (1976a, 41; 1981, 40) as she is lying on the flowerbed, and these sounds prepare her to be reconciled with the bedouin. The "sounds of the night" also conclude the first story, representing the voice of the "lands of the jackal."

Now we may sum up with certainty: "Nomad and Viper" was intended by its author to be read after "Where the Jackals Howl," and in its light. Many details in the second story should be interpreted through that reciprocal bond (of course, in relation also to the other details of the story). That connection clarifies the special significance attributed to the bedouin, the psychic processes undergone by Geula, and the meaning of light and darkness.

Such conjunctions of themes and motifs are found throughout the book. The stories are linked together in varying degrees. Thus, for example, "Before His Time" is more closely connected with the stories preceding it (in particular "Where the Jackals Howl") than with those following. In contrast, "Redeeming the World" is mainly bound up with the story following it, and only a few motifs connect it with the preceding one (the two protagonists fail to reach their destination in time to transact the business for which they went to town; both are perturbed by "rounded" women [92, 118]).

A major portion of the stories present an encounter with someone who stands for the world of nature, the "lands of the jackal," and the story follows the protagonist's reaction to that encounter. Thus, for example, after "Nomad and Viper" we have "The Way of the Wind," ending, like the preceding story, with the death of the young protagonist. Still, despite the possible similarity between the endings of these two stories, there is, in fact, a dialectic contrast between them. Gideon, the paratrooper hanging from the high tension wires, suddenly identifies the figure of a beast in his brother, hurrying to his rescue: "With wide open eyes Gideon stared at the wolf's fangs bristling in Zaki's mouth. Dread attacked him as though he had looked into a distorting mirror and seen the human visage wiped from his own face" (57) (Zaki has previously been compared to a jackal, a monkey, and a cat). Realizing that a potential wolf exists within himself, he seeks to flee it. He can only do so by committing suicide. Thus, in contrast to Geula, who desires to become part of the world of the night and dies in that desire, Gideon dies because of his wish to flee from that world.

In most of the stories the plot takes place in the same geographical setting, a kibbutz in northern Israel with mountains to the east, where the enemy lurks, and with the sea to the west. The last story in the book, "Strange Fire," transports the encounter to Jerusalem. It seems to me that Oz sought to disentangle his subject from the restricted area of the kibbutz in order to indicate its universality. The geographical structure of the kibbutz and its social structure (the founding generation, the generation of its children, etc.) appear repeatedly, and with them certain typical characters: the ideologue, a member of the founding generation, the young kibbutz member who has taken part in reprisal raids and been decorated for heroism, refugees from World War II. And around the kibbutz are the jackals. They appear in all the stories, sometimes in the center of the picture, and sometimes just in outline. In "Strange Fire" the narrator remarks with the venerable wisdom of Agnon: "Muffled and distant the cry of the jackals is heard. Words flee from him. Something that is not words seeks to be uttered but cannot be. True, the jackals don't belong to the body of the story. They are not immanent, Dr. Kleinberger would remark, and he is correct. But how could we dispossess them from the story. They stand in its basement and turn its wheels" (168). Against the background of that conflict between landscapes and society, as I have pointed out, there is a constant struggle between society and the powers of the "antagonist" (that word appears in most of the stories, and all of them are accompanied by other terms relating to struggle and war).

In addition to those general connections there are, as noted, other, local connections. They are not cut from the same cloth. Sometimes figures from contiguous stories have similar traits (both Geula and Gideon in "Nomad and Viper" and "The Way of the Wind," for example, have "poetical" experiences; the main protagonists of "Redeeming the World" and "A Hollow Stone" are characterized by the hatred that guides their acts), and sometimes the plots contain similar components (both protagonists of "All the Rivers" and "Redeeming the World" go to the city to transact some business, and both of them fail in that task because they reach their destinations too late). Even marginal descriptive details recur (e.g., the description of the bare bulbs and peeling paint in "Before His Time" and "The Trappist Monastery"). Some of the stories are connected to each other by a simile or metaphor: in addition to the example cited at the beginning of this appendix, see, for example, the comparison with an ape that links "The Way of the Wind" with "Before His Time." In other instances the repeated detail appears in two stories but not in the same stratum of the text. One of the main characters in "The Way of the Wind" is Shimshon, Gideon's father. The following story begins with Shimshon the bull (the adjective "potent," applied to Shimshon, is also applied to the bull). Another example: the main protagonist of "Before His Time" is Dov ("bear" in

Hebrew) Sirkin; Itcheh, the central figure in the following story, is compared twice to a bear (76, 79).

Such connections are not only built between adjacent stories, but they exist throughout the entire volume. "Before His Time," the fourth story in the book, harks back to the first story, "Where the Jackals Howl," in most of its motifs, and Geula, the female protagonist in the second story, appears in it as well; hatred explains the behavior of figures like Geula (the second story), the man who would reform the world (the seventh story), and Batya Pinski (the eighth story); a metaphorical description of rivers flowing to the sea is found in "All the Rivers" (the sixth story), and in "A Hollow Stone" (the eighth story). Since the entire book is arranged as a single unit, connections of that sort can also arise between stories at opposite ends. Thus, for example, the description of the fish in "A Hollow Stone," the eighth story, is a counterpart to the description of the jackals in "Where the Jackals Howl" (cf. 14, 145). The encounter between Lily Dannenberg and her future son-in-law in "Strange Fire" is obviously parallel in meaning and detail with the encounter between Matityahu Damkov and Galila, which begins the book.

The fact that the book is written as a closed structure of symbols allows the author to interpret the symbols of one story in another one, or to relate to those symbols as the sequence of narratives develops. The protagonist of "Redeeming the World" stands "helpless in front of the night libertine voices. He wishes to hear an echo of his thoughts in them, whether by playing on the words 'wind,' 'breath,' and 'spirit,' or by identifying the real crying of the jackals with the jackal cry which is a familiar symbol of the destruction of the kingdom and of the madness and death that lie in wait for every man" (120). The wordplay on "wind," "breath," and "spirit" hints at the double meaning of the word "wind" in "The Way of the Wind": the Hebrew *ruah* refers to both the soul and the natural phenomenon of wind. Enough has already been said about the meaning of the jackals in this book. Shimshon Sheinbaum dismisses his son's books and sketches contemptuously: "Here you'll find no wheedling poems about a flower that's been plucked or a jackal caught in a trap" (49). The author is ironic about himself (a trapped jackal appears in "Where the Jackals Howl" and "Before His Time"), but that irony boomerangs against the character, indicating the implied author's attitude toward Shimshon.

I have previously mentioned the constant power struggle between the forces of nature and human society (or that between the different psychic forces). The internal organization of the book also determines the ordering of this key issue. The book has a decidedly thematic organization: it begins with stories in which an uncompromising struggle is waged between the two camps, and it ends with two stories in which that struggle is resolved in synthesis, in mutual accommodation.

The first stories of the book pose the question of who is stronger, the lands of the jackal or human society, or, in the words of the main character in "Before His Time," who will have the last laugh, the members of the kibbutz or the jackals. The encounter between the two worlds is destructive, and the kibbutz member is unconditionally defeated in it, among other reasons because the jackals appear within his very being and he cannot find a compromise between them and the framework of the society in which he lives. "Redeeming the World," the seventh story, is typical: its protagonist tries in vain to fight against the night voices, but they "come to him and pounce on him" (120). Therefore, "a person wants to turn on the radio and stifle those evil voices. The radio breaks out in nasal song, and the room fills with the groans of a drunken bash. The man shuts the radio, and the first voices come back and attack him" (121). The protagonist of the story, who cannot make a compromise between the contradictory forces within himself, sees no alternative but suicide.

As noted, in the last two stories the nature of the relation between the rival powers changes. The destructive encounter gives way to one which, while still imbued with tension and confrontation, also promises reconciliation and fecundation. "A Hollow Stone" is one of the most complex stories in the volume. The story describes a sudden storm that attacks a kibbutz and lays it waste. In parallel, a kibbutz member, Batya Pinski, is described: she is secluded in her apartment, taking care of her tropical fish. Batya is presented as an evil witch whose actions are guided by hatred and the urge to destroy. It is easy to interpret the storm as a projection of her destructiveness. In fact the story moves in another direction entirely. The key to its contents lies, it seems to me, in the parallel established between the processes taking place in the weather outside and in the aquarium. After the storm at night the skies are clear in the morning: "Brilliant, polished clarity, a blue desert. It was a long time since we had seen such a clear sky as on that morning when we went out to assess the damage, and our feet stumbled over the corpses of inanimate objects" (124). A similar process takes place in the aquarium. The narrator explains how the filter keeps the water clean: "In that way a constant flow is maintained, and the apparatus absorbs turbid water from the bottom and spurts it out in a thin stream above the surface. The pollutants are trapped by the fibrous materials, and the water of the aquarium is purified and keeps its marvelous clarity" (145). Later he remarks:

"The width distracts one from the depth, but the hidden depths send up wave after wave of soothing darkness. The darkness of the depths gives the surfaces their purity and clarity, the clarity which reflects images like polished glass" (146). Thus, the darkness of the depths is not the opposite of clarity, but rather its source. It is impossible to miss the similarity between that process of clarification and the rare, brilliant clarity that follows the storm. The focus of the story, therefore, is the question of the status of the forces of destruction and evil in the world. The answer offered is that these natural forces are not the polar opposite of culture. On the contrary, in its own way, nature can purify culture and contribute to its inner strength and well-being. Paradoxically, it turns out that Batya Pinski, who is analogous in the story to the aquarium and its fish, fulfills in the kibbutz the function of filter in the aquarium.[2]

A similar conception also characterizes "Strange Fire," which concludes the book.[3] On the one hand, this story harks back to the plot of the first one, strengthening the inner structure of the volume. Yet the story does not simply ask which of the two rival forces is stronger. It seeks, rather, to point out their fertile conjunction (a detailed discussion of this story appears in Chapters 3 and 5). The synthesis achieved in this story is more evident than in "A Hollow Stone," for the phenomena of "dialectics" is constantly discussed; those phenomena are hinted at time and again, both by the features and experiences of the main characters, and by short descriptions of their surroundings (e.g., the night birds and the day birds, the olive trees and the decorative shrubs).

The struggle between the forces of nature and the city is embodied here in the olive tree that has overpowered the gatepost attached to it. The author uses the sight of the olive trees to describe a state of affairs parallel to the relations between the dark depths of the aquarium and its external clarity: "In aggressive hunger they send out their root hairs into the depths of the earth. . . . The treetops are caressed in the wind with a noble and moderate mien, but unseen their roots

---

2. Implicitly, the hollow stone in the aquarium, which merges life and death, is depicted as the philosophers' stone. The search for this main alchemic symbol is found throughout Oz's work.

3. In the Am Oved edition of *Where the Jackals Howl*, another story was added, "Upon This Evil Earth." This story can be seen as a kind of renewed interpretation and summary of the stories in *Where the Jackals Howl*, and it concludes the nine original stories of the book. That change brought about further editorial modifications. In that edition "Strange Fire" appears after another story that also takes place in the vicinity of Jerusalem, "The Trappist Monastery."

seek moisture with passionate powers" (158). That reciprocal relationship is expressed in various ways in the story. Dr. Kleinberger teaches his friend that "the alternation between degeneracy and purity is like that between day and night. They seem to be contraries, but in fact one draws the other out, and neither can exist without the other" (149); and later he attacks a certain author for not attaining "the unity of opposites" (166). The doctor's writing is also viewed as a process that strives for the "marvelous unity of opposites" (173). Another aspect of that unity is illustrated by the old madwoman, known as "One Meaning": "The blessing of the sky above and the blessing of water beneath, from Frankfurt to Jerusalem. One meaning to all deeds, to those that build and those that destroy" (163).

Thus, the dark world of the depths is not only a source of destruction and ruin but also an infinite reservoir of life and creativity. The effort to repress that world, to ignore its existence, gives rise to sterile, degenerate life, or else it ends in a destructive outburst of the forbidden powers. A person can, in contrast, live in awareness of those powers and the wisdom and creativity stored up in that world, and try to purify their destructiveness and be nourished by them like the olive trees that probe the depths with "passionate powers." That conception continues to be found throughout Oz's works.

# BIBLIOGRAPHY

(H): Sources in Hebrew

Agnon, S. Y. 1942. "Sefer Hama'asim" (in *Elu Va'elu*). Jerusalem: Schocken. (H)
Alter, Robert. 1977a. "Afterward: A Problem of Horizons." *Triquarterly* (39), Spring.
———, 1977b. "Fiction in a State of Siege." In *Defence of the Imagination*. Philadelphia: Jewish Publication Society.
Aschkenasy, Nehama. 1986. *Eve's Journey*. Philadelphia: University of Pennsylvania Press.
Avigur-Rotem, Gavriela. 1990. "The Spy as a Metaphor." *Alei-Siah* (27/28), Summer. (H)
Balaban, Avraham. 1986. *Between God and Beast*. Tel Aviv: Am Oved. (H)
———, 1988a. *Toward Language and Beyond*. Tel Aviv: Am Oved. (H)
———, 1988b. "Secularism and Religiousness in Modern Hebrew Prose." *Moznayim* (5–6), August–September. (H)
———, 1989. "Elections and Literature in Israel." *Midstream* (2), February–March.
———, 1990. "Language and Reality in the Prose of Amos Oz." *Modern Language Studies* (2), Spring.
———, 1991. "Oz Breaks the Vessels." *Ma'ariv*, 5 April. (H)
Barzel, Hillel. 1974. *Metarealistic Hebrew Prose*. Tel Aviv: Massada. (H)
———, 1981. *The Best in Hebrew Prose: Essays on Modern Hebrew Novels*. Tel Aviv: Yahdav. (H)
Ben-Baruch, Yosef. 1982. "The Lands Beyond the Fence." *Alei-Siah* (13/14), Spring. (H)
Ben-Dov, Nitza. 1990. "To Know a Woman, To Know a World." *Alei-Siah* (27/28), Summer. (H)
Bergman, Samuel Hugo. 1977. *A History of Philosophy* (Jacobi, Fichte, Schelling). Jerusalem: Bialik Institute. (H)
Blackburn, Simon. 1984. *Spreading the Word*. Oxford: Oxford University Press.
Bonwick, James. 1956. *Egyptian Belief and Modern Thought*. Indian Hills, Colo.: Falcon's Wing Press.
Buber, Martin. 1958. *I and Thou*. Trans. Ronald Gregor Smith. New York: Scribner's.
———, 1967. *Between Man and Man*. Trans. Ronald Gregor Smith. New York: Macmillan.
Burge, Tyler. 1979. "Individualism and the Mental." *Midwest Studies in Philosophy*, vol. 4.

Campbell, Joseph. 1973. *The Hero with a Thousand Faces*. Princeton: Princeton University Press (Bollingen Series XVII).

Cirlot, J. E. 1983. *A Dictionary of Symbols*. Trans. Jack Sage. New York: Philosophical Library.

Cohen, Joseph. 1990. *Voices of Israel*. Albany: State University of New York Press.

Cooper, J. C. 1984. *An Illustrated Encyclopedia of Traditional Symbols*. London: Thames and Hudson.

Culler, Jonathan. 1982. *On Deconstruction*. Ithaca: Cornell University Press.

Felman, Shoshana (ed.). 1982. *Literature and Psychoanalysis*. Baltimore: The Johns Hopkins University Press.

Ferguson, Francis. 1957. *The Human Image in Dramatic Literature*. New York: Doubleday.

Ferguson, George. 1961. *Signs and Symbols in Christian Art*. Oxford: Oxford University Press.

Fletcher, Angus. 1982. *Allegory*. Ithaca: Cornell University Press.

Foster, John Burt. 1981. *Heirs to Dionysus*. Princeton: Princeton University Press.

Freud, Sigmund. 1954. *The Origins of Psychoanalysis*. Trans. Eric Mosbacher and James Strachey. New York: Basic Books.

———, 1960. *The Ego and the Id*. Trans. Joan Riviere. New York: Norton.

———, 1961a. *Beyond the Pleasure Principle*. Trans. James Strachey. New York: Norton.

———, 1961b. *Civilization and Its Discontents*. Trans. James Strachey. New York: Norton.

———, 1962. *Three Essays on the Theory of Sexuality*. Trans. James Strachey. New York: Basic Books.

———, 1965. *The Interpretation of Dreams*. Trans. James Strachey. New York: Basic Books.

———, 1969. *An Outline of Psychoanalysis*. Trans. James Strachey. New York: Norton.

Fuchs, Esther. 1987. *Israeli Mythogynies*. Albany: State University of New York Press.

Gertz, Nurit. 1980. *Amos Oz—Monograph*. Tel Aviv: Sifriat Poalim. (H)

———, 1983. *Generation Shift in Literary History: Hebrew Narrative Fiction in the Sixties*. Tel Aviv: Hakibbutz Hameuhad. (H)

Hall, James. 1979. *Dictionary of Subjects and Symbols in Art*. New York: Harper and Row.

Hartman, Geoffrey, ed. 1979. *Deconstruction and Criticism*. London: Routledge and Kegan Paul.

Heidegger, Martin. 1962. *Being and Time*. Trans. John Macquarrie and Edward Robinson. New York: Harper and Row.

Jacobi, Jolande. 1974. *Complex/Archetype/Symbol in the Psychology of C. G. Jung*. Trans. Ralph Manheim. Princeton: Princeton University Press (Bollingen Series LVII).

Johnson, Barbara. 1980. *The Critical Difference: Essays in the Contemporary Rhetoric of Reading*. Baltimore: The Johns Hopkins University Press.

Jung, C. G. *The Collected Works*. Trans. R.F.C. Hull. Princeton: Princeton University Press (Bollingen Series XX).

    1953a. *Two Essays on Analytical Psychology*, vol. 7.

1953b. *Psychology and Alchemy*, vol. 16.
1954. *The Practice of Psychotherapy*, vol. 16.
1956. *Symbols of Transformation*, vol. 5.
1958. *Psychology and Religion: West and East*, vol. 11.
1959a. *The Archetypes and the Collective Unconscious*, vol. 9I.
1959b. *Aion*, vol. 9II.
1960. *The Structure and Dynamics of the Psyche*, vol. 8.
1963. *Mysterium Coniunctionis*, vol. 14.
1964. *Civilization in Transition*, vol. 10.
1968. *Alchemical Studies*, vol. 13.
Jung, C. G. 1973. *Memories, Dreams, Reflections*. Trans. Richard and Clara Winston. New York: Pantheon Books.
Jung, C. G., and C. Kerenyi. 1963. *Essays on the Science of Mythology*. Trans. R.F.C. Hull. Princeton: Princeton University Press (Bollingen Series XXII).
Kripke, Saul. 1980. *Naming and Necessity*. Cambridge: Harvard University Press.
―――, 1982. *Wittgenstein on Rules and Private Language*. Oxford: Blackwell.
Langton, Edward. 1949. *Essentials of Demonology*. London: Epworth Press.
Lonergan, Bernard. 1976. *The Way to Nicea*. Philadelphia: Westminster Press.
Lurker, Manfred. 1980. *The Gods and Symbols of Ancient Egypt*. London: Thames and Hudson.
Neumann, Erich. 1963. *The Great Mother*. Trans. Ralph Manheim. Princeton: Princeton University Press (Bollingen Series XLII).
―――, 1969. *Depth Psychology and a New Ethic*. Trans. Eugene Rolef. New York: Putnam.
―――, 1973. *The Origins and History of Consciousness*. Trans. R.F.C. Hull. Princeton: Princeton University Press (Bollingen Series XLII).
Nietzsche, Friedrich. 1966. *Thus Spake Zarathustra*. Trans. Walter Kaufmann. New York: Viking.
―――, 1967a. *On the Genealogy of Morals* and *Ecce Homo*. Trans. Walter Kaufmann. New York: Vintage Books.
―――, 1967b. *The Birth of Tragedy* and *The Case of Wagner*. Trans. Walter Kaufmann. New York: Vintage Books.
Norris, Christopher. 1982. *Deconstruction: Theory and Practice*. London: Methuen.
Oren, Yosef. 1983. "A Genetic Look at the Israeli Situation." *Ha'aretz*, 25 February. (H)
Otto, Rudolf. 1958. *The Idea of the Holy*. Trans. John W. Harvey. Oxford: Oxford University Press.
Oz, Amos. 1961a. "Participation is No Substitute for Equality." *Davar*, 20 February. (H)
―――, 1961b. "A Crack Open to the Wind." *Keshet* (11), April. (H)
―――, 1962a. "Purple Coast." *Davar*, 5 May. (H)
―――, 1962b. "Before His Time." *Keshet* (4), July. (H)
―――, 1962c. "The Trappist Monastery." *Amot*, October. (H)
―――, 1963a. "Where the Jackals Howl." *Keshet* (2), January. (H)
―――, 1963b. "The Way of the Wind." *Keshet* (3), July. (H)
―――, 1963c. "Strange Fire." *Moznayim* (1–2), December. (H)

———, 1964a. "Nomad and Viper." *Ha'aretz*, 7 February.
———, 1964b. "A Hollow Stone." *Me'asef Ledivei Sifrut*, December. (H)
———, 1965a. *Where the Jackals Howl*. Ramat Gan: Massada. (H).
———, 1965b. "The Strong Weaknesses of the Founding Generation." *Davar*, 9 July. (H)
———, 1965c. "Literature from Main Street to the Suburbs" (interview with Yitzhak Betzalel). *Masa*, 13 August. (H)
———, 1966a. *Elsewhere, Perhaps*. Tel Aviv: Sifriat Poalim. (H). English: 1973. Trans. Nicholas de Lange. New York: Harcourt Brace Jovanovich.
———, 1966b. "A Conversation on *Elsewhere, Perhaps*" (interview with Yehoshua Kenaz). *Shdemot*, December. (H)
———, 1967. "Fathers and Sons in Our Modern Literature." *Shdemot*, July. (H)
———, 1968a. *My Michael*. Tel Aviv: Am Oved. (H). English: 1972. Trans. Nicholas de Lange. New York: Alfred A. Knopf.
———, 1968b. "The Long Journey into Language" (interview with Shoshana Pilus). *Hotam*, 5 June. (H)
———, 1968c. "Writing is the Conjuring Up of Spirits" (interview with Yifat Nevo). *Davar*, 19 July. (H)
———, 1971a. *Unto Death*. Tel Aviv: Sifriat Poalim. (H) English: 1975. Trans. Nicholas de Lange. New York: Harcourt Brace Jovanovich.
———, 1971b. "For Me Writing Is the Conjuring Up of Spirits" (interview with Naomi Gutkind). *Hatzofe*, 2 July. (H)
———, 1971c. "Zionism, the New Left and the Palestinian Problem." *Davar*, 19 September. (H)
———, 1972. "We Have Lost the Ability to Dream." *Al Hamishmar*, 5 May. (H)
———, 1973a. *Touch the Water, Touch the Wind*. Tel Aviv: Am Oved. (H) English: 1974. Trans. Nicholas de Lange. New York: Harcourt Brace Jovanovich.
———, 1973b. "The Figure of the Author as the Tribal Witchdoctor" (a conversation with Oz). *Bahugim Lesifrut*, April. (H)
———, 1974. "My Michael: The Fifties, Jerusalem" (interview with Azriel Kaufman). *Kolno'a*, September. (H)
———, 1975. "With Amos Oz" (interview with Alon Yarden). *Bamahane Nahal*, 3 December. (H)
———, 1976a. *Where the Jackals Howl*. Tel Aviv: Am Oved. (H) English: 1981. Trans. Nicholas de Lange and Philip Simpson. Toronto: Bantam Books.
———, 1976b. *The Hill of Evil Counsel*. Tel Aviv: Am Oved. (H). English: 1978. Trans. Nicholas de Lange. New York: Harcourt Brace Jovanovich.
———, 1976c. "Amos Oz Talks about Berdyczewski." *Alei-Siah* (4), September. (H)
———, 1977a. "We Will Make Peace with Them While We Are Awake" (interview with Nurit Baretzki). *Ma'ariv*, 30 December. (H)
———, 1977b. "Observations and Interpretations." *Proza* (12–13), February–March. (H)
———, 1978a. *Soumchi*. Tel Aviv: Am Oved. (H) English: 1980. Trans. Amos Oz and Penelope Farmer. New York: Harper and Row.
———, 1978b. "An Interview with Amos Oz." *Galie Tzahal* (IDF Broadcasting), 14 April. (H)

———, 1978c. "A Conversation with Readers at Ariel Bookstore" (recording notes in Oz's archives in Arad). Jerusalem, 21 July. (H)
———, 1978d. "Like a Gangster in a Brawl but a Bit in a Dream." *Ma'ariv*, 18 August. (H)
———, 1979a. *Under This Blazing Light*. Tel Aviv: Sifriat Poalim. (H)
———, 1979b. "Poland Defeated Russia in the Land of Canaan." *Ata*, October. (H)
———, 1979c. "A Religious Rumor" (unpublished). Oz's archives, Arad. (H)
———, 1979d. "Good Advice to a Member of the Knesset" (unpublished). Oz's archives, Arad. (H)
———, 1979e. "A Conversation with Amos Oz." *Hahevra Lehaganat Hateva*, December. (H)
———, 1980. "If Kafka Were a Member of Kibbutz Beit Alfa" (discussion with A. B. Yehoshua, Amos Oz, Dan Shavit, and Alexander Barzel). *Ma'ariv*, 2 May. (H)
———, 1982. *A Perfect Peace*. Tel Aviv: Am Oved. (H) English: 1985. Trans. Hillel Halkin. New York: Harcourt Brace Jovanovich.
———, 1983. *In the Land of Israel*. Tel Aviv: Am Oved. (H) English: 1983. Trans. Maurie Goldberg-Bartura. New York: Harcourt Brace Jovanovich.
———, 1987a. *Black Box*. Tel Aviv: Am Oved. (H) English: 1988. Trans. Nicholas de Lange. New York: Harcourt Brace Jovanovich.
———, 1987b. *The Slopes of Lebanon*. Tel Aviv: Am Oved. (H) English: 1989. Trans. Maurie Goldberg-Bartura. New York: Harcourt Brace Jovanovich.
———, 1987c. "The Scouts and the Brothers." *Davar*, 22 May. (H)
———, 1989a. *To Know a Woman*. Jerusalem: Keter. (H) English: 1991. Trans. Nicholas de Lange. New York: Harcourt Brace Jovanovich.
———, 1989b. "Amos Oz: To be I—He" (interview with Hilit Yeshurun). *Hadarim* (9), Spring. (H)
———, 1991. *The Third Condition*. Jerusalem: Keter. (H)
Ramras-Rauch, Gila. 1989. *The Arab in Israeli Literature*. Bloomington: Indiana University Press.
Rank, Otto. 1959. *The Myth of the Birth of the Hero*. Ed. Philip Freund. New York: Vintage Books.
Rusch, G. William. 1980. *The Trinitarian Controversy*. Philadelphia: Fortress Press.
Schelling, F.W.J. 1936. *Philosophical Inquiries Into the Nature of Human Freedom*. Trans. James Gutmann. Chicago: Open Court.
Scholem, Gershom G. 1965. *Major Trends in Jewish Mysticism*. New York: Schocken.
———, 1987. *Origins of the Kabbalah*. Ed. R. J. Zwi Werblowsky. Trans. Allan Arkush. Philadelphia: The Jewish Publication Society; Princeton: Princeton University Press.
Schopenhauer, Arthur. 1948. *The World as Will and Idea*. Trans. R. B. Haldane and J. Kemp. London: Routledge and Kegan Paul.
Schwaller de Lubicz, Isha. 1978. *Her-Bak: Egyptian Initiate*. Trans. Ronald Frazer. New York: Inner Traditions International.
Shaked, Gershon. 1970. *A New Wave in Hebrew Fiction*. Tel Aviv: Sifriat Poalim. (H)

———, 1985. *Wave After Wave in Hebrew Narrative Fiction*. Jerusalem: Keter. (H)
Shalev, Mordechai. 1968. "*My Michael* by Amos Oz." *Ha'aretz*, 9 August. (H)
Shoham, S. Giora. 1980. *Salvation Through the Gutters*. Tel Aviv: Tcherikover. (H)
———, 1982. *Love as Bait*. Tel Aviv: Ramot. (H)
Skura, Meredith Anne. 1981. *The Literary Use of the Psychoanalytic Process*. New Haven: Yale University Press.
Spinoza, Baruch. 1982. *The Ethics* and *Selected Letters*. Trans. Samuel Shirley. Indianapolis: Hackett.
Tillich, Paul. 1962. *Religiousphilosophic*. Stuttgart: W. Kohlhammer.
———, 1974. *Mysticism and Guilt-Consciousness in Schelling's Philosophical Development*. Trans. Victor Nuovo. Cranbury, N.J.: Associated University Press.
Vries, Ad de, 1981. *Dictionary of Symbols and Imagery*. Amsterdam: North-Holland.
Yehoshua, A. B. 1963. *The Death of the Old Man*. Tel Aviv: Hakibbutz Hameuchad. (H)
Zilberman, Dorit. 1991. "Oz for the Gentiles and for Us." *Moznayim* (5), February–March. (H)

# INDEX TO THE WORKS

"A Crack Open to the Wind," 29, 33–39, 46, 48, 49, 84, 87, 136, 141 n. 2, 183, 239, 246
"A Hollow Stone," 52, 65, 73, 183, 185, 186, 246, 247, 248–49
"All the Rivers," 13, 64, 66, 100, 103 n. 26, 140, 146, 246, 247
*A Perfect Peace*, 1, 5, 8, 14, 23, 24, 27, 30, 41, 42, 64, 65, 66, 67, 70, 71, 74, 76, 81, 85 n. 15, 86, 93 n. 20, 100, 110–30, 131, 135, 140, 142, 143, 154–58, 159, 160, 181, 183, 184, 192, 196, 202, 206, 211–29, 233, 234
"Before His Time," 2, 13, 18–19 n. 9, 26, 33, 48–63, 70, 72, 75, 87, 88, 89, 91, 95, 98, 140, 183, 229, 242, 243, 245, 246, 247
"Crusade," 21 n. 10, 86, 98, 181
*Elsewhere, Perhaps*, 5, 7, 8, 16 n. 5, 6, 20, 22, 23, 24, 25, 27, 29, 30, 36, 41, 42, 64, 65, 66, 67, 69, 70, 71, 73, 74, 75, 84, 86, 98, 104 n. 27, 106–10, 115, 119 n. 34, 129, 135, 140, 143, 146–54, 157, 158–59, 181, 183, 195–211, 213
"Hill of Evil Counsel, The," 14 n. 2, 22–23, 36, 64, 66, 73
*In the Land of Israel*, 7, 80 n. 1
"Longing," 13, 14
"Late Love," 14, 71
"Mr. Levi," 13, 36, 157 n. 14
*My Michael*, 14 n. 2, 19, 20, 24, 36, 42, 64, 66, 70, 71, 86, 135, 140, 141, 142, 143, 159, 160, 164, 166–76, 181, 205, 229
"Nomad and Viper," 146, 181, 185–86, 242, 243–45, 246
"Purple Coast," 4, 33, 39–48, 51, 52, 53, 54, 88, 140, 141–42, 146, 151, 152, 183
"Redeeming the World," 73, 186, 245, 246, 247, 248
*Slopes of Lebanon, The*, 7
*Soumchi*, 13, 17, 20, 21–22, 52, 66, 74
"Strange Fire," 24, 64, 65, 71, 72, 74, 81, 86, 100–103, 140, 146, 184, 185–95, 245–46, 247, 249
*Third Condition, The*, 6, 23, 24, 47, 65, 70, 76, 81, 82 n. 6, 86, 121 n. 36, 130–36, 181, 184
*To Know a Woman*, 6, 64, 66, 132, 140, 141, 183–84 n. 2
*Touch the Water, Touch the Wind*, 70–71, 74, 115 n. 30, 140, 142, 173 n. 24, 183
"Trappist Monastery, The," 13, 14, 52, 61, 64, 70, 81, 86, 87–94, 95, 98, 101, 242, 243, 246, 247, 249
*Under This Blazing Light*, 7, 8, 59

*Unto Death*, 68
"Upon This Evil Earth," 24, 66, 81, 82n.6, 86, 98, 100, 103–106, 107, 146, 249
"Way of the Wind, The," 14, 24, 73, 100, 140, 183, 186, 245, 246, 247
*Where the Jackals Howl*, 1, 13, 19n.9, 23, 27, 33, 48, 63, 64, 65, 66, 67, 70, 71, 72, 73, 100, 103, 104, 106, 107, 110, 140, 143n.3, 146, 154, 181, 195, 198, 200, 201, 241–50
"Where the Jackals Howl," 24, 26, 42, 52, 63, 64, 69, 73, 89, 95–100, 135, 142, 143–46, 183, 186, 242, 243–45, 246, 247

www.ingramcontent.com/pod-product-compliance
Lightning Source LLC
Chambersburg PA
CBHW031548300426
44111CB00006BA/212